The Land of Piceno

The Life and Times of Le Marche, Italy

Phoebe Leed and Nathan Neel

Rondini Press

The Land of Piceno

The Life and Times of Le Marche, Italy

Copyright 2020 by Phoebe Leed and Nathan Neel
Rondini Press
rondinipress@gmail.com

ISBN 978-1-7358532-0-8 Paperback
ISBN 978-1-7358532-1-5 Hardcover
ISBN 978-1-7923-5087-0 Ebook

Library of Congress Control Number 2020918506

Cover and interior design and typesetting by Jane Tenenbaum
Typeset in Dante Monotype

Contents

Baedeker's Central Italy
Guide 1909 — Le Marche

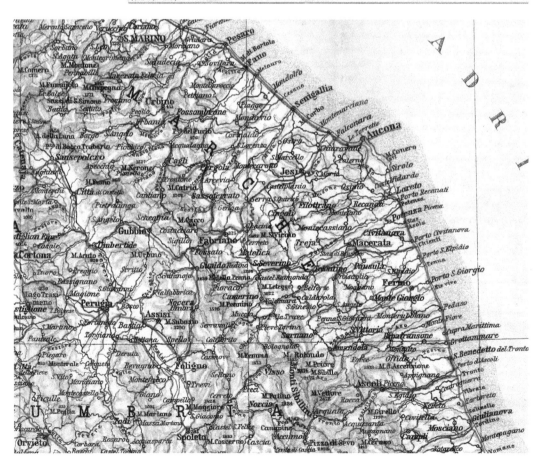

Overture

The present manuscript exists in a space between history, travel literature, legend, and love letter. Here is a biographical sketch of a place, *la Terra Picena*, as if it were a living person. From this perspective, myths and fairy tales can carry as much weight as documented fact. Our goal has been to recount what are for us the major stories associated with the Land of Piceno, some of them personal. We make no pretense of writing a comprehensive history, a voluminous task. Instead, among other things, we hope to recreate the experience of standing on the steep mountainside at the mouth of the Grotta della Sibilla, gazing out towards the blue haze that is the Adriatic Sea.

We wondered how to explain the phrase *terra picena* to readers who had never heard of this corner of the world. Piceno land, Picenum, the land of the Piceni—but who were these Piceni? Simply put, the *Terra Picena* is an imprecisely defined area in central Italy, corresponding more or less to today's Le Marche region with some of northern Abruzzo included. From high in the Apennine Mountains, a series of parallel rivers flows down to the Adriatic Sea, not 56 km/35 mi east as the crow flies, from snow-clad peaks to rolling pastures, through terraced hillsides of grapes and olives, to the palms and orange trees on the coast. Well adapted for habitation (except perhaps for the earthquakes), humans have survived here for thousands and thousands of years, despite the onslaughts of marauding invaders. A prehistoric culture of heterogeneous people, called "Piceno" by the ancients who encountered it, flourished in the millennium before the birth of Christ, until it fell under Roman domination. Most of what the Piceni left behind is an unwritten record of grave goods, the dead buried with their jewelry, weapons, banqueting and barbeque accessories, and even chariots.

An unrelenting consciousness has been imposed on our brains through all the visits through all the years: this is a very ancient land. You can't put a shovel in the earth without revealing traces of our predecessors. We were forced to ask, what is so ancient about the ancient world? The word "ancient" is in fact a distancing concept, as if to imply a time before time. The 2,000 years since Rome's rule is a small portion of the existence of modern humans.

Nowadays, this land is unheralded, little known—with no Michelangelos, no gondoliers, no Vatican, to attract attention. But these mountains have sheltered Neolithic shepherds, hermits and necromancers, brigands opposing the Unification of Italy, and partisans who fought the German occupation during WWII. In Ascoli Piceno's Piazza del Popolo, you can see Roman ruins in the basement bathrooms of the Art Nouveau Caffè Meletti, next to the 13th century Palazzo dei Capitani later worked on by the Renaissance architect Cola dell'Amatrice. Medieval troubadours spread tales of an enchantress who ruled a mysterious realm deep within Monte Sibilla, luring knights to their eternal damnation. Cousin Ada takes us to the Templar stronghold of Castignano; in a church she kisses her fingers and touches the hem of Mary's dress painted by Vittore Crivelli in the late 1400s. Driving the back roads that link the hilltop fortresses, we stop to poke around a deserted gristmill poised over a torrent filled ravine. As they had in the Middle Ages, country women were still bringing their grain here to be ground into flour as recently as the 1960s.

Certain themes arise again and again. Above all is the nexus of *mare, colle,* and *montagne*—sea, hills, and mountains. At a traditional Easter lunch in Pozza, a remote village in the heart of brigand territory known for a nearby partisan graveyard, a fellow at the next table strikes up a conversation. From Ancona, he wants to know how foreigners like us came to find this spot. We explain how Nathan's maternal grandparents were Marchigiani (people from Le Marche), and that while visiting our relatives we had explored many of the nearby nooks and crannies. Our new friend offers us a *piconi*, a cheese pastry that is a seasonal local specialty, and launches into an impromptu summary of the beauty of the landscape, the Adriatic coast he lives on, the hillsides covered with vineyards, and finally the rough Sibillini Mountains—all within an hour's drive.

Le Marche became a romantic refuge for us with its dramatic landscape, ancient ruins, and locavore charms. Local is another of those recurring themes manifesting itself on many levels—like a geographical/historical force. On the outskirts of a small town an elderly woman runs a grocery store off of her living room which could only be called a hole in the wall. But the simplicity of the space belies the fresh eggs (that remind us of how food tasted when we were children before massive food industrialization) and the delicious sheep's milk cheeses from nearby farms. A noted local winemaker sells only in bulk out of a cave behind his house. You bring your own five-liter bottle, he fills it with red or white for less than ten dollars. They say Pope John Paul II was enamored of his grape.

In our time of relentless centralization and globalization, Le Marche offers a strong current in the opposite direction. The older, lifetime residents will talk about how much has been changed and lost, but to us from America, with its endless chain stores and Starbucks on every corner, these unique local enterprises offer a fantastic journey. Economists have written about the *modello Marchigiano*, of small family-based firms and factories and craft production. The availability of high quality artisanal products like ceramics, shoes, hats, and musical instruments persists, although Amazon is making inroads here, too.

But there is no changing the geography of Piceno, a landscape made for isolated independent activities. The mountains, a longtime border, create resistance. There is no superhighway or train over them from Ascoli Piceno to Rome. Moving north or south inland is hampered by the hills and river valleys. It is often faster if farther to go down to the coastal superhighway and then turn inland. Over the millennia authority from afar has often asserted itself. If many times in the past Piceno was ungoverned or self-governed, there were also times when it came under the scope of other powers. Ancient Rome comes to mind, but there was also

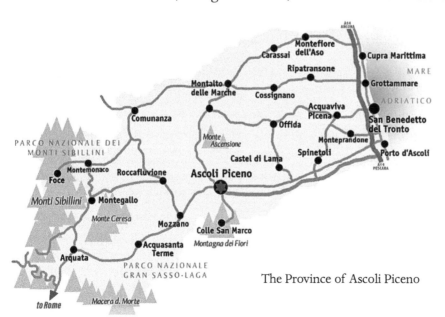

The Province of Ascoli Piceno

the pope, the Holy Roman Emperor, the Austrians, Spanish, and French before Piceno became part of a modern nation state—based in Rome.

We have tended to concentrate on the southern area around Ascoli Piceno, because Ascoli was the main city of the Piceni. (The name Askl/Asculum/Ascoli apparently has pre-indo-european linguistic roots and means "settlement.") Plus, many of Nathan's relatives live in Ascoli and in the mountainous district of Montegallo, "Mount Rooster," above it. We first came to Le Marche more than thirty years ago to find long-lost relatives, descendants of great-aunt Rosa, who never left the family home, and great-uncle Domenico, who returned to it from America. We call them *cugino/a*, cousin, *zia*/aunt, *zio*/uncle, but they are in fact second cousins, second cousins once-removed and beyond, as we follow the intertwined genealogical branches out to their furthest twigs, sharing plenty of great meals and conversations along the way. Because of this family connection, we have hiked the trails, researched the archives, visited the churches and archaeological sites of this particular zone. And so we start with an overwhelmingly broad picture of the geological formation of the Italian peninsula, the migrations of humans around the Mediterranean and across Europe, and by the end we have narrowed it down to the story of a tiny village in the Sibillini Mountains.

But for those who are unfamiliar with Picenum, as the Romans called it, they first need to know how to get there.

Le Marche and its Provinces

Via Salaria in Blue, Augustan Era Map
Historical Atlas of William R. Shepherd 1926

1

Take the Salt Road

To reach the *Terra Picena* from Rome, take the Salt Road. In prehistoric times the Sabine people, centered in the Apennine Mountains around Rieti, made their way down to the marshes at the mouth of the Tiber River on the Tyrhennian Sea, where they gathered salt. Their route crossed the Tiber at the first place above this estuary where both swampy riverbanks firmed up enough to support a settlement. This ford was shared with two other tracks, the Via Latina from the south and the Via Veientana which led north to the Etruscan city of Veii.

View of the Salario Bridge, Giovanni Battista Piranesi, 1754

Around this intersection, at the *Forum Boarium* (Cattle Market), the city of Rome ultimately arose. During the Age of Augustus, in the first century after the birth of Christ, the Romans paved the Salt Road and it became the consular road known as the Via Salaria. It may have the oldest origins of all the consular roads, and Edward Lear, in 1846, called it the "loveliest."

Salt played an important role in the economies of the ancient world, and this is a region where cooks still use it not by the pinch but by the handful. Until the 20th century, salt was rare, precious, and hard to find. Essential for human existence and for the domestication of animals, it served as a form of money; the word "salary" is derived from "salt." Using salt, meat can be preserved without refrigeration, milk can be turned into cheese, produce such as olives can be held over from one harvest till the next. Salt was also harvested on the Adriatic coast, and inland sources existed as well, along the Tronto River—it is not clear from which direction the salt trade first arose.

The Via Salaria (SS4) sets out from Rome not far from the Termini train station. Once, the road exited through the ancient Servian Wall by way of the Porta Collina, which it shared with the Via Nomentana. On the morning of July 19, 390 BC, Brennus, king of the Senone Gauls, led his rampaging army through this open and undefended gate. During the Second Punic War (217 BC) Hannibal, with 2,000 Numidian horsemen, got this far but no further; he withdrew instead into Picenum (as the Romans later named the region) to replenish his supplies. In AD 410, the Goths under King Alaric entered Rome through the Porta Salaria, in the third century Aurelian Wall, and undertook the "Sack of

Rome." In AD 537, this was the site of various skirmishes between Belisarius, general of the Byzantine Empire forces besieged in the city, and the Gothic army of Witigis. The Porta Salaria was damaged during the taking of Rome in 1870, in the last battles of the Risorgimento and the Unification of Italy. While the gate was rebuilt at that time, it was finally demolished in 1921. The remains of the Porta Collina were demolished in 1872 in order to build the Ministero delle Finanze, at the corner of Via XX Settembre and Via Goito.

Beyond the gates the Via Salaria is still a city street. On the right is the Villa Albani. Completed in 1763, it once housed the fabulous collections of antiquities amassed by Cardinal Albani and catalogued by J. J. Winckelmann, the first professional art historian. When Henry James visited in 1873, he greatly admired the sculptures but described the grounds as "Overformal and (as my companion says) too much like a tea-garden." Mounted on the enclosing wall is a plaque commemorating the assassination on this spot of Massimo D'Antona, professor of labor rights, on May 20, 1999 by the Red Brigade. Across the street is the Augustan Age mausoleum of Lucilio Peto and his sister Lucilia, a travertine *tumulo* capped with verdant green.

Running north through a 19th century residential area, including an Art Nouveau enclave with a glittering mosaic of peacocks over a church door, the Via Salaria passes the Villa Ada, once the Villa Savoia, estate of the former royal family of Italy. Here on July 25, 1943, Prime Minister Benito Mussolini was stripped of his office by King Victor Emmanuel III and was promptly arrested and imprisoned. Lined with early Christian catacombs and necropoli, the road meets the Aniene River, crossing it on the Ponte Salario. A haunting Piranesi engraving from the mid 1700s shows the oft-rebuilt Roman arches surmounted by a tower, perhaps added in the eighth century. Most of this was destroyed in a series of wars and today's bridge is unremarkable—yet remnants of the ancient floodways can still be seen. Not far upstream, the two Saccopastore Neanderthal skulls, male and female, were casually dug up in a gravel quarry in 1929 and 1935. Recent analysis has dated them as being 250,000 years old, the earliest signs of Neanderthal presence in Europe.

For a while the road follows the Tiber River. About 16 km / 10 mi from Rome, somewhere on the hills above Settebagni stood the town of Crustumerium (or Crustuminum). In The *History of Rome,* Livy relates that around 750 BC the first Romans, led by Romulus, offered asylum to fugitives, slaves, runaways, vagabonds—whoever they could get to increase the population of the new city. These men needed wives but the surrounding communities despised the mob and rejected all matchmaking overtures. So Romulus and his gang resorted to subterfuge. They planned a big festival and invited their neighbors, among them the inhabitants of Crustumerium, who may or may not have been Sabines. Drawn by the tales of the marvels of the city, they came to Rome for the day. Once everyone was distracted by the festivities the Roman men swept in to abduct the young women and drive out the families. The distraught victims were eventually reconciled to their fate with promises of marriage and husbandly devotion. However, the neighboring settlements, including a Sabine contingent, launched a series of attacks on Rome to regain their daughters. In one of these the men of Crustumerium, acting on their own, were defeated. The Sabine forces were able to enter Rome, and were fighting a pitched battle between the Palatine and Capitoline Hills when the kidnapped women, now Roman wives and mothers, stood between their husbands on one side and their fathers on the other and insisted on an end to the hostilities. From this pact arose the population of Rome. Roman settlers moved into the desirable fertile land of Crustumerium, while the families of Crustumerium moved into Rome to be with their daughters. Or so goes the Roman version of "The Rape of the Sabine Women."

Crustumerium was already in ruins, a lost city, when another epochal event transpired in the valley below it. On the flatland of Marcigliana, where the Allia River (a ditch now known as the Fosso della Bettina), enters the Tiber, the Battle of Allia took place on July 18, 390 BC. The Senone Gauls (the Latin name Gaul comes from a Greek word meaning salt; the Greeks called them Keltoi, or Celts) had descended from the North, looking for land to settle on near the Etruscan city of Clusium (Chiusi). The Etruscans called upon the Romans to judicate the matter. When the Roman ambassadors violated international law by taking up arms with the Etruscans, the Gauls marched on Rome. The Roman and Gallic armies met at the Allia. Accounts vary widely as to the size of these armies, whether one or the other was outnumbered, but the outcome was devastatingly clear. The Romans were routed; some fled to the nearby Etruscan town of Veii, many drowned trying to swim across the Tiber weighed down by their armour, and a handful made it back to Rome. From there they and the rest of the Roman populace escaped as best they could. The city gates were left open and the next day the Gauls entered Rome unopposed. They burned and sacked the city, departing only when the Romans paid them a large sum of gold. The Senone Gauls returned along the Via Salaria and made their home on the Adriatic Coast, as northern neighbors of the Piceni; their presence is still remembered in the name of the town of Senigallia.

None of this history is visible to the casual eye. The roadside is cluttered with shabby gas stations, garden supply lots, punctuated with new office buildings and supermarkets; prosperity marked by the towering presence of construction cranes. Travelling in packs, the cars press close, bumper to bumper, using the center line as a third lane. A double row of plane trees, which restricts the width of the road, recalls a slower era. Every so often, at a discreet pull-over on the grassy narrow shoulder, a scantily dressed woman waits for customers.

After Settebagni, the landscape opens up, the wide green fields dotted with red poppies, farmhouses shaded by umbrella pines, greygreen olive trees rising up the gentle hillsides. In spring, the wildflowers bloom on the banks of the two-lane road, white and purple Dutch irises and bright yellow broom. At Monterotundo the traffic crawls through town past new apartment blocks and a beauty parlor advertising "Tattoo/Piercing." Brand new suburban villas follow a rosy stucco tavern in decay. Heavy purple wisteria frames the doorways of shops and houses, cactuses grow in gardens.

The Tiber and the AI superhighway veer off to the north while the Via Salaria turns east towards Rieti. Suddenly the traffic thins. The road rises through olive groves and vineyards, heading for the high, bare slopes. The view opens up across the fertile valley to a fortress town on a hilltop, and then far ahead the snowcapped Apennines. For years, a series of little billboards for Monini olive oil, depicting a sturdy man's hand crushing a fistful of olives, dotted the upper fields, but they have been replaced. Just to the north lies the Abbey of Farfa, founded in the mid-sixth century, whose power extended throughout central Italy for over a thousand years. At San Giovanni Reatino laundry lines hang on medieval stone walls.

The Sabine capitol Rieti sits in a basin on the Velino River, ringed by mountains. Giuseppe Garibaldi and his wife Anita were reunited here in early spring 1849; on April 25 Garibaldi and his Red Shirts Brigade descended on Rome to defend the newly declared Republic.

Margaret Fuller, the Cambridge transcendentalist and feminist intellectual, gave birth to her only child here on September 5, 1848. The father was the Marchese Giovanni Ossoli, an officer in the Roman Civic Guard. The couple wanted to conceal the existence of their baby, presumably conceived before their secret marriage; Rieti was far enough away from Rome, but not too far. Fuller enjoyed the picturesque setting, and the delicious and inexpensive figs, olives, almonds, peaches, grapes, and salads, but she mistrusted the locals. The boy was baptized on November 5, and two days later his parents went back to Rome, leaving little Angelino behind with a wet nurse. Fuller was the only American journalist in Rome reporting on the French siege of the city for Horace Greely's newspaper, the *New York Daily Tribune*. When the Republic fell, Fuller described Garibaldi, Anita, and 4,000 volunteers retreating from Rome on July 2, 1849; the French entered the city on July 3. On July 12, Fuller and Ossoli left by carriage for Rieti, no doubt on the Via Salaria. They found Angelino sick and weak; his wet nurse had saved her milk for her own baby and fed Angelino only wine and bread. By the end of August the baby was well enough to leave Rieti for Perugia. In 1850, returning to America, the little family drowned in a shipwreck off of Fire Island, NY. Angelino's body was retrieved, but not his parents; nor did Fuller's friends, including Henry David Thoreau, ever find the manuscript of her *History of the Italian Revolutions*.

One year, we decided to spend a few days in Rieti instead of just circling around it on our way to and from Fiumicino airport. The first thing we did was sign up for Rita Giovannelli's "Rieti Underground." She is a local guide and writer, and her tour provides a great experience of Rieti's peculiar history.

Much of the Rieti basin was once a marshy lake, prone to the flooding of the Velino River and to outbreaks of fever, perhaps malaria. The walled city was perched on a vulnerable hillock in the middle, with a long Roman bridge carrying the Via Salaria above streams and bogs up into town center. In 271 BC the Romans decided to improve the situation by cutting a channel which diverted the excess water into the Nera River valley, creating the Cascate delle Marmore, the tallest man-made waterfall in the world. The swamps were drained and Rieti thrived on the exceptionally fertile farmland. But after the fall of the Roman Empire the drainage system silted up and the floods returned. Rita points out metal rings at doorframes along a main street, where barges tied up to unload supplies on thoroughfares turned seasonally into waterways, the Venice of central Italy. Not until 1601 was the drainage system successfully reopened, the water controlled and redirected. Rieti still supplies Rome with untreated mountain drinking water; Romans in our tour group express their gratitude. The Cascate delle Marmore are now turned off and on, alternating between hydroelectric power plant and tourist destination.

The Roman bridge was used into the early 20th century, and blocks of it remain visible in the river next to the modern replacement. The first new bridge was completed in 1936 but was bombed by the retreating German army in 1944. Turning down a side street, Rita takes us through a door in a massive stone wall and down into a labyrinth of vaulted chambers. Once these spaces had been open alcoves under the ancient viaduct, where tradespeople set up shops and storehouses. At the end of the 16th century, the town government decided that the area had become too dangerous—the hangout of robbers and murderers—so they walled up the arched openings. Renaissance palaces were built on top of the Roman level, with access into the caverns below. In one place, a trapdoor opened so they could throw grapes down into vats to be crushed. Rita makes a final dramatic presentation of children's shoes left behind when the space was used as an air-raid shelter during WWII. We climb up a stone staircase and emerge dazzled into a sunny palace courtyard.

Nearby, in the Piazza San Rufo, a low circular stone monument marks the geographical center, the "bellybutton," of Italy. Further along the Via San Rufo stands the house where St. Francis visited an Arab doctor and heard an angel playing the lute to soothe his pain. The Sacred Valley of Rieti hosts a nest of St. Francis sites, connected by the 80 km/50 mi Cammino di Francesco. The saint's first trip here was in 1208, when he surmounted a crisis of faith at Poggio Bustone. He returned many times, establishing five Franciscan monasteries, four of which survive, and many local miracles are attributed to him. In Grecchio, he set up the first living crèche, which is re-created every Christmas. In September 1225, he was persuaded to come to Rieti to be treated by the pope's physicians for his painful and worsening eye problems. When their treatments failed, he was taken to the nearby hermitage of Fonte Colombo where they cauterized his temples with red-hot irons, which also did not seem to help. Neither did piercing his ears with hot pokers at La Foresta. St. Francis left Rieti in April 1226, returning to Porziuncola near Assisi, where he died on October 3.

The old Via Salaria winds through Rieti, past the third century AD Roman arch; the present road goes into a long tunnel and emerges on the further, harsher side. Forested slopes rise above the lush valley; on a hilltop a cluster of medieval buildings surround the church tower.

At Caporio di Cittaducale, on the left, a roadside café serves as a stop for the Rome-Ascoli Piceno bus. For generations, the Cameli (now "Start") line carried Ascolanis to the Holy City to see the pope, to look for work, and to emigrate to America. The bar is suddenly crowded with passengers knocking back espressos, fresh-squeezed blood orange juice, ordering one of the many kinds of tramezzini sandwiches or porchetta panini. The now refilled bus departs and the 94-year-old retired plumber resumes his daily bantering with the friendly woman behind the counter. Every April when we stop there on our drive in from Fiumicino, she says, "Ah, the *rondini* (swallows) are back, it must be spring!" with a kiss on each cheek.

At Terme di Cotilia, a strip of porchetta stands line the right side; the tempting smell of the roast pork mixes with the sulpherous fumes of the waters in the bright blue pools on the left. Once sacred to the Sabine goddess Vacuna, pilgrims would come to consult the oracle at these abundant natural springs. The Romans built lavish baths on the site and there is still a thermal spa center offering a host of cures and treatments.

According to church legend, St. Vittorino was martyred here in AD 96. The first bishop of nearby Amiterno, he was hung upside down over the sulpherous water for three days, until he died of the poisonous fumes. The town between Caporio and Terme di Cotilia is named after him, and there is a church dedicated to him on the Via Salaria. On the site of a small shrine, the more imposing edifice was constructed in 1613. Almost immediately it began to disappear into a sinkhole, a geological feature the plain of San Vittorino is known for. A spring now pours from inside the half-drowned, overgrown church; the water is said to have healthful, even miraculous, powers.

Following the Velino River valley, the Via Salaria makes its way through little towns; the stone storefronts press close, the fortress watchtowers rise above. Olive groves spread over the rippling hills; an old woman in black skirt and cardigan turns over the soil in her kitchen garden with a hoe. Near Castel Sant'Angelo, archeologists identify the Lago Paterno with the *Lacus Cutiliae*, sacred to Vacuna. Pliny and other ancient historians describe this lake as having a floating island also known as the bellybutton of Italy. According to legend, the Sabine rites of *Ver Sacrum* (Sacred Spring) which were practiced here gave rise to many of the Italian peoples, including the Piceni. Thus, the Sabine tribe was considered the Mother of Italy.

At Antrodoco, the riverbed is mostly pebbles and weeds, with only a trickle of water down the middle, but the town follows its wide, sinuous curves. A plaque commemorates the first battle of the Italian Risorgimento March 7–9, 1821. Called Interocrium by the Romans, this is in fact a major intersection because here the Via Salaria splits in two. One branch, at various times in its history called the Via Caecilia, the Via Sabina, and sometimes the Via Salaria, goes east through the Gole di Antrodoco, the gorges of the Vomano River, towards L'Aquila in Abruzzo—Samnite territory. The other branch, the ancient and present day Via Salaria, turns sharply north.

The Velino River has sliced deep into the limestone mountain. Stone and stucco houses cling to the left side of the road, their doors one step from the white borderline; the churches are below, in the valley. This is where winter lingers, leaving behind the temperate climate of the softer western slopes. The geological layers are laid bare, slabs of rock angling sharply skywards, carrying with them bands of poplar, beech, and pine trees.

A series of tunnels cuts through this difficult terrain, emerging onto a wide plateau. Dandelions brighten the pale green fields. Pastures hold cows, sheep, goats, horses. Lumber is stacked by the farmhouses, piles of logs lie at the mouths of gullies; the forests are young, planted and harvested. In August 2009, archaeologists announced that they had found the remains of the Roman town of Falacrinae and the villa of the Roman Emperor Vespasian near the town of Cittareale, on the north side of the Via Salaria. Vespasian is remembered not only for invading Britain and putting down the Jewish Revolt in Judea (his son Titus destroyed the Second Temple), but for using the spoils of war and graft to build the Colosseum and the Galleria del Furlo, a tunnel used by the Via Flaminia on the northern reaches of *Terra Picena*. According to Suetonius in his *De Vita Caesarum*, Vespasian died here in AD 79. "During his ninth consulship Vespasian visited Campania, and caught a slight fever. He hurried back to Rome, then went on to Cutilae and his summer retreat near Reate, where he made things worse by bathing in cold water and getting a stomach chill. Yet he carried on with his imperial duties as usual, and even received deputations at his bedside; until he almost fainted after a sudden violent bout of diarrhea, struggled to rise, muttering that an Emperor ought to die on his feet, and collapsed in the arms of the attendants who went to his rescue" (Suetonius, p. 251). His son Titus, who had succeeded him as emperor, died in the same place as his father in AD 81. The current excavations have revealed a 15,000 sq.m /161,459 sq.ft first century villa with a multicolored mosaic floor made from North African marbles. The nearby site of Falacrinae, a long lost Roman town, has been identified by an inscription celebrating the participation of a resident of Falacrinae in the Social War of 91–88 BC.

An aboveground cemetery contained within its alcoved walls is silhouetted against the skyline of snow-covered peaks. A plain stone church with a rectangular bell tower sits alone on the shore of the man-made reservoir, the Lago di Scandarello.

The Velino has turned aside and the Tronto, here a lively brook, comes down through Amatrice, a quiet place perhaps best known for spaghetti *all'Amatriciana* made with the local *guanciale* (pig jowl) and pecorino cheese. It was also the birthplace of Renaissance painter, sculptor, and architect Cola Filotesio, known as Cola dell'Amatrice; many of the Renaissance buildings in Ascoli Piceno bear his mark. He not only grew up here, but after the Spaniards destroyed Amatrice in 1529, he planned the town that rose from the ruins. Unfortunately, at one point while living in Ascoli he had to flee for political reasons. He and his wife were being pursued by soldiers who were perhaps mainly interested in the beautiful young woman. To save her honor and Cola's life, she threw herself off a cliff; according to one version, into the Chiaro stream bed near the city gates of Ascoli. The tragedy of his wife's death clouded the rest of Cola dell'Amatrice's life.

We once had the pleasure of taking part in a festival in Amatrice—a donkey race. Each local township sponsored a donkey named after their mayor, and the goal was to come in last. Before the race each group paraded down the main street in traditional garb; everybody else in luxurious Renaissance court dress, our crew from Montegallo wearing the coarse garments and high boots of brigands. This splendid town center was destroyed by the earthquakes of 2016–17.

Having crossed the watershed between the Tyrrhenian and Adriatic Seas, the Via Salaria follows the Tronto down the steep eastern side of the Apennines. By the time it passes Accumoli, the mimosa and forsythia are in full bloom. Every so often, clusters of pre-fab structures and modular units sadly provide temporary shelter to the inhabitants and businesses of earthquake damaged towns like Grisciano and Pescara del Tronto. Grisciano is the namesake of pasta *alla Griscia/Gricia*, which is basically what *all'Amatriciàna* was before tomatoes arrived from the Americas.

Then, like an illustration of a fairytale, the fortress of Arquata looms above. The fortification of this hill and the construction of the castle were begun sometime in the 11th–12th centuries. The Neapolitan Queen Giovanna II D'Angio lived here from 1420–1435. Rumor has it that her ghost still prowls the castle's rooms. (At her castle in Naples she was said to choose her lovers from amongst her soldiers, and then dispose of them by way of a trapdoor that led to caverns teeming with hungry crocodiles.) The fortress dominates this vital mountain pass, the intersection of four modern regions—Lazio, Umbria, Abruzzo, and Le Marche—and traditionally served as border guard and tollhouse. Many Marchegiani friends and relatives have told us that the sight of this landmark on their drive back from Rome tells them they're almost home.

At Trisungo, in Le Marche, the Rome-bound bus waits at the Bar Bleu to pick up connecting passengers. Opposite the bar a small road goes up the hill beside Arquata, skirting the edge of the fortress town itself, on its way to our Montegallo, to Castelluccio di Norcia, up through the Sibillini Mountains. This is one of the north-south routes, ancient tracks of the prehistoric Apennine culture, which at one time stretched the length of Italy. These networks of pastoral migrations, trade routes, seasonal harvesting, and pilgrimages were of prime importance in the land of Piceno, perhaps even more so than the road to Rome. A branch of the Via Salaria, called the Salaria Gallica, led from here through Amandola, Urbs Salvia, Jesi, to the coast near Senigallia.

Descending from Arquata, the Tronto has carved a deep, harsh, serpentine gorge, the sandstone walls pitted with strange circular holes and caves, and the village of Favalanciata tucked into the face. Seeing this stretch it is not so surprising that parts of the Via Salaria were abandoned after the fall of the Roman Empire. In this region of earthquakes and landslides, heavily eroded by rain and rivers, regular maintenance was a necessity. The Romans were famous for their roadbuilding technology, and when their state control of the area was finally destroyed by the Goths, the consular road fell into ruins as well. The paving stones and mile markers were dragged off for other uses. It is said that from the ninth until the 19th century there was no direct route from Antrodoco to Ascoli. An 18th century traveler who wanted to go from Perugia, on the eastern side of the mountains in Umbria, to Ascoli Piceno, would go south by way of Rieti, L'Aquila, and north along the coast. Natural disasters large and small still close the road with a certain frequency.

The town of Quintodecimo takes its name from a Roman milestone marking fifteen miles to Ascoli; the stone itself was repurposed and built into a local dwelling. Along this narrow stretch, on the morning of July 11, 1809, a troop of the occupying French forces marched from Ascoli towards Arquata, searching for a band of brigands they had been informed was in the area. It was, however, a trap. The brigands and the mountaineers of Montegallo were eager to avenge the maltreatment they had suffered at the hands of the French, which included mass arrests and executions. The Napoleonic Kingdom of Italy had just annexed the Papal States and the locals preferred the pope. As the French soldiers and some Ascoli officials advanced along the Via Salaria, they found the road blocked and on the heights above them were armed rebels. When they tried to retreat the road was closed behind them. The brigands held the right bank of the Tronto, the mountaineers the left; more than a hundred of the trapped men were slaughtered.

Roman soldiers bathed in the sulpherous hot springs of Aquasanta Terme. At the dark bottom of the ravine cut by the Tronto River, these strangely bright bluegreen waters pour out of the rocks, a warm, foul-smelling mist rising out of the mineral encrusted grottos. The modern spa is closed for renovations; workmen are plastering and painting the low-lying buildings, which resemble an abandoned set for Fellini's 8½. You can take a glorious dip for free in the recently established riverside park, Lu Vurghe.

A travertine bench outside the Bar dello Sport is remembered as the spot where Garibaldi smoked a cigar in 1849. Aquasanta Terme is a center of travertine quarries, still in operation. Ascoli Piceno is known as "the city of travertine," since so many of its buildings were built with this stone, and polished slabs of it pave the luminous Piazza del Popolo.

The new road floats above the valley, soaring around the curves of the mountains. Down below, the old road stays close to the river. Along it you can see the former posthouses, the mileage markers, the little stone towns that were once major crossroads. Slabs of travertine are stacked in several stone yards, and under the elevated highway is a quarry, slicing the rock from the back of the pit. Looking up you can see another quarry at the top of the mountain, hollowing out the peak while leaving a crowning wall to face the unsuspecting traveler. At Garrafo and Ponte d'Arli stand single arch Roman bridges, and the area's only remaining water-powered gristmill operates nearby.

At the Fluvione River another important route heads north into the mountains, also a tributary of the Salaria Gallica. At this crossroads, Taverna Piccinini, Piceni remains have been unearthed. Later, the Romans made it a way station for changing horses; their single arched bridge still crosses the Tronto. Nearby Mozzano has a natural salt spring, recognizable by a patch of discolored rocks on the riverbank. Just a trickle now, but women of previous generations would collect this water and boil it down for the salt.

On the left is a massive plane tree, its trunk empty and twisted, called the *Albero del Piccioni*. Local folklore insists that this tree was a hideout for the brigand Giovanni Piccioni and his men, used to ambush wayfarers in the mid-19th century. Historically, Piccioni was no highwayman but a reactionary resistance leader fighting against the new Republic. The only anecdote which links this tree with these "brigands" concerns a battle which took place near it in 1849. During the fight, the head brigand's horse was slashed across the neck with a saber. Seeing the horse vomiting blood, one of the Republican soldiers yelled, "The Piccioni's horse is shooting flames from its mouth!" The Republican forces were thrown into a panic as this cry spread; they dropped their arms and fled. In fact this plane tree was first mentioned in 1109, as a boundary marker, and took its name from the owner of the property, the noble Piccione Parisani.

In the valley below is a big electrical power plant, now outfitted with solar panels. The Romans quarried travertine here and presumably brought it down the Via Salaria to build their Ascoli Piceno, of which many remnants remain.

The main road from Rome no longer passes through the center of Ascoli Piceno. Travelers continuing on to the Adriatic coast stay on the *autostrada*, which loops high above the riverbed on the southern edge of the city. The highway is lined with acacia trees blooming with white panicles; it looks down on the many medieval towers, the domed churches, and the rock walls of the Fortezza Pia. The breeze carries the sweet smell of the flowering sambuca bushes and currents of gossamer from the poplar trees, like snow in a shaken paperweight.

From here the distinctive highly defensible placement of the city is clear. Two rivers, the Tronto and the Castellano, tumbling down from their sources in the mountains above Amatrice, come together to create a triangular peninsula, a natural fortress protected on two sides by deeply etched gorges. The Piceni, and later the Romans, reinforced their position with massive city walls on the third side, the approach from the mountains. The Visigoths, led by Alaric in AD 410 and later by Ataulf, seeing this impregnable position, bypassed Ascoli in favor of the easier pickings of Rome. Popular tradition has it that Alaric was put off not just by the sight of the city walls, but by a vision of the headless St. Emidio, patron saint of Ascoli, atop them.

The ancient Via Salaria enters Ascoli Piceno from the mountain side, through the Porta Romana. Stretches of the Roman wall remain; there are also several massive blocks of sandstone, remnants of the earlier Piceno wall. Ascoli was a highly developed city long before the Romans conquered it and superimposed their classic urban grid. The Augustan Age *decumus maximus*, the principal east/west street, followed the present day Corso Mazzini. However, the Via Angelini—Via XX Settembre—Corso Vittorio Emanuele was perhaps the older, equally important road, judging by the location of the Roman theater and other significant ruins. Given the role played by the theater in the Ascoli uprising during the Social War (90–89 BC), it is thought that this was the heart of the Piceno city.

It is unclear which route the oldest Via Salaria followed, through the Piazza del Popolo or through the Piazza Arringo, both now closed to traffic. It may have turned north and crossed the Tronto at the Porta Solestà. The Roman bridge is still there, beneath the modern road surface. It is possible to go inside this structure, into the void where defective concrete, supplied by a contractor two thousand years ago, crumbled. The Italian countryside is littered with massive blocks of Roman concrete that survived the demolition of the edifices they supported; in this unique case, it was the concrete that failed. In the Fascist 1930s the debris was removed, and the bridge rebuilt with a new road suspended over the old paving stones. Mariolina Massignani, an Ascolana historian, took schoolchildren through this passageway on fieldtrips, exhorting them, "Remember this, this is your history, don't let anyone take it away from you!" (She and her husband Carlo Cappelli led the effort to open up this tunnel.) This possible branch of the Salaria then follows the northern bank of the Tronto, past an Iron Age necropolis and the early Christian tombs at Sant'Emidio alle Grotte.

If the Via Salaria followed either the Roman *decumanus maximus*, or the main east/west street of the Piceni, it would have crossed the Castellano River at the Ponte di Cecco. In the 14th century, Cecco d'Ascoli was said to have created his bridge in one night with the aid of the Devil; in fact it was built with the local travertine in the first century AD. During WWII, the Germans bombed it to rubble as they retreated up the Italian boot, but it has been rebuilt stone by stone. Too narrow for cars, it serves as a haunt for local teenagers. This route continues to the Abruzzo side of the Tronto, past the site of WWII partisan resistance at the Via Erasmo Mari barracks. After around 1400, the Via Salaria used a new bridge over the Castellano at Porta Maggiore, at the end of Via Vitt. Emanuele. The Ponte Maggiore was also destroyed and rebuilt after WWII. This major thoroughfare goes past the train station and out of historic Ascoli, crosses the Tronto and as the Via Salaria Inferiore rejoins the other possible Via Salaria, the Via delle Zeppelle, heading into the modern district of Monticelli.

Developed in the early 1980s, this is an unattractive stretch of road interrupted by dangerous intersections. On both sides are blocks of concrete apartment buildings as high as fifteen stories, public housing set in parking lots with minimal landscaping. Many of the working class people who live here (including some of our relatives) are the children of *contadini* from the surrounding mountains. In many cases the families still own the ancestral property and farm it in the summer. They certainly know what good food and wine is. The Mondo Pizza, facing one of these parking lots, is better (and cheaper) than any of our so-called gourmet pizzerias. The MaxiTigre supermarket, crowded with housewives, could compete with any Whole Foods in the huge selection of locally made salamis and pecorino cheeses, the bundles of all sorts of fresh bitter greens, the citrus from Sicily, the wine from nearby vineyards whose slopes were cultivated since before the Romans took them over.

Beyond Ascoli, today's Via Salaria follows the Tronto down to the Adriatic. The river itself is barely present, its water dammed, diverted, controlled—a trickle threading down the valley. But the broad alluvial plain is still there. Now that disastrous flooding is no longer feared (though floods do happen), it is being filled in with factories, warehouses, shopping centers. The *autostrada* drives straight towards the sea while the Via Salaria meanders along the north bank, through modern town centers, under double rows of plane trees. In one nondescript stretch of shops a building site is fenced off. Construction has been delayed by the discovery of seventy-six Roman graves from the second–third centuries AD. The rectangular excavations are visible through the chain link; the bones, the swords, the jewelry, have been removed for further study. A year later the metal skeleton of a new building rises on the spot. Nearby, at Colle Vaccaro, the expansion of a school unearthed a Piceni necropolis, a treasure trove of grave goods from the sixth century BC; our cousin Anna Maria Ferri was involved in the excavation. One warm spring day we meet her at the Archaeological Museum in Ascoli Piceno, where she was working. Dressed in tight jeans and a black sleeveless T-shirt with a sequined butterfly on it, her dark curls flying, Anna takes us to an exhibit of a little girl dug up here. Hovering over the panel of clay, Anna points out part of the cranium. Judging by the baby teeth she was about six years old. The corpse is bedecked with jewelry; earrings, a *torque* necklace, a bronze spiral bracelet, metal studs, rings still circling her finger bones. Anna also shows us the partial remains of a Piceno baby, a blob of clay wrapped in plastic inside a wooden box a little larger than the one that Christmas clementines come in. Under Anna's guidance, we could make out bits of bone and the curve of a *fibula* pin.

The undulating floodplain stretches out towards the mountains on the other side of the Tronto. Who knows what these fields cover? How many more bodies lie under the surrounding buildings, under the present day road, and beyond?

Vineyards climb the slopes almost to the doors of 18th and 19th century villas. In one honey-colored enclave of stone farm buildings, now converted to a B&B, a peacock perched on a garden shed spreads his magnificent fan. These country homes belonged to patrician Ascolanis, who would come to supervise the harvest. Their family names, redolent of the Guelph/Ghibelline strife of the Middle Ages, now grace the labels of Rosso Piceno and Falerio wines.

Higher up, on the sharply fluted ridges on both sides of the valley, the ever-present hilltop fortress towns keep watch; to the north, Appignano, Spinetoli, Monsampolo, Montepradone, Aquaviva; to the south, Folignano, Maltignano, Ancarano, Controguerra, Colonnella. The Tronto serves as the boundary between the modern regions of Le Marche and Abruzzo, as earlier it divided the Papal States from the Bourbon Kingdom of Naples, and before that the Romans chose it as the southern border of Picenum. The ancient land of the Piceni however included these southern hills, and the river valleys beyond, extending towards Teramo, containing the Neolithic settlement of Ripoli, the fortress of Civitella del Tronto, and the massive Piceni necropolis at Campovalano.

The Tronto and the Via Salaria reach the Adriatic Sea at Porto d'Ascoli, the Roman Castrum Truentum, in a tangle of ramps serving the *autostrada* and the coastal *superstrada* toll road, about 210 km/130 mi from Rome. Here was the last Italian outpost of the Liburni pirates, who navigated these waters nine centuries before Christ. Just to the north is San Benedetto del Tronto, a palm-lined resort where the Miss Italia pageant was formerly held, and Cupra Marittima, site of a shrine to the pre-Roman goddess Cupra. Prehistoric amber merchants, Mycenaean adventurers, Roman navies, and Saracen invaders used these ports. Now the long straight coastline from Ancona to Pescara is an almost unbroken stretch of hotels, seafood restaurants, beaches covered with umbrellas for rent, little towns that fill up with vacationers every August, their places reserved a year in advance. Across the water, just out of sight beyond the blue gray mist, is the Dalmatian shore, ex-Yugoslavia, the old Ottoman Empire. The Adriatic Sea flows into the Ionian Sea through narrow Strait of Otranto at the heel of the boot. Here is Greece, with the Aegean just around the corner, and then the Mediterranean, the marine highway leading to Troy, to the Levant, to Egypt, Carthage, Sicily, Spain...

"Charmed magic casements, opening on the foam
Of perilous seas, in faery lands forlorn."
—*Ode to a Nightingale*, John Keats, 1819

Sibillini Mountains seen from Colle Turano (Amandola)

⚬⚬⚬ *2* ⚬⚬⚬

Terra Picena: The Lay of the Land

The jagged Sibillini Mountains, split by rivers racing towards the Adriatic Sea, loom large over terraced hillsides and broad farmlands. Yet these mountains, and the whole Apennine range, and all of Italy, were once at the bottom of the sea. This primordial ocean, called Tethys, separated the continents of Laurasia, to the north, and Gondwana, to the south. Its oldest form, Paleotethys, was created in the Paleozoic Era, about 320 million years ago. The collision and interaction of the Eurasian and African-Arabian continental plates eliminated this first body of water; subsequently the Neotethys Sea began forming in the early Mesozoic Era, about 251 million years ago. Continuous tectonic movement stretching over tens of millions of years pushed up the sedimentary rock that had

Monte Vettore

formed on the seabed, creating enormous mountains, as high as the Himalayas. Eons passed, and these peaks were worn down by erosion, shattered by earthquakes. The Apennines, the youngest mountain chain in Europe, are about 1.6 million years old and about 1,400 km/870 mi long. The western slope down to the Tyrrhenian Sea is softer, more gradual, than the steep eastern descent to the Adriatic; the peninsula is less than 240 km/150 mi from coast to coast—as the crow flies, to be sure. Sharp slabs of rock, mostly sandstones, limestones, and clays, have been pushed skywards at acute angles by the pressure of the colliding tectonic plates. This phenomenon was noted by, among many others, Ovid, Boccaccio, and Leonardo da Vinci, who first used the term "folding" to describe rock formation. Fossilized shells, including ammonites, have been found high up on the mountainsides and gathered by the bucketful. Giovanni Arduino (1714–1795), often called the father of modern geology, was inspired by these traces of earlier life that surrounded him in the hills of central Italy.

Monte Vettore (2,476 m/8,123 ft) is the highest peak in the Sibillini Mountains and the second highest in the Apennines; the highest is Corno Grande (2,912 m/9,553 ft), in the Gran Sasso Massif in nearby Abruzzo. A gigantic block of limestone, Mt. Vettore is snowcapped much of the year. Close to the summit lies the glacial Lago di Pilato, the only natural lake in Le Marche, one of the few alpine type lakes in the Apennines. The neighboring Monte della Sibilla (2,175 m/7,136 ft) has a striking knife-edge that runs up to its crowned peak. At the bottom of the cliffs between them lies the Gola del Infernaccio, a dramatic gorge cut through this rock by the Tenna River on its way down to the Adriatic. A dozen or more similar rivers run virtually perpendicular from the mountains to the sea, virtually parallel to each other ("like the teeth of a comb" is the common description), neatly dividing the territory into even smaller parcels. In northern-most Le Marche the Foglia River reaches the sea at Pesaro. Below it the Roman Via Flaminia follows the course of the Metauro down to Fano. The Esino River above Ancona, historically considered by many the northern boundary of the *Terra Picena*, is 45 km/23 mi long, while to the south the Tronto is the longest at 115 km/71.5 mi. Between them run the Musone, the Potenza, the Chienti, the Aso, and more, each with a mouth on the Adriatic, and to the south the Vibrata and the Salinello in Abruzzo. These river valleys, isolated from each other by imposing ribs of rock, determined in many ways the future development of Piceno.

The ongoing collision of the Eurasian and African plates has caused frequent earthquakes, transforming the landscape; more than 90 percent of the Marchigiano territory is at a constant seismic risk. Over the millennia they have been seen as the expression of divine will, for example influencing the outcome of the decisive battle between the Piceni and the Romans in 268 BC. The patron saint of Ascoli Piceno is St. Emidio, protector in case of earthquakes. The 1997 Colfiorito earthquake did tremendous damage to the area around Camerino and of course to the Basilica of St. Francis in Assisi, Umbria. The devastating 2016/17 earthquakes are a recurring theme in this book.

Much of the *Terra Picena* is what is called karst topography. It is largely composed of limestone, derived from layers upon layers upon layers of compressed shells. Acidic groundwater erodes it, forming deep fissures, caves, tunnels, hot springs and sinkholes. This creates the setting for local legends of grottos inhabited by supernatural beings, and lakes that appear and disappear overnight. On the Umbrian side of the range, the Piano Grande of Castelluccio is a vast empty lake basin, drained by underground fissures, filled only with brilliant flowers every spring.

The Frassassi cave complex, tunneled out by the Sentino River near Genga and still not fully explored, is among the most extensive in Europe. The most famous of the Frasassi caves was only discovered in 1971 when three members of a spelunking club from Ancona dropped into the enormous Grotta Grande del Vento/Great Cave of the Wind. Explorations of this karstic system had begun in 1948, but with this discovery of one of the largest underground caverns in the world, a new phase was launched. Since 1974 it has become a major tourist attraction; the parking lot, filled with tour buses in the summer, is lined with souvenir and snack stands. A guided tour takes you deep into the mountain, where daylight has never penetrated and the temperature is a constant 14 C/57 F. Within vast voids, colored spotlights illuminate stalactites said to resemble the Madonna and other figures; boardwalks zig-zag over pools of glowing water. The lightshow was created by Carlo Cesarini da Senigallia, a TV set designer with local roots, famous for his work on Italian variety shows like *Canzonissimma*. In 1987, Maurizio Montalbini, also from Senigallia, set a world record for complete isolation by spending 210 days alone in one of the untouristed sections of Frasassi.

When you emerge you can't help but see the surrounding mountains as mere shells containing boundless caverns, some of which have been frequented by humans since the dawn of our existence, some of which have yet to be discovered. This sense, of another world of tortuous passageways and magnificent spaces concealed under the visible mantle of pastures and vineyards, informs many

of the legends of the region. As a practical example, the Gran Sasso National Laboratory in nearby Abruzzo is the world's largest underground research center, built almost a mile/1,400 m below the surface.

Calanchi of Castignano

Calanchi, or elephant's feet, are a dramatic feature of the landscape. In the flanks of the outcroppings of relatively soft rock, rain has carved deep gullies, leaving ribs like the toes of the largest beast known. This form of erosion, exacerbated by deforestation, is similar to the badlands of the American West. Here however the cliffs are topped by brick-walled medieval fortresses, or, in the case of Offida, by the Santa Maria della Rocca, a magnificent Romanesque/Gothic church built in 1330.

Travertine, extensively quarried and used, is the only local rock that was not directly created in the ancient seabed. It is formed where natural springs rich in carbon dioxide percolate through the limestone, dissolving it. When this mineral laden water comes to the surface the carbon dioxide is released and the calcium carbonate recrystallizes into travertine. It is a hard durable stone, in contrast to the widely used sandstone tufo. However, tufo has its own special characteristic; it is softest when initially quarried, and then hardens after being exposed to air, for example, after being carved into decorative doorframes.

Unlike other parts of Italy, there are no volcanos here. The area has however been affected by massive volcanic eruptions around Naples, and the blankets of ash created by them.

The *Terra Picena* ends at the coast of the Adriatic. This shore has changed significantly over time; the Adriatic Sea was at one time the Great Adriatic Plain, dry land as far south as the Gargano promontory. With

Portonovo

the alternating Ice Ages and interglacial periods the sea level has risen and fallen, invading and draining the river valleys. Once the coastline was irregular, with many potential harbors, especially in the mouths of the rivers. But gradually these indentations were filled in with sediment washing down from the hills, a process speeded up by deforestation. The Romans harvested the lumber, and then recognized the resulting problems and replanted the slopes. In historic times the one true harbor has been at Ancona, where the rocky Conero peninsula, though reduced by erosion, still forms a sheltering arc. The rest of the coastline runs straight, smooth, and unprotected, down 350 km/218 mi to the Gargano.

The Adriatic Sea is for the most part less than 200 m/660 ft deep, shallower than the Tyrhennian. From Ancona across to Zadar or Split on the Balkan peninsula is less than 240 km/150 mi; further south, at Otranto, the distance to Albania is less than 80 km/50 mi. On a clear day the opposite coast is visible. This long narrow body of water, fed by freshwater Alpine streams from the north, is less salty than the rest of the Mediterranean, and unlike the larger sea it has tides. Since earliest times it has been a source of prodigious amounts of fish. The variations in salinity allow a range of species to find their ideal environment, and the tidal margin between high and low water supports crustaceans and other shellfish.

Le Marche gets the hot *sirocco* wind, which picks up moisture and sand as it blows across the Mediterranean from the deserts of North Africa, and also the *bora* from the northeast, cold and damp from the Balkans and Russia. The Romans noted that the wood from the Adriatic coast was wetter than from the Tyrhennian, less valuable for building.

The mist rolls in from the sea in the afternoons. In Recanati, an inland town with views from the Adriatic to the Sibillini peaks, the poet Giacomo Leopardi (1798–1837) gazed from his window towards his *monti azzurri* and wrote:

"What sweet dreams were inspired in me by the sight
Of that distant sea, those blue mountains…"
—*Le Ricordanze*, vs 21:24

3

The First People

At some point, early humans entered this landscape. The vertical environment, that is, the short distance from sea level to mountaintop, was and is particularly well suited for habitation. It was relatively easy for life forms—flora and fauna—to adapt to the climatic changes brought about by a series of ice ages and interglacial warming periods. When the climate got cold living beings could settle along the more temperate shore. When global warming melted the glaciers, raising the sea levels, flooding the coastal plains and the river valleys, they moved up to the higher cooler slopes. As Secondo Balena says, "…if during glaciations the whole peninsula was a refuge for Europe, this became a refuge within a refuge. A place particularly adapted for living" (*Ascoli nel Piceno*, p. 46).

In Europe the earliest humans, probably of more than one type, date back something like 800,000 years. Our ancestor, *homo heidelbergensis*, appeared about 500,000 years ago (Tattersall, Schwartz, *Extinct Humans*, pp. 165–170). Most of the evidence regarding these early humans consists of their stone tools. Almost every town museum here has some, and the Museo Archeologico Nazionale delle Marche in Ancona has a lot, displayed on the second floor. The oldest ones, dating back to the archaic humans who lived here as much as 350,000 years ago, are tear-shaped hand axes of the Acheulean type. (Tool types were named after the sites where they were first identified—in this case, St. Acheul in France). The heavy stone cores have been chipped away on both sides, producing a double-sided sharp edge. These are the first tools ever made to a standardized pattern, showing premeditation on the part of the maker. They have been found all over Italy; in Le Marche on Mt. Conero at Ancona, in the riverbeds north to south, and especially in the Valle della Vibrata in northern Abruzzo. This type of Paleolithic tool was made for hundreds of thousands of years, with little variation—one archaeologist complains of their "unimaginable monotony" (James Shreeve, *The Neandertal Enigma*, p. 21).

During the Third Ice Age, in the Middle Paleolithic Era, the Neanderthals, a species of humans native to Europe and Eurasia, established themselves here. The museum cases are full of the innovative Mousterian tools associated with them (named after the Le Moustier site in France). Scrapers, blades, razors, spear points, borers, awls, denticulate saw blades; they serve all sorts of purposes. The great technological leap of this era is called the Levallois prepared core technique. A suitable rock was chosen; the glass-like flint found in the Apennines was good because it was brittle and flaked easily. This core was chipped into the desired form and then one heavy blow on the prepared end, perhaps with a wood or bone hammer, and a flake splits off, flat on one side and sharp all the way around. This flake could be used as is, or further worked to perform a specific function. The remaining core would yield further flakes; the earth of Italy is full of them and the debris from preparing the initial core. The tools are surprisingly colorful—bright ivory, or a rich red-brown like toffee or dried blood. After WWII, while rebuilding the Porta Cartara bridge in Ascoli Piceno (bombed by the retreating Germans) two Mousterian stone blades were found in the Castellano River. Did they come from a nearby site, or had they

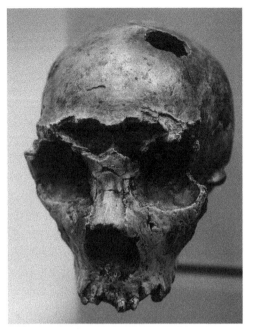

Saccopastore Neanderthal Skull (copy)
National Museum of Natural History,
Washington, DC

been washed downriver from elsewhere? As with so much of Italy, it is not practical to think of digging up part of the modern city, down through Renaissance churches, medieval palaces, Roman ruins, Piceni necropoli, in hopes of locating a seasonal Neanderthal camp.

Italy is rich in Neanderthal sites. More than 350 of them are spread throughout the peninsula, from the seashores to high in the mountains. Some of the most studied ones are south of Rome at Monte Circeo. Actual skeletal remains, sometimes consisting of only one tooth or a fragment of a skull, have been found at thirteen sites in Italy (Kuhn / Bietti, "The Geography of Neandertals and Modern Humans," Peabody Museum Bulletin 8, p. 57). Only France has produced more; the total number of identified Neanderthal individuals worldwide is less than 300. The two Saccopastore skulls found near Rome are dated to 250,000 years ago, the oldest in Europe. In 1993, in Altamura, Apulia, spelunkers found a complete human skeleton embedded in a cavern wall. Now considered to be a Neanderthal, the man had apparently fallen into a karstic shaft and, unable to get out, had starved to death 130,000–170,000 years ago. The femur of a Neanderthal child was found in a rock shelter on Gran Sasso in Abruzzo. The last Italian Neanderthals were perhaps the Uluzzians, named after a site on the Uluzzo Bay on the Ionian Sea where two Neanderthal teeth were found with transitional tools. Uluzzian stone tools have been found in southern Italy, up to the Gargano promontory which was rich in suitable stone, and in Tuscany, but, so far, not in between (Millikin, *The Neanderthals in Italy*, pp. 60, 67).

Not many Neanderthals were alive at any one time, perhaps only a few thousand in all of Italy. They were migratory hunter-gatherer-foragers, following game and other sources of food, apparently moving around in extended family groups of at most forty to sixty adults and children. There are traces of them in all parts of the peninsula, but it cannot be determined which of these were separate groups, which a single group roaming long distances. Some sites contain large quantities of their stone tools, or lots of animal bones that show signs of being broken or scraped by them, but this does not mean that a large population had settled there. It may indicate a spot that was visited year after year, millennium after millennium, where there was a good source of stones, or a watering hole frequented by desirable animals. In some cases floodwaters deposited heaps of debris, washed down through the eons. It is also hard to tell whether sites were used for an extended period of time, or on a regular seasonal basis, or only briefly or sporadically. Wild animals, like hyenas and cave bears, may have lived in places like the Grotta Salomone in Abruzzo between visits by Neanderthals.

Descriptions of the Neanderthal way of life are by necessity an act of imagination. The vast gaps in our knowledge should not be assumed to signify that nothing existed there. Neanderthals apparently used fire, cooked meat, did leatherwork. Analysis of neck and throat bones supports the theory that they could speak (Juan Luis Arsuaga, *The Neanderthal's Necklace*, pp. 258–268). What can ever be known about forms of art, music, culture, spirituality, that leave no permanent record? For instance, does the lack of grave goods mean that the Neanderthals did not deliberately and meaningfully dispose of their dead? A few possible burials have been found, but social rituals performed before tossing the corpse into a crevasse would leave no evidence. What can be known for sure from a collection of stone tools, a wheelbarrow full of fossilized bones, scorched rocks in a cave? Did they sing as they chipped out their stone blades? Did they tell stories around the fire? We will never know how a Neanderthal felt at the sight of the new moon over Mt. Vettore, the stars glittering in an enormous swath above the snowy peaks.

Perhaps with the Neanderthals we begin to see the first traces of human patterns of behavior that continue to this day. Of all the winding pathways, tracks, trails, and roads, including the Via Salaria, that make their way through these mountains and down to the sea, followed through the millennia by hunters and pilgrims, shepherds and farmers, armies and tourists, how many of them were also used by the Neanderthals? Despite earthquakes and erosion, a mountain pass like Colfiorito may remain the best way to cross the range, the Vibrata River valley the best way to the coast. Unlike the territory to the south, Piceno has plentiful sources of water year-round. If Ascoli Piceno was regarded as prime real estate by the Piceni and everybody thereafter, why not by the Neanderthals? The Romans soaked in the hot springs at Aquasanta Terme; maybe the Neanderthals did too—after all, the apes of Hokkaido recognize the pleasures of a warm bath!

The Arrival of Modern Humans

Sometime around 40,000 years ago, modern humans (*homo sapiens*, formerly known as Cro-Magnon) made their way into Italy. They had originated in Africa and probably came by way of the Middle East though some might have crossed the Straits of Gibraltar and traveled along the northern coast of the Mediterranean. They found the Neanderthals already here. Current thought holds that we share a common ancestor (*homo heidelbergensis*), the two branches diverging somewhere around half a million years ago. Neanderthals and modern humans may have co-existed in Italy for at least 4,000–6,000 years, although the technical problems in dating artifacts from that era make it difficult to say in what fashion (Jean-Jacque Hublin, "Modern-Nonmodern Hominid Interactions: A Mediterranean Perspective," Peabody Museum Bulletin 8, p. 171). Some sites may have been used by modern humans in alternation with the Neanderthals, or even at the same time. The imprecise nature of the dating means that they could have been contemporaneous, or separated by thousands of years. The search continues for proof of interbreeding between the two species.

The anatomically modern humans did not represent the invasion of a highly advanced culture. Their tool kit was not significantly different from the Neanderthals', but with time the tools of both groups changed and developed, perhaps inspired by their competition for food and other resources. The later Aurignacian (named for a site in southwestern France) tools, characterized by greater specialization, the use of bone and antlers, and a broader array of sizes and uses and techniques, are associated with modern humans, but some sites have produced these tools with Neanderthal skeletal remains. "Over the long term, the indigenous populations may have had nearly as profound an influence on the new arrivals as newcomers had on them, not so much as a font of fresh ideas but as a competitive stimulant. One could even speculate that the impressive artistic and technological developments of the European Upper Paleolithic may in part be a consequence of the competition between modern humans and indigenous archaic" (Kuhn/Bietti, "The Geography of Neandertals and Modern Humans," Peabody Museum Bulletin 8, p. 72).

For the Neanderthals, central and southern Italy may have served as a *rifugia*, a place where a group continues to exist long after it has disappeared from the rest of its range. These pockets of survival are characterized by favorable physical conditions and by isolation from malignant outside forces. The secret hideouts in the mountains may have been just as appealing to them as to subsequent inhabitants. The Iberian peninsula—and particularly Gibralter—is considered the last holdout of the Neanderthals, but the Uluzzian culture of Italy may well be another. All we have to go on are the tools, which cannot tell us who made them. They held onto this territory for several thousand years after the new people had taken over northern Italy (Kuhn/Bietti, p. 71). A refuge, but not necessarily in isolation or untouched by the invaders. It could have been that the two species of hominids were now inhabiting the same ecological niche, with an increased number of humans vying for the same resources, hunting the same animals, eating the same plants. A slight advantage on one side—greater speed, for example, or a more developed language—or a small disadvantage on the other—perhaps a lower rate of reproduction—could have fatally tipped the balance. A refuge, and maybe also a dead end: for it may have become impossible to leave the peninsula, surrounded on three sides by water and blocked at the top by the new people.

The Neanderthals disappeared from Italy sometime between 30,000 and 25,000 years ago, when northern Europe was covered with glaciers. Italy resembled the Russian steppes, with herds of reindeer, bison, elk, and giant deer. The Neanderthals vanished as the last Ice Age approached its peak, even though they were physically well adapted to the cold, more so than the newcomers. The modern humans must have had other advantages, perhaps their ability to build seasonal shelters (Mussi, *Earliest Italy*, p. 373).

Around 35,000–30,000 years ago, there was an enormous volcanic eruption in the Phlegrean Fields, the largest eruption in the Mediterranean zone in the last 200,000 years. Aside from the massive changes to the terrain around Naples, airborne volcanic debris (Campanian Ignimbrite) spread over about 500 sq. km/200 sq. mi. Beyond that, clouds of ash blanketed a much wider area. Layers of it have been found on the Adriatic side of the Apennines in Abruzzo and Le Marche. In some places in Italy, Aurignacian (Upper Paleolithic) sites were covered, and no subsequent traces of Aurignacian industries were found above the ash layer. "In central Italy, some human groups probably perished, while others were able to flee and resettle elsewhere. Animal life was similarly affected" (Mussi, p. 210).

The small bands of hunter-gathers, who used Aurignacian or Uluzzian tools, must have suffered. There is no archeological record of human settlement in Italy for 1,000 to 5,000 years, the population non-existent or too small to leave any identifiable trace. We speak of 5,000 years as a brief interlude, a minor interruption in the forward march of progress, but it is as long as our entire recorded history.

The first wave of people who reinhabited the Italian peninsula 28,000–25,000 years ago probably came from southeastern France. They brought a new type of tools, the Gravettian, characterized by a wide variety of microliths, very small flint or chert blades. The museum cases in Ancona display heaps of these, like so many disposable razor blades. They also used eyed bone needles, presumably to make clothing. This was the culture of the Laschaux cave paintings of animals like bison, cattle, and deer; the walls of the Chauvet cave in southern France show lions, wooly rhinos, leopards, mammoths, and bears (Tattersall/Schwarz, *Extinct Humans*, p. 236). The oldest cave paintings of this type in Italy are in the Grotta Paglicci at the Gargano peninsula in Apulia, depicting horses and handprints in red ochre. This cave also contained the oldest Aurignacian and Gravettian remains in Italy.

During the Last Glacial Maximum the climate pushed the European humans south, concentrating them in the more habitable regions below the Alps. At the peak of this Ice Age, 18,000 years ago, the Italian peninsula may have been isolated from the rest of the continent by a band of glaciers, the humans on it cut off from the rest of the world.

There is a theory that art and ritual are symbolic responses to stress. When human groups are few and far between, social and territorial markers are not necessary. Loads of stuff are of limited value to hunter-gatherers always on the move; knowledge of routes and survival skills are more important. Competition over territory and resources calls for ways to distinguish between friend and foe, to leave signs of ownership or control. Another source of stress may have been the climate change itself, the alteration of the land and the disappearance of certain animals. It has been noted that cave paintings generally depict animals which were not common (Mussi, p. 367).

The first burials in Italy are dated to around 25,000 years ago; art on a wide scale appears three thousand years later. There is a gap in the record, during the isolation at the height of the Ice Age, and then by 13,000 years ago an exponential increase in the number of sites. Things began to warm up, Italy was no longer closed. Groups of people came in from the north, bringing their technologies and cultural markers. There was a boom in art, personal ornaments, and burial goods. In 1884, a stone was discovered in the Chienti Valley that had been engraved with the figure of a woman. Her breasts and pubic triangle are clearly delineated, and her arms are crossed over her belly; however, this body bears the equine head of what may be the extinct European ass. This enigmatic object, the Pebble of Tolentino, dates back to the Upper Paleolithic, and can be seen in the Ancona Museum (Mussi, p. 340). Hunting and gathering remained the primary mode of subsistence but with the addition of a more sophisticated stone tool kit—hence the name "Neolithic" (New Stone Age).

The Pebble of Tolentino
Museo Archeologico Nazionale delle Marche

With the end of the last Ice Age (12,000–8,000 BC) Italy assumed roughly the shape and climate that it has now. The glaciers melted, raising sea levels, turning the Mediterranean from an inland lake into a sea, flooding the Great Adriatic Plain. As lowlands became open water, as steppes turned to marshes, as prey retreated into the mountains, humans ventured ever higher, following ibex, chamois, and wild boar.

Neolithic Cultures

But another influence was arriving on the southeastern shores. Sometime around 5000 BC settlers came by sea from the Balkans and beyond that, the Middle East, bringing with them a tradition of settled farming. The arrival of these settlers in Apulia did not signal the absolute beginning of agriculture in Italy. The difference was that these new arrivals came equipped with a complete agricultural system with generations of experience behind them. They built huts with stone wall footings, had stone axes with their edges ground smooth, stored seeds, and they came in boats, bringing with them domesticated cattle, sheep, goats and pigs. Most useful from an archeologist's point of view was the development of pottery, whose shards are read like the tea leaves of time (David H. Trump, *Central and Southern Italy Before Rome*, pp. 30–32).

In 1943 during WWII, the RAF was flying photographic missions over the Tavoliere plain near Foggia, inland from the Gargano peninsula. Seen from high up dark circles were visible in the crops where the vegetation had scorched less quickly in the summer heat. The circles turned out to be traces of ditches surrounding a compound of huts. At another nearby site in Passo di Corvo three concentric ditches 3 m/10 ft deep enclose a 250 m x 150 m/800 ft x 500 ft area with a hundred compounds—the largest Neolithic site in Europe. Obsidian knives of almost surgical quality (the edge of an obsidian flake can be a molecule thick) were found indicating trade with the Lipari Islands or Sardinia since obsidian, a volcanic glass, is not found on the Italian mainland. The find of a few shards of their pottery in a cave at Frassasi suggests further trade, perhaps for high quality stone axes; a trek of more than 130 km/80 mi leads to the nearest site where this pottery is commonly found.

Apulia was the first center of this Neolithic culture; the new people may have taken advantage of the Tremiti Islands to hopscotch across the Adriatic. At first these settlers kept a stable frontier zone between themselves and the hunter-gathers to the north, with some sort of trade-exchange-theft taking place across it. Within a few generations, overpopulation and the need for fresh soil due to its depletion from overuse apparently caused waves of migrations and resettlements. It took about 800 years for them to reach the central Adriatic coast. By 7,500 years ago the hunter-gather culture had disappeared (Mussi, p. 374).

With the Neolithic Age comes a greatly increased human footprint on the land. As humans and their animals stayed longer in one place, as the population grew, their refuse piled up. Forests were burnt to clear land for pasture or agriculture. Designated places were established to dispose of the dead. Archaeology depends on the rubbish heaps, the cemeteries, the foundations of houses, the ditches built to pen in animals or to serve as boundaries or lines of defense. Broken bits of pottery come to define whole cultures. Long distance travel or trade is traced through obsidian blades. The bones of the animals cut apart, cooked, and eaten, are examined to determine how many wild species were still being hunted, how many young male sheep were raised solely to provide meat.

Neolithic culture in central Italy was very local. The small self-sustaining villages traded with their closest neighbors, in this way also securing an exchange of mates outside the family circle. Not much in the way of weaponry from this era has been found. Unlike their contemporaries in the Balkans and central Europe, there is no massive evidence of organized religion such as Stonehenge. While domesticated animals and cereal crops were present, many of the older ways of living persisted. The major factor continued to be the environment, the seasonal difference between the seacoast and the nearby mountains. Paleolithic and Mesolithic (the transitional Middle Stone Age) hunters probably followed herds of wild animals from their winter home on the coastal plains to their summer pastures high in the Apennines; Neolithic herders traveled the same route with their domesticated flocks. This rhythm of seasonal pasturage, the *transumanza*, continues up to the present day.

On the southern edge of the *Terra Picena* lies the Valle della Vibrata, the Vibrata River valley. On the hills between the Vibrata and the Tronto Rivers are a series of hilltowns—Tortoreto, Corropoli, Controguerra, Ancarano—and a history of human settlement that goes back to the lower Paleolithic. Acheulean and Mousterian stone tools have been unearthed; no place in Italy is richer in prehistoric remains (Thomas Eric Peet, *The Stone and Bronze Ages in Italy and Sicily*, p. 100). There are those who seek to be the first human ever to set foot someplace, or at least to be the first white man in 700 years, or what-have-you. These places hold the opposite fascination; people have lived here since the earliest days. Nowadays the Valle della Vibrata is filled with ugly, low-lying buildings, the blight of modern human industry—and yet looking down into it you can still see why it has always attracted settlers. The broad fertile plain cradled by the gentle hills, the bright river tumbling down from the snowcapped mountains, give rise to a sense of ease, of comfort, the human scale of having everything you need close at hand. Only later did the increasing threat of invaders, coming up the valley from the sea, drive the inhabitants to build fortified towns on the crests of these hills.

We circle Corropoli, an enticingly compact hilltown, looking for any mention of the archaeological site of Ripoli. Finding nothing we take the highway that follows the valley down to the Adriatic. The tree-lined road, the gaudy stores along it, have a sea-side feel; the air is softer. The Vibrata River is swollen by the recent rains and the melting of the snow higher up, and it surges, tumbles, over its usually dry bed. Antonio M. Radmilli's *Guide to Prehistoric Italy* (1978) says that Ripoli is 3 km/2 mi along the road towards the coastal town of Alba Adriatica, and we have already come that far. The signposts are crowded with the names of auto body shops, olive oil factories, all the small enterprises that now cover the floodplain. Approaching a rotary intersection, about to turn back, suddenly we spot a small brown rectangular sign, with the stylized broken white columns that denotes an archaeological site, and the name Ripoli.

The side road goes off to the right, past one lone newer building on the edge of green fields; an old tumbledown stone farmhouse is set in a hollow on the gentle slope down to the Vibrata. At the bottom of the fields a short classic stretch of country lane shaded by a canopy of pines runs parallel to the river and then turns back to the highway. Is this really the place, this peaceful verdant rectangle, we wonder, and then we see the street sign where this road joins the *autostrada*—Via Radmilli, named for the noted archaeologist who led excavations here in 1960–'65 and 1970–'71.

At a nearby gas station, we ask the woman running the extensive café/bar about the site. "There's nothing there anymore," she says. "They took everything away a long time ago." The older Ripoli finds are in the Ancona museum and in the Pigorini collection in Rome; the most recent are in the regional museum at Chieti.

When Neolithic culture spread northward, it found an ideal setting here. Between 1865 and 1873, Doctor Concezio Rosa excavated fifteen settlements containing 336 hut-foundations (Peet, p. 100). The most extensive Neolithic village was found at Ripoli, which gave its name to a widespread culture characterized by a particular type of pottery, buff ware with black and red geometric designs. The site also contains traces of prior Mesolithic habitation, and was lived in through the Bronze and into the Iron Age.

The long history of archeological excavation here has created the most extensive plan of a later Neolithic settlement in Italy. The Neolithic level contained over fifty structures. There were groups of three to six wattle and daub huts, with sunken floors and round or oval floor plans. A distinct necropolis, separate from the habitations, had been established by the mid-Neolithic. A total of forty-six bodies were found in the trench graves, between two and fourteen people per grave, lying on their sides in a crouched fetal position. The dead were buried with funeral goods of pottery and tools made of stone and bone. The most famous tomb, found in 1913, is that of the "Woman with Dog;" a young woman buried with an apparently domesticated dog lying at her feet.

The Neolithic cultures spread little farming villages across the coastlands and hillsides of the *Terra Picena*, their hearths like so many stars scattered across the night sky. Some rose and vanished in the course of a few generations; some, like Ripoli, endured at least 500 years. The largest early-mid Neolithic villages, in the Adriatic lowlands, sometimes contained 200–300 people, but more likely 100. They raised cattle and pigs, sheep and goats, and hunted red and roe deer. They grew cereals—barley, wheat, and emmer, a type of wheat of which one variety, durum, is used today to make pasta. Although the Neolithic peoples of Italy used wild grapes and olives, no traces of wine or olive oil have been found (Malone, *Italian Neolithic*, p. 268).

The Neolithic, Copper, and Bronze Age cultures of Italy are known by the names of the places where distinctive types of artifacts were found. To list some of those most pertinent to the *Terra Picena*— Ripoli, Lagozza, Rinaldone, Gaudo, Remedello, Conelle—the names roll off the tongue like a necromantic incantation.

Among the finds at Ripoli were artifacts of the Lagozza type. The Lagozza culture was named after a site near the Lago di Varese in northwest Italy. It is the only mainland Italian branch of the western Neolithic, which can be traced through central France, southern Spain, and back to North Africa. Around 3000 BC, these people built pile settlements—*pallafitte*—along the Po River and the northern Italian lakes, such as Lago di Como and Lago di Garda, either over the water or on the marshy banks. They made plain black highly burnished pottery, of the type found at Ripoli. Some Ripoli ware is a hybrid, showing an ongoing exchange between the two cultures. Lagozza people also had spindle whorls and loom weights, the first signs of the manufacture of textiles. While the loom weights found at Ripoli are of a different form, they may have learned spinning and weaving from the northerners. The widespread exchange of goods and techniques, the combinations of pottery styles, imply not only trade but the movement of people into the territory. The Lagozza culture traveled a long distance, leaving traces along the eastern side of the Apennines from north of Milan as far south as Bolognano, near Pescara in Abruzzo. Pottery of the Ripoli and Lagozza styles have been found there in the Grotta dei Piccioni, a cave visited by the Ripoli people presumably for religious purposes. Within it eleven circles of pebbles contained animal bones, some of them marked with red-ochre-stained clay; in two of these circles were found the remains of a newborn and two children between six and ten years old.

Until the Final Neolithic Age, very few arrowheads were found at these sites. At this time they start to show up in large numbers and in a wide variety of styles. Stone mace heads and axe-hammers more suited to warfare than hunting appeared (Trump, p. 67). The large ditch that surrounds Ripoli may have served a defensive function in a period that became increasingly violent.

At the beginning of the second millennium BC another way of living appeared. This culture is referred to as Rinaldone-Gaudo, after two major archaeological sites. Rinaldone is near Montefiascone in Tuscany. Gaudo, south of Naples near Paestum, was discovered in 1943 when a bulldozer working on a new airfield opened the ceiling of a rock chamber tomb. They were a migratory pastoral people, who came perhaps from the steppes of Anatolia on horseback, speaking an indo-european language. Not given to establishing permanent settlements, virtually all that remains of them are their necropoli and the contents thereof. They had a distinctive method of burial; inhumation in individual or communal rock cut chamber tombs found dispersed and isolated all through the territory; their form is reminiscent of the stone post-and-lintel dolmans of central Asia. The tombs were reused over time, as the shepherds passed and repassed through these places. Some, but not all, of the people buried in them, crouched in a fetal position, are described as "round-headed," in contrast with the "long-headed" people who had been living here throughout the Neolithic period. Grave goods typically consisted of dark burnished *buccero* pottery, flint blades and arrowheads, stone axe heads, and, most significantly, objects made of worked metal, such as copper daggers. These newcomers brought with them the science of metalworking, as well as a widespread use of offensive weapons not associated with the agricultural communities.

These were not the peaceful shepherds featured in so many Christian nativity scenes. Always on the move, always looking for new pastures, they had much in common with the hunters. As these shepherd/warriors ranged through the center of the Italian peninsula, they carried with them what came to be called the Apennine culture. They survived by means of the *transumanza*, the long-distance herding of sheep, goats, and cattle from lowland winter meadows to mountain summer pastures. Many of the sites associated with them, like the caves at Frasassi, the Grotta del Mezzogiorno, the caverns of Grotta Salomone and Grotta Sant'Angelo, are caves that contain springs. Some have seen the periodic use of these places as proof of religious cult practice but seasonal use following the routes of the *transumanza* would also make sense. These places provide reliable shelter and water, and perhaps only later was a religious significance overlaid on this practical reality. Similarly, the many small clay vessels found in some of these caves have been interpreted as votives, religious offerings. Or the tiny jars could have been used to store and transport a valuable substance, such as rennet, the stomach lining of grazing animals used in cheesemaking (Salvatore Puglisi, *La Civiltà Appenninica*, p. 57).

The Grotta Sant'Angelo and the Grotta Salomone are two interconnected caverns in a vast system of caves in the karstic Montagna dei Fiori, Mountain of the Flowers, in northern Abruzzo, the southern reaches of *Terra Picena*. The region is known as *Tra i Due Regni*, between the two realms, that is between the Papal States and the Bourbon Kingdom of Naples. For centuries the wild borderland between north and south, these mountains are now part of the Parco Nazionale del Gran Sasso e Monti della Laga, one of the largest of Italy's national parks, established in 1991.

The Salinello River has carved a deep gorge between Mt. Fiori and Mt. Campli, with a dramatic waterfall just below the entrance to the Grotta Sant'Angelo. A small road leads to a substantial parking lot and picnic area. This is still a pilgrimage site, dedicated to the worship of Michael the Archangel. Within it is the medieval hermitage of San Michele, with an altar built in 1236. The Grotta Salomone also looks out on this valley; the cave itself suffered a massive collapse in the 1960s. Stone Aurignacian tools made from the local flint, dating back 25,000 to 20,000 years BC, were discovered in the cave along with the bones of cave bears, stambecks, and horses. The people who made these tools probably came to Piceno from the southern plains of eastern Europe, crossing the great Adriatic plain when it was still land and not sea. A type of scraper or plane found here has also been found in the settlements of the Val Vibrata; the Vibrata River flows down from the northern side of the Monte dei Fiori, down past Ripoli to the Adriatic. It is thought that the same people who lived in those settlements in the Neolithic era also frequented these caverns. Within the Grotta Sant'Angelo, nine pits were found containing flint, pottery, and the carbonized bones of at least nine juvenile humans, possibly connected with cannibalistic or sacrificial rites.

The Apennine Culture

The shepherds' relationship with the agriculturists was double-edged; they could descend as a raiding party to rob and pillage but they also needed the villagers, who fired pottery and stored grain. Over time a mutually beneficial if uneasy trade developed, with exchanges of animals, of food, of mates, of exotic items brought from afar, like amber and metal, traded for useful items produced in settled communities. Eventually this led to the development of a more homogenous culture, the patchwork of the isolated Neolithic villages stitched together by the traveling bands.

This Apennine culture extended from the Tuscan/Emilian plain as far down as northern Calabria. To the north the vast pastures of the Po River valley encouraged the shepherds to stay put, while southernmost Italy, dominated by the Sila Massif, lacks a reliable year-round water supply. A uniform type of dark burnished pottery is found throughout the Apennine zone, with local variations in decoration and handle styles. One of their distinctive contributions was an early kitchen appliance, the milk boiler. Used to make cheese, it consisted of a perforated funnel suspended within a pottery cooking vessel; this allowed the foam of boiling milk to rise up through the holes, reliquify, and drain back down (Puglisi, pp. 34–41). This was the northern style, found in Le Marche; a southern style was found throughout Apulia, Campania, etc., much like today's two versions of stovetop espresso makers. These milk boilers continued to be used into the twentieth century in rural areas. The dividing line between the two forms, and between many styles of pottery decoration and handles, ran just south of the *Terra Picena*.

The Apennine culture is not defined so much by territory or settlements or ethnicity, as it is by the range of influence. New people had come bringing their customs, skills, and artifacts, but they did not conquer or supplant the indigenous peoples—rather they intermingled and transformed the culture. Indo-european came to form the basis of most of the subsequent Italic languages, with some exceptions like Ligurian and Etruscan.

In the central section of the Apennine range many of the routes of the *transumanza* were centered on a series of low altitude passes. These were not the *tratturi* of further south, the wide highways and pastures traversed by enormous herds as they made their way from the high basins of Abruzzo and Apulia to the broad swampy coastal plains of Campania and the Maremma. Here the valleys are narrower, the high plateaus smaller, the paths more tortuous. From the Adriatic side the Sentino and Esino rivers lead to Umbria. The Colfiorito pass (750 m/2,500 ft) cuts through the mountains on the border between Umbria and Le Marche. Here is the source of the Chienti River, carving a route which leads down to the Adriatic near Civitanova Marche, with settlements along it dating back to the 10th century BC. The Colfiorito pass connects to the mineral-rich land that came to be called Etruria. Follow the Tronto up to its source and then the Velino down to Rieti and the flatlands of Lazio beyond. The sites on these east-west routes have more in common with each other than with those further to the north or south. The mountains in places form a barrier, in others create a shared network of ongoing contacts and influences.

Picenum is situated to make the best of both worlds. The coastal plains and river valleys were broad enough to support farming. The mountains were near enough to provide summer pasturage; on the western side of the Apennines, this distance between sea and mountains is much wider. A plentitude of springs and rivers made water available year-round. Starting in the 14th century BC, a "sub-Apennine" culture developed, basically agricultural with pastoralists who moved relatively small herds of animals relatively short distances between summer and winter pastures. This compromise spread throughout the area of the preceding nomadic Apennine influence, and formed the basis of the Piceno culture.

The tradition persists even today in the *commune* of Montegallo, a township of twenty-two villages in the Sibillini Mountains above Ascoli Piceno. On a Sunday morning in late April, a dozen or so cows and an unruly mob of sheep are driven from their winter home at Giuseppe Monti's Azienda Agricola in Roccafluvione to their summer pastures above Balzo. The herd is accompanied by a party of local horse riders, many in American cowboy gear. With a certain amount of drinking and shouting they make their way along the two-lane highway up through Uscerno. Giuseppe's young son Manuele poses for a photo on horseback in his gaucho hat, with the snow mantled Mt. Vettore as a backdrop. The distance is about about 15 km/9 mi, and takes a couple of hours. At the end the riders gather for an outdoor lunch of grilled sausages, fresh ricotta, bread, and red wine in a field below the 15th century fortress/church Santa Maria in Lapide. The kindergarden teacher is here, and the post office manager, and the families that run the bed and breakfasts, the restaurants, the grocery stores of Balzo, Montegallo's government seat (870 m/2,854 ft above sea level). They hope to make the roundup into a tourist attraction, to help maintain a way of life in these mountains. In a less dramatic fashion, the flocks of sheep, often attended by Albanian or African shepherds and large white Pastore Maremma dogs, are moved ever higher on the slopes as the season warms up.

Copper, Bronze, and Iron Ages

The Old Stone Age/Paleolithic Era, when humans made flaked and chipped stone tools, had been followed by the New Stone Age/Neolithic Era, whose stone tools were ground smooth and polished. Next came the Copper, Bronze, and Iron Ages, defined by the metals used. These eras however, cannot be rigidly defined in time, certainly not in central Italy. The transition from the Copper to the Bronze Age was more of a technological and economic development. Copper was the first metal to be utilized by humans. Although not commonly found, it is easy to recognize in its natural state, and could be worked as a soft type of stone. It was first hammered to make small personal ornaments in Anatolia and Mesopotamia between 8500 and 7500 BC, but the real technological breakthrough was the discovery that it could be melted and cast. In Picenum the Copper Age dates to the fourth and third millennia BC. To make bronze, tin is added to copper. Bronze melts at a lower temperature so it is easier to work with and less likely to develop flaws during casting. Now metalworkers could go beyond recreating stone objects in another medium to making a vast assortment of objects which were only possible with the new technology.

Stone tools continued to be used long after metal ones had made their appearance, simply because stone was more plentiful and easier for the individual to craft. Òtzi the Iceman, found frozen in the Italian Alps in 1991 and dated at 3350–3120 BC, carried both a flint dagger and a copper ax. A cache of Rinaldone Copper Age flint daggers found in Osimo were carefully carved with decorative rivets to more closely resemble metalwork. While Italy is littered with stone tools, Copper Age metal objects have been recovered primarily in tombs. Unlike stone, metal could be melted down and reworked. Stone tools just wore down; some of the microliths, identified as specialized miniature blades, may have been merely the last precious scrap of obsidian remaining. Early and Middle Bronze Age metal objects have been found primarily in hoards, not graves, reflecting the increased trade economy. Some, like the twenty-five unused Remedello bronze daggers found at Ripatransone, may have been a merchant's stock. Others are collections of scrap metal, perhaps gathered by itinerant metalworkers in exchange for new items and on the way to be recycled. The metal trade was presumably a hazardous business; these hoards were hidden by people who never returned to retrieve their treasures.

For a society to sustain a metalworking industry, more is required than the basic technical knowledge. Neolithic communities were self-sufficient, the farmers could make whatever tools were required. With the advent of metal, a whole new system was needed. The raw materials had to be acquired—not much copper can be found in the *Terra Picena*, but over the mountains, in Etruria, is the mineral rich Monte Amiata. Prospecters had to locate the sites, miners had to extract the ore, traders had to get it to the artisans who ran the foundries. These specialized workers, and the commercial relations between them, spread new types of tools and weapons, new styles of pottery, and new forms of burial.

The Copper Age is marked by many fragmented cultures and the increased use of weapons. Unlike ancient Greece, whose people were a more or less homogeneous ethnic group, Italy was a mixture of cultures, languages, and ethnicities. Outsiders from all points of the compass arrived and intermingled with those already there, creating unique hybrids in each specific place.

To the north, in the central plains of the Po River valley, was the Terramare culture. In the 19th century, farmers had dug into large mounds of rich dark soil (*terra mara*) for use as fertilizer. The highly organic nature of this earth was in fact the legacy of the domestic refuse of villages dating back to the Middle and Late Bronze Age (c 1700–1150 BC). These people apparently came from the Danube region, present-day Hungary, across the Alps by way of the Brenner Pass. Some sixty villages have been excavated, laid out in a quadrangular plan which presaged the famous Roman grid. The houses were made of wood, often on wooden piles although they were not built over water. (The relationship between the Terramare and Pallafitte cultures remains unclear). The settlement was generally surrounded by a large ramparted ditch or moat, which diverted a local stream around the dwellings. This running water may have served a defensive or a sanitary function, or both. The villages were apparently burned down with some frequency, perhaps as a public health measure, which contributed to the richness of the soil. They brought with them the ability to make things from bronze, and also a different way of dealing with the dead—cremation. The bodies were burned and the ashes were then buried in simple clay urns, without much in the way of grave goods.

Around 1200 BC, the Terramare villages were abandoned, perhaps in as little as one generation. Overpopulation, political upheaval, environmental problems; the cause or causes are mixed and uncertain. One theory holds that rising water levels, which included the Po River valley, drove these people out, and that many of them came to live in the *Terra Picena*. And perhaps some ended up in Rome, taking with them their history of urban planning. There is no evidence of invasions or colonization, just a wide sphere of cultural influence.

In our territory both the Apennine culture sites and the agricultural settlements show signs of contact with the Terramare culture. As the shepherd/warriors settled down, they adopted a number of its features. There have been major finds of Terramare type material at the Grotta Sant'Angelo in Abruzzo, in the Sentino River valley at Frassasi, Genga, and Pianello, and at San Paolina di Filottrano inland from Ancona. This last, unlike the others mentioned, was not a cave location, but an open air village perched above the Musone River. It consisted of oval huts and contained an unusual clay-lined pit, perhaps a water reservoir for the dry season.

In 1878, Guglielmo Allevi, one of the pioneers of modern archaeology in Italy, undertook the exploration of a site near his hometown of Offida. As usual, the first word had come from farmworkers, who reported a ditch where blocks of metal had been found. When he saw them Allevi recognized these as the bronze tablets used by ancient metalworkers. Above this ditch was a field where the farmers, when plowing, often ran up against buried tree trunks. Allevi systematically excavated a small portion of this area using the newly developed scientific procedures. What he found was a series of large tree trunks lined up to create a platform, or as he described it, *una zattera*, a raft, which had once floated on the surface of a now vanished lake. There were no signs of the support columns used in the Pallafitte settlements on the northern lakes; it resembled instead some constructions of the Terramare culture in the Po region, which could rise and fall with the water level. Allevi analyzed the layers of soil and carbon deposits, the fragments of ceramic and metal and flint, and concluded that this had been a village of around two hundred people that lasted for centuries. The many bronze tablets and objects which he took to be molds led him to believe that this had been a center of metalworking and commerce in the Early Bronze Age, whose inhabitants had originally come from the Terramare culture to the north. It may be one of the oldest examples of this industry found in Italy. The site must have been abandoned suddenly, since so much precious bronze had been left behind. Invaders would have scooped up this booty, so it was probably an overwhelming natural disaster, a flood or mudslide that destroyed and buried everything. Allevi published his findings in 1889, in his book *Offida Preistorica*, with an appeal for further investigation of this intriguing site. A hundred years later local historian Carlo Cappelli, following Allevi's description, located it—unmarked, unprotected, unexamined. His pamphlet *"La 'Zattera' di Guglielmo Allevi"* repeats Allevi's appeal.

The Sentino River springs from its source in the mountains between Umbria and Le Marche, near the cliff-lined Scheggia pass which leads to Gubbio. It flows down past Sassoferrato and ancient Sentinum, site of the decisive Roman victory over the Samnites and Senone Gauls in the Third Samnite War. In the Regional Park of Gola della Rossa and Frasassi it cuts a dramatic gorge through limestone cliffs. But before the river takes this plunge, on the left bank of the flat valley floor lies Pianello di Genga, site of a vast urnfield cemetery. Traces of human occupation go back to the Neolithic Era, but the necropolis was established sometime in the Final Bronze Age, around 1200 BC. It is notable because the bodies of the dead were incinerated and the ashes buried in covered pottery urns. The prevailing funereal custom in the region up until this point had been the burial of the intact body. This phenomenon, the urnfield, has a history that leads back through the Terramare people to Central Europe and the urnfields of Hungary. The culture of Pianello shows a merging of Terramare type burial rites and metalworking skills with the Apennine style of pottery. The site has been described as proto-Villanovan, that is, leading up to the Villanovan culture that made the transition from the Bronze Age to the Iron Age. Villanova is the name of a specific site near Bologna, but this type of settlement spread throughout central Italy, especially on the western side of the Apennines, in the places that came to be called Etruscan. Here at Pianello di Genga, more than a thousand burials have been brought to light in excavations starting in the early 20ᵗʰ century. While some bronze razors and *fibulae*/pins were recovered, there was no widespread panoply of grave goods. The Ancona Museum has an exhibit of several of the mud-colored urns, capped with their distinctive biconical bowl-like covers, carefully placed in a mound of dirt. More evocative is a photo from the dig itself showing rank upon rank of these jars tumbled on top of each other lining the side of a trench.

So large a necropolis was presumably used by the inhabitants of a number of settlements in the surrounding area, but the countryside has not been extensively investigated. The urns could also have been brought here seasonally by the migratory bands that ranged across the mountains and plains. Pianello is now a pleasant stretch of meadowlands studded with small industrial buildings, including one owned by the appliance manufacturer Ariston/Whirlpool. Despite these you can feel the mysterious attraction of the place; to bring the remains of the departed here, to this green peaceful basin on the lip of the awe-inspiring canyon, the river hurtling down into the sunless chasm between gray perpendicular cliffs, where the spirits of the dead can rest forever in this paradise on the edge of the inferno.

Down in the Gola della Rossa, pitting the limestone walls of the gorge are several caves which have yielded up traces of Bronze Age use—the Grotta dei Baffoni, the Grotta del Mezzogiorno, and the Grotta della Santuario. This last once contained Apennine and sub-Apennine finds; it now holds a neat octagonal chapel built with the site's own travertine in 1828 by the architect Giuseppe Valdier for Pope Leo XII, who was originally from nearby Genga. Also nestled into the overhanging rockface is the Santa Maria *infra Saxa*, "in the rocks," a shrine mentioned as already in existence in 1029.

The Misa River empties into the Adriatic at Senigallia. It is a short run, only about 35 km/20 mi, from its source near Arcevia. Here in these foothills are a series of archaeological sites revealing traces of human activity going back millennia. An open-air site at Ponte di Pietra has produced evidence of flint working from the late Paleolithic Era. In the Cava Giacometti, the deepest level of excavations contained Neolithic Era potsherds of both the Ripoli and Lagozza types, and higher levels had proto-Apennine ceramics more than 3,000 years old; this spot was inhabited for more than a thousand years. Monte Croce Guardia was a later proto-Villanovian settlement with wood framed huts from the end of the Bronze Age. And it is possible to visit one much-studied Copper Age site, the defensive ditch at Conelle, which dates back to the third millennium BC.

Around Arcevia the fields unroll down the slopes from the heights above, like bolts of cloth, bright yellow, velvety green. Rain clouds hang low on the rocky crags. While all the archaeological finds have been taken to the Ancona Museum, the ditch itself still exists. By the side of a small country lane, surrounded by a fence with an unlocked gate, the site is unattended. A large metal roof protects the middle of the ditch and a walkway spans it, so you can look down into the unremarkable trench. On the earthen path, a wet stone glints. A distinctive reddish brown, like toffee, the edges are chipped into sharp planes, much like the piles of flint tools on display in Ancona.

No ruins remain of the settlement at Conelle, obliterated by centuries of agricultural use, but indirect evidence suggests that a village was sited on this peninsula of land created by two streams, the Torrente Aquaviva and the Fosso di Montefortino. Judging from the size of the site, it could have held 200–400 inhabitants. Conelle di Arcevia lacks a known cemetery; possibly the people who lived there used the one at Pianello di Genga, about 20 km/12 mi away on today's roads. Fragments of plaster marked with traces of thatch suggested wattle and daub huts with wooden structures. The defensive position is similar in concept to the location of Ascoli Piceno between the Castellano and Tronto Rivers. On the third side, however, instead of building a wall a ditch had been dug in the gravelly soil. Only a slight depression hinted at its presence before it was excavated by Salvatore M. Puglisi, 1958–1969. The ditch measured more than 100 m/328 ft long, 8 m/26 ft deep, and 4–7 m/12–23 ft wide. Thought to have been originally created as a defensive barrier in perilous times, over the centuries it was gradually refilled with the village's debris, an archaeologist's treasure trove of trash. This mother lode was created between 3500 and 2900 BC, when a top layer of dirt and gravel was laid down, presumably to bring it up to the level of the surrounding land.

The contents of the ditch attest to a variety of activities. Wild boar and deer were hunted; deer horns were used to make hoes, scythes/reaping hooks, and other tool handles, boar tusks were fashioned into ornaments. Cows, sheep, and especially pigs were raised for meat. The cows provided milk, and were also used as work animals, pulling carts. Sheep, and more rarely goats, also provided secondary products such as milk and cheese. A large number of loom weights indicate that weaving was done here, presumably of wool. Dogs were probably employed guarding the herds as well as for hunting. The many grindstones indicate the cultivation of grains that were then cooked and eaten. There were remnants of all stages of stone manufacture, from pebble to finished arrowhead. The many ax-hammers indicate a high level of woodworking, necessary to provide handles for so many tools. Potsherds show distinct local characteristics but also affinities with products of Abruzzo, Emilia Romagna, and Lazio. One of the most interesting connections is with the Balkan coast of the Adriatic, indicated by certain types of ceramics and stone tools. The many arrowheads, spearheads, flint daggers and ax-hammers found could have been used for hunting but seen in conjunction with the ditch it seems likely that they were also used as weapons. After all, only 32 km/20 mi east, near Osimo, a group of Rinaldone warriors from Umbria were buried with their flint daggers and battleaxes. Very little metal was found at Conelle, probably because it was too valuable to throw away. One fragment of copper that was unearthed, which ultimately originated in central Europe, was linked to the Remedello culture, groups of nomads who spread out from the Provence region of France. They traded with agricultural communities, and penetrated into the Po River plain. Archeologists suggest that their influence may explain differences in the development of Bronze Age cultures between the northern Po region, which was oriented towards continental Europe, and the central-southern areas of Italy (Carlo Cappelli notes that this north/south distinction has never disappeared in Italy, *La Civiltà Egeo-Appenninica*, p. 81).

Early Greek Influences

The Myceneans, archaic predecessors of the classical Greeks, left some traces in Piceno; two ceramic fragments in the Ancona area, one at Treazzano di Monsampolo in the Tronto valley. Forty pieces were discovered in Tolentino, which sits in the mountains close to the Colfiorito pass, on a major trade route between the Tyrhennian and Adriatic sides of the peninsula.

In Castel di Lama, in the Tronto River valley between Ascoli Piceno and the coast, a ceramic fragment was found in 1984 during the excavation for a skating rink. This "enigmatic" potsherd was in the midst of material from the Apennine culture, and dates to around 1400 BC. It is from the edge of a pot or vase, of Apennine type with a bit of typical Apennine decoration on it but also several indecipherable symbols. This locally made pottery, not something brought from far away, shows that the maker had at least been exposed to the idea of writing, had perhaps seen other jars with the contents or the name of the owner written on them, and had copied it.

Carlo Cappelli includes this precocious exposure to writing in his list of Aegean cultural influences on the Piceno area which predate the Greek colonies of the second half of the eighth century BC. The technological level achieved by Piceno's metalworking industry, one of the oldest in Italy, and a certain artistic quality, similarities in styles of jewelry, indicate that Piceno was integrated in the network of Mycenean merchants. Another Mycenean contribution may be the early cultivation of grapes and olives. The presence of war chariots in Piceno graves might lead back to the Myceneans, while a type of stone hut, the *caciara*, found on the Adriatic coast and up into the mountains above Ascoli mirrors the construction of Mycenean tombs (see photo p. 186). The Piceni matriarchal goddesses Ancaria and Cupra resemble similar Cretan and Aegean divinities and the role of women in Piceno society partakes of the more matriarchal aspects of the Greeks, in contrast to the patriarchal culture of the Apennine shepherds. Most importantly, the contact with the Myceneans exposed the peoples of Picenum to an urban civilization, with social stratification, an artisan class, and the more sophisticated political organizations and trade networks made possible by writing.

The Late Bronze Age civilization of Mycenae arose on mainland Greece around 2000 BC. Known for its warlike nature, massive citadels, and metal weapons as grave goods, this culture also established major sea trade routes in the eastern Mediterranean, including an outpost at the southern port of Taranto. Imported Mycenaen pottery has been found there, and the designs were soon adopted throughout the region. The Mycenaens were looking for metal ore, and had contact with Sicily, Sardinia, the Lipari Islands, and the Tuscan copper mines. And the trade went both ways. Three pieces of Apennine ware handles were found at Troy VI and VII, the level associated with the Trojan War. Of a type characteristic of Picenum, they were probably shipped through Taranto.

Sea trade and land trade operate differently when it comes to cultural exchanges. A Mycenean tomb from the 17th century BC contained a Baltic amber necklace; the Amber Road already stretched from the Baltic Sea to the Adriatic and beyond, but it did not bring Mediterranean cultures and peoples to the northern lands. There were too many points of transfer along the road, the goods travelled the whole way but not the people. Merchant marines however carried a crew from the place of origin to a series of foreign ports, going ever further in search of raw materials and markets. The ancient ships stayed close to the land, harboring overnight and resupplying as needed. Mycenean merchants set up trading posts, *emporae*, along the coasts of the Mediterranean. Traders settled at the more important ones, perhaps ultimately creating a colony which replicated their culture, directly exposing the peoples of the host lands to their particular ways of doing things. And they took goods, ideas, and people from those countries back to their own.

The sea trade in the Adriatic was determined by the water currents. The Mycenean merchant ships were flat bottomed, had one large sail, and oarsmen who were primarily used to maneuver the craft into and out of harbors. The currents in the Adriatic carried the boats up along the Dalmatian coast, with its many islands and inlets, and then across to the Italian side at the level of the natural harbor of Ancona. From there the boats passed the Po Delta and the mouth of the Adige River and reached the Venetian lagoon. The return trip however stayed along the Italian coast, riding the currents south to the Gargano peninsula, where the Tremiti Islands serve as stepping stones, or all the way down the boot heel. In that era the Piceno rivers were not silted up, and these estuaries, especially the Tronto, offered comfortable harbors.

The Mycenean civilization fell apart around 1200 BC, soon after it conquered Troy. This mysterious and catastrophic collapse severely damaged the trade networks. The merchants of Taranto, cut off from Greece, took over the sea trade. Hostile neighbors in Lipari made the Tyrhennian Sea less welcoming and led traders to concentrate on the Adriatic. Here various pieces of the local patchwork began to fall into place. Up until this point the Myceneans had been taking copper ore back to Greece to fabricate into objects, while in the Po valley the people of the Terramare culture had been importing their metal from beyond the Alps. Now the far-ranging bearers of the Apennine culture connected the merchants of Taranto and the metalworkers of the Terramare with the ores of Monte Amiata in Etruria. From a northern Adriatic port somewhere near today's Rimini, the Tarantine ships picked up the products of the Terramare and perhaps Apennine industries and traded the bronze tools, weapons, and ornaments throughout southern Italy. And here we begin to approach historic record. In the late first century BC Dionisius of Halicarnassus, writing to reassure the Romans that they descended from the heroic ancient Greeks, describes their ancestors as the Enotri and Ausoni who landed in Apulia seventeen generations before the Trojan War (C. Cappelli, *ASKL*, p. 11). That would have been around the 13th–12th centuries BC, and would still have made them latecomers.

And, out of this melting pot, arose the culture that came to be called *Piceno*.

Picus viridis, European Green Woodpecker
Sergey Ryzhkov

4

The Piceni

Noi abbiamo un grande fantasma che ci perseguita da molti decenni: sull'Adriatico,
nel centro dell'area adriatica, questo fantasma sono i Piceni.

We have a great phantom that has haunted us for many decades: on the Adriatic,
in the middle of the adriatric zone, this phantom is the Piceni.
—Massimo Pallottino, 1975

A small band of 20-year-olds, boys and girls, make their way through the heavily forested mountains. All were born in the same fateful year, their lives pledged to a god. In earlier times these children might have been sacrificed but now they are only expelled from their families and sent out in the springtime to make a new life in a new place. They bring with them sheep, chickens, and other livestock. At the head of the group someone carries a standard; perched on it, guiding them, is a *picus*, a woodpecker sacred to Mars the god of war.

In Roman mythology, Picus was the extremely handsome son of Saturn and first king of Latium, known for his horsemanship. According to Ovid, one day when Picus was out hunting, the witch Circe, daughter of the sun god Helios, caught sight of him and was seized with a great passion. She sent a ghost boar across his path; he pursued it deep into the forest to where she was waiting. But Picus spurned her advances because he had already given his heart to a certain nymph. In a jealous rage the sorceress transformed him into a woodpecker whose magnificent plumage reflected the luxurious garments of the young man. When his hunting companions chased Circe down she set off an earthquake and turned them all into wild animals (Ovid, *Metamorphoses* 14, lines 308–440). Plutarch says that "they regard this bird as sacred to Mars… For it is a courageous and spirited bird and has a beak so strong that it can overturn oaks by pecking them until it has reached the inmost part of the tree" (Plutarch, *Roman Questions*, 21). The deity Picus was linked to agricultural practices, especially the use of manure, and augury, interpreting omens by observing birds. The woodpecker chosen by Ascoli and its soccer team as a mascot is black and white with red details.

The *Ver Sacrum*, Sacred Spring, was a ritual described by the ancient Romans and Greeks as the source of the Piceni people. The Piceni were said to have originated in Sabine territory, perhaps at the Lago di Paterno, of Sabine stock. And while the youths headed for new territory, they ended up near Ascoli Piceno, where humans had been living for quite some time already.

The ritual was perhaps an effective form of population management, more humane than killing the excess infants. Maybe it describes the process of leaving behind exhausted agricultural soil for more fertile sites. Or it can be seen as the mythification of the age-old migratory culture of the shepherds. The ancient writers Strabo, Pliny, and Festo cite this origin story of the Piceni, or Picentines, or Picenti, as they are variously called. On the other hand, the historian E.T. Salmon says "These prehistoric inhabitants of the region were probably very heterogeneous, but can be called collectively Picenes, a geographical term which has no ethnic implications." He describes them as "probably an amalgam of the population settled since Bronze Age times in northeastern peninsular Italy and enterprising immigrants who had been crossing into Italy from equally early times from the Illyrian side of the Adriatic" (E.T. Salmon, *The Making of Roman Italy*, p. 30 and fn 149). Some scholars avoid "tribal" names altogether, and refer to a generalized mid-Adriatic culture. We do not know what, if anything, they called themselves.

The Via Salaria enters Ascoli Piceno through the remnants of the Roman wall, at the Porta Gemina; the twin Roman arches still stand to the side of the modern road. Stretches of the Roman travertine foundation are surmounted by a patchwork of Roman and medieval stonework. Across the road is a row of large sandstone blocks that barely rise above ground level. This is all that remains of the city wall built by the Piceni. As Carlo Cappelli writes in *ASKL*, the date of its construction has not been fixed; we can only trace references to when it was already in existence. Archaeologists have dated it to between the third and second century BC. Earlier scholars assumed that it could only have been built under Roman rule, with their urban technology. However, the counter argument is that the Romans would never have permitted Ascoli, a city that was forced to join the Roman federation but remained independent, to construct such a massive defensive work. Perhaps it was built as protection against raids by the Gauls at the end of the fourth century BC. Like the walls that followed and like the walls or stockade fences that perhaps preceded it, it served an obvious function. Its course completes the third side of the triangle that is the fortress city of Ascoli Piceno, running from the heights above the Tronto River, up to the hilltop of the Annunziata crowned by the Fortezza Pia (rebuilt in 1560 on a site that had been fortified since the time of the Piceni), and then down to the cliffs cut by the Castellano River. The city's location is both a highly defensible promontory and an unavoidable crossroads, controlling the trade route across the Apennines from the Tyrhennian to the Adriatic, linking the Etruscan, Piceni, and Greek merchants and cultures. These few sandstone blocks are among the rare traces found so far of the Piceno city Askl, now covered by more than 2000 years of subsequent habitation.

The story of the Piceni lies almost entirely in the realms of archaeology, in a wealth of objects, much of it held in museum basements and warehouses, seen only by experts and students. The people themselves left no record of their name or history. We know as much as we do because for the most part they were buried, not cremated, with an array of imperishable things made from metals and ceramics. What you see in the museum exhibits of the Piceno culture are primarily grave goods, and small hoards of weapons found in non-cemetery settings. The few stone statues and the stelae with enigmatic drawings and inscriptions are thought to be funeral monuments. Beyond this, there are sites identified as dwellings or workshops by postholes, dry stone footings, chunks of wattle and daub walls, roof tiles. But the items on display, the luxurious accessories of the upper ranks, represent only a narrow band of the culture and are not the daily implements of the farmers, laborers and perhaps slaves who worked to produce this prosperity. We have the ceremonial jewelry and not the cloth garments, the banqueting vessels and not the humble daily kitchenware. Much of this lopsidedness is inevitable, but the abundance of minutiae can be overwhelming while the big picture is elusive. The study of the Piceni sometimes seems like an endless list of styles of vases, of varieties of pins, of types of helmets—because that is what remains, and from these things everything else must be deduced.

The Piceni Era spanned almost a millennium. While the onset of the Iron Age in Italy is set around 1000 BC, many features of the Bronze Age remained, especially in Picenum, which had no iron ore. The Piceno culture arose directly from the peoples and cultures already present in the area. The three main components were the Apennine, the proto-Villanovan, and the transadriatic. The migratory shepherd/warriors of the Near East had settled down into the pre-Apennine network of villages with a shorter-range *transumanza*. The proto-Villanovans, distinguished by their use of cremation as a funeral rite, had roots across the Alps in the Bronze Age cultures of central Europe. The Adriatic *koine* (the network of shared cultural markers) connected the peoples on both sides of the sea, the Italian coast with the Balkan, the Liburni pirates with the merchant vessels of Greece and Magna Graecia.

Phases of Piceni Culture

Delia Lollini, the *grande dame* of Piceno studies who directed and wrote up many of the important post-war digs, defined the seven chronological phases of Piceno culture (*Popoli e Civiltà dell' Italia Antica*, Vol. 5, *La Civiltà Picena*).

The first phase, Piceno I, is set at 900–800 BC, although modern dating techniques have suggested that some of the objects associated with this phase may be as old as 1000 BC. The finds, while spread over a broad area of what came to be called Picenum, are concentrated along what was then the Adriatic coastline, somewhat inland from today's shore. Some dwelling sites have been found, and a number of necropoli. The dead were characteristically buried in a crouched fetal position, in a trench, often within a layer of gravel. The grave goods were sparse, maybe just a single object such as a bronze *fibula* (pin) of a type found both throughout the Italian peninsula and on the opposite Balkan coast. The graves contained no ceramics; potsherds have been found at the dwelling sites. At this point in time Fermo, south of Ancona, was a Villanovan outpost, the only such place that did not subsequently become an Etruscan settlement. The evidence shows direct contact between Fermo and the Villanovan culture of Tuscany and Lazio, rather than with that of Bologna to the north, highlighting the pattern of east-west trade along the river valleys that crossed the Apennines.

In Piceno II (800–700 BC), sites are found as far north as the Foglia River, including the necropolis at Novilara, and also well inland such as at Tolentino. The skeletons are sometimes stretched out full length, and ceramic vases are now included in the grave goods. There is evidence of an active local metalworking industry, with an abundance of bronze ornaments in styles that are either unique to the Piceno zone or especially widespread here. And iron objects make their first appearance, including swords and hunting knives. While some of the grave goods are in a Villanovan style, the influence is not as strong as one might expect given the presence of Fermo; instead, the necropolis of Fermo shows the influence of the Piceni. The cultural *koine* of the Adriatic reveals itself in the shared forms of *fibulae* on both the Italian and Balkan coasts. Where these styles orginated is not clear. Metal ornament styles from other parts of Italy are also present.

During Piceno III (700–580 BC), the culture began a development called "Orientalization," influenced by increased contacts with the Etruscans and, either through them or independently, with the Greeks. Characteristic sites, such as Fabriano, Pitino di San Severino, and Matelica, are located in the mountainous inland regions, positioned to take advantage of the always important passes across

the Apennines. These were intense points of contact with the Etruscans on the western side of the peninsula. The "orientalized" Piceni tombs (sometimes capped with a *tumolo*, a mound of stones) are rich
with Etruscan objects and objects imported by way of Etruria, whose ships dominated the Tyrhennian
Sea. All the graves are burials, generally with the body in an extended position, except at Novilara where
two cremations have been found and the burials are in the fetal position. Some of the 300 tombs there
were apparently marked by the stone slabs inscribed with pictures and writing known as the Novilara
stelae. At this point Fermo ceased to exist as a separate cultural entity, and was subsumed into the Piceno
koine.

This was a culture of luxury, of heaps of ornaments, equipment for banquets, laminated bronze
breastplates, helmets, and shields. Ceramic vessels appear in ever-greater panoply of local forms, some
unique to a single necropolis; on the other hand, there are painted vases imported from Apulia. The
local metalworking industry produced cast bronze objects, especially jewelry. Laminated bronze objects
include breastplates (*dischi-corazza*) with elaborate incised or raised embellishments, and containers
with highly original decorations. Iron had come into general use for tools and weapons such as axes,
lance points, knives, and a type of sword also found on the Balkan peninsula. Almost all the *fibulae*
found are still made of bronze, in a notable variety of styles.

Piceno IV-A (580–520 BC) continues this outpouring of ornaments, in a vast array of forms and
styles. The women were buried with loads of jewelry, mostly bronze. The sheer quantity implies a
local system of mass production. The men were buried with many weapons, mostly iron. Banqueting
equipment included iron spits and bronze laminated graters. Some tombs, male and female, contained
two-wheeled chariots with iron wheels and horse bits of iron or bronze. Ceramics were being made
using the pottery wheel. While there are few traces of the Piceni north of the Esino River in this era,
their necropoli are found as far south as Pescara, Abruzzo, including one at Campovalano where the
tombs are surrounded by circles of stones. Two presumably funereal statues date from this period, the
Warrior of Capistrano and the Head of a Warrior of Numana, as do the South Piceni or proto-Sabellic
inscriptions that have been found. Now there is evidence of Greek commercial ships plying the Adriatic,
putting the Piceni in direct contact with the culture of Golden Age Greece and Magna Graecia without
the intervention of the Etruscans. Imported materials are abundant—Greek vases, amber from the
Baltic Sea, sea shells from the Indian Ocean, the carved ivory and ostrich egg found in Belmonte Piceno.
Trade continued to flourish with Etruria, Apulia, and the opposite coast of the Adriatic.

Archeological evidence is scarcer regarding Piceno IV-B (520–470 BC). This phase is distinguished
by a certain type of *fibula*, the Certosa, and by the growing dominance of Greek ceramics, with impressive examples of black vernice, black-figured, and then red-figured vases. Under this artistic onslaught,
local ceramics rapidly lost their originality. The most characteristic weapon of this time is the iron
scimitar. Glass beads have been found in the women's tombs, as well as bone cylinders closed with a disc
with a bronze tack through it, whose use is unknown.

Piceno V (470–385 BC) is noted for the presence in tombs and dwellings of red-figured Attic vases,
often very large and of high artistic quality.

The last of these phases, Piceno VI (385–268 BC), shows the final dissipation of the independent
Piceno culture, the disappearance of its characteristic traits. The ceramics in the graves for the most part
reflect styles from other places. The weapons fall mainly into two categories, lances and swords. These

swords are of a Celtic type, as are many of the toilet articles and ornaments; by now the Gauls were a strong presence. Lollini ends her timeline of Piceno culture when the Romans won the Picenean War.

The Sites and the Objects

Ancona is the only true harbor on this stretch of the coast between the Po River and the Gargano peninsula. A rocky arm of Monte Conero reaches around the ample basin; from this spit you can see the sun both rise and set over the sea. The city's name comes from the Greek *ankon* "elbow"; Greeks from Syracuse established a colony or trading post here around 390 BC. But the highly desirable location had been occupied since long before that. The Duomo di San Ciriaco is set on the highest point, above the city, the port, the expanse of the Adriatic. This medieval church was built on the site of a fourth century BC Greek temple dedicated to Venus or Aphrodite, according to ancient sources, perhaps replacing a sanctuary honoring the Piceno goddess Cupra. Remnants of the Greek temple are still visible in the crypts under the church. The Museo Archeologico Nazionale delle Marche di Ancona is housed in the Palazzo Ferretti, a 16th century residence a short walk downhill. Gazing out the windows on its upper floors, you can see Trajan's Arch, built by the Romans in AD 114–115, forlorn on the jetty and dwarfed by the massive ships that crowd this active commercial port.

In the 19th century, archeology became a field of study and a collecting craze, pursued in many cases by educated amateurs, wealthy landowners with a hobby. Many of the early finds, including some of the most famous, were fortuitous. Agricultural laborers turned up objects of interest which they brought to the landowner, or to a local dilettante, who thus amassed a fascinating collection. Unfortunately, the object was stripped of its context—except perhaps for a more or less precise notation as to where and when it had been found. At first most of these materials ended up in Rome, and a large collection remains there in the Pigorini Museum. Later many of the local treasure troves were sent to Ancona to establish a museum under the auspices of the new Italian state.

In June 1944, Allied planes chasing the Germans up the boot targeted the strategic harbor. Unlike Rome and Florence, Ancona was not a protected cultural site. Bombs severely damaged the museum in its previous location, destroying irreplaceable Piceni masterworks and rare evidence from the prehistoric past. (Zia Costanza remembers hearing the bombing from Abetito, her tiny village in the mountains above Ascoli.) A huge labor of restoration was undertaken in the '50s, led by Director Giovanni Annibaldi. The museum opened in the Palazzo Ferretti in 1969. In 1972, an earthquake severely damaged the building and it remained closed to the public for sixteen years, until 1988 when Director Lollini reopened the Piceni exhibit. Other sections—the Paleolithic and Neolithic Eras, the Bronze and Iron Ages—followed. Replicas of the Roman gilt bronzes from Cartoceto di Pergola, life size statues of two horses, their riders, and two standing women, crown the edifice.

After the war, the archeological exploration of Piceno took off. (Mussolini's Fascists were only interested in the Roman past, dismissing other cultures as not sufficiently glorious.) New technologies such as dendrochronology enabled more precise dating and analysis of every fragment of material. This boom culminated in the year 2000 with the exhibit *Piceni Popoli d'Europa*," which was shown in Frankfurt and Rome. Much of the material came from the Ancona Museum and local museums in Le Marche, with significant additions like the Warrior of Capistrano from Abruzzo, and objects on loan from other European museums. *"Eroi e Regine/Heroes and Queens,"* the catalogue of this exhibit with some additional later updates, is a fascinating collection of essays by the experts (many cited below) covering all aspects of what is known about the Piceni. Unlike Alessandro Naso's otherwise exhaustive *I Piceni*, which stops at the modern day provincial boundary of the Tronto River, it also discusses the important finds and sites in Abruzzo, including the necropolis at Campovalano.

Here, in this series of ornate rooms with their heavily frescoed ceilings, are the objects that define the Piceno culture. The museum guards linger on the landings, charged with keeping an eye on us, the only visitors, but they had rather continue their gossiping. The windows are open, the breeze off the Adriatic warm and humid; the sea glints a long way below us.

Picenum was notable for the vitality and originality of its metalworking, despite having little in the way of the raw materials. Perhaps the most ubiquitous Piceno item is the *fibula*, the most com-

Piceno *Fibula* found in Colle Vaccaro
Photo Anna Maria Ferri

mon ornament worn by Piceni women. The *fibula* is a brooch much like our safety pin, used to fasten garments and as decoration. The basic form is an arc, a spring, a needle, and a clasp or catch plate to hold the needle closed. The oldest ones, dating to the Late Bronze Age, were found in the lake villages of northern Italy, and in Mycenaean Greece. It is not clear who came up with the idea first, and a similar pin was developed apparently independently in northern Europe.

Most of the *fibulae* here are bronze, although there are also iron, silver, and gold ones. The wide array of styles, many of them named after sites in Le Marche, can be linked to very specific places and eras, even when found far afield. The earliest is the violin bow, the top piece a simple arc. Later variations have double strands of bronze twisted together, or serpentine ribbons, or multiple knobs on the arc, or animal heads. Some have swollen bodies like leeches or wind filled sails, the surfaces covered with incised designs. Some are iron inlaid with bronze, in imitation of the "orientalized" Etruscan inlays of gold and silver. Amber, bone, and glass beads could be threaded on the arc. Another version, popular in the tenth–eighth centuries BC, has the pin attached to the back of flat metal spirals, sometimes as big as saucers, a style found also on the Balkan peninsula. The Certosa *fibula*, with its doubled bilateral spring, is found throughout Europe and is used to reliably date archaeological strata. The Certosa is a small pin while other types are over a foot long. Further ornaments could be hung from the needle, including seashells from as far off as the Red Sea, wild boar teeth set in bronze, bronze pinecones. *Fibulae* found in Cupra Marittima carried tweezers and implements for cleaning the fingernails and ears.

Elaborate, sometimes massive, *pettorali* could also be suspended from a *fibula*, worn, as the name indicates, on the chest. Bronze plaques are fringed with chains, linked with rings, dangling charms in the form of open hands, stylized human figures, little jars, stars. The more elaborate versions, with double tiers decorated with birds or horses' heads, are rare and clearly belong to elite burials. Single tiered ones are more common but are also found only in certain contexts, often in graves with loom weights, spindles, and other implements of the weaving industry. Thus, these luxury ornaments may indicate that the deceased was the matriarch of the family, who organized the home-based work of spinning and weaving. In antiquity textile production was primarily a domestic industry, work done by women to supply their household. However, high-ranking women in powerful families managed workshops that made fabric for domestic, commercial, and ritual use.

Another characteristic ornament is the *torque*, an open-ended bronze neck ring. Perhaps the most famous example is worn by "The Dying Gaul," a fourth century BC Hellenistic statue on display at the Capitoline Museums in Rome (see photo p. 76). In Picenum, the *torque*'s turned back ends are often decorated with human or animal heads or pinecones. A beautiful one from Belmonte Piceno turns the ends into seahorses, and mounted on the circle are two winged sirens, their arms wide, wearing their own little necklaces. It is attributed to itinerant Greek artisans working for Piceni clients in the late sixth century BC.

Piceno *Pettorale*
Museo Archeologico Nazionale delle Marche

Women's Graves

One day, we drive east out of Ancona on the Viale della Vittoria, a tree-lined boulevard bordered by a calm and orderly series of villas, many with Art Nouveau details. At the end of the avenue is the Fascist-era war memorial, a white columned temple gazing out across the Adriatic. Turning south to Monte Conero, the massive rocky peninsula that has attracted mariners for millennia, the road follows the cliff edge for a while and then curves inland. This rolling countryside of fields and pastures is where a number of the major Piceni necropoli were found, and in them many of the things on display in the Ancona Museum.

Numana has been inhabited at least since the Bronze Age. Tombs found there date to the ninth century BC. One burial consisted of a biconical cremation urn set in a bed of sea gravel, accompanied by bronze items such as a pin, a razor, a knife, and a whetstone; the deceased was presumably male. Lollini considered this grave to be one of the earliest evidences of the Piceno civilization. Between the seaside towns of Sirolo and Numana there are four cemeteries dating from the late seventh century to the fifth century BC, containing more than 1,500 tombs. Most of these are simple trench graves, but there are also more than ten monumental circle tombs. This type of burial is found throughout central Italy, from Abruzzo in the south to Etruria, Umbria, and Romagna in the north. One or more burial trenches were encircled with a ditch and probably covered by a mound of pebbles. The *tomba a circolo* is not associated with any particular ethnic group but rather with a wealthy social class.

At the "*I Pini*" site, the remains of a woman dating to the end of the sixth century BC were found buried in one of these circle tombs, 40 m/130 ft in diameter, ringed by a trench 4 m/13 ft wide and almost 2 m/6.5 ft deep. Within this circle were a number of trenches, one the grave of an early fifth-century BC boy. The site was excavated in 1989 using systematic modern technology, including removing whole intact layers of earth to be taken apart and analyzed in the laboratory. Numana has a small museum displaying many of these local finds. Excavations continue; in 2020 a fully outfitted warrior was unearthed nearby.

In the center of the circle was the tomb of the "Queen of Numana," consisting of three sections. In the first were more than 200 objects, including banqueting equipment such as iron knives, spits, and andirons, and Piceni, Etrurian, and Greek metal and ceramic vessels. The bone, ivory, and amber decorations of a wooden *kline*/small reclining bed serve as rare and significant indication of the spread here of Greek banqueting practices. In the second section were two two-wheeled chariots, the bronze and iron wheels and other parts marking where the wooden structure had been. The third section contained the remains of two mules, which had presumably pulled these chariots. Chariots and banqueting equipment are more typical of male burials. That these high status objects were also sometimes buried with women, and even children, indicates that social position was hereditary within the aristocratic clan, not earned by each individual during his/her lifetime.

Below the chariots was the body of the woman, covered in jewelry. She was buried with an unprecedented number of *fibulae*, around a thousand of them, with another 600 or so ornaments made of bone, amber, and glass beads, containers for personal toiletries, and the remnants of two pairs of sandals. At the nearby burial complex known as the *"Circolo delle Fibule,"* nine tombs yielded up more than 2,000 *fibulae*: 500 pins buried with one woman, 350 with another, 200 with a third. While some of these pins may having been serving a function of holding together the clothing and various layers of funeral winding sheets, Maurizio Landolfi (*"Regine e Principesse picene vestite e coperte di bronzo e ambra," Non Solo Frivolezze*, p. 76) suggests that these women may have been buried with all the ornaments each had acquired in her lifetime, carefully arranged on and around the body. Some of these ornaments, with their pectoral tiers, arrays of pendants, multiple bronze spirals, are so heavy that it would seem they could only have been intended for occasional ceremonial use, if not solely for funeral rites. Such a wealth of *fibulae* is not found in other Italian burials, nor in the Greek tombs of the era. At the most, an early seventh century Etruscan tomb at Corneto Tarquinia contained seventy-four *fibulae*, and one at Cervetri had twenty-three mainly gold ones (along with many other precious objects).

The human figure is not often depicted in Piceno art, and only in a stylized way, for the most part without much detail. The figures that hang from *pettorali* and *fibulae* reveal little more than how women fixed their hair. A fragment of a limestone statue, a headless woman's torso, was found at Capestrano in Abruzzo; it is presumed to be part of a funeral stele. One braceletted arm is crossed between her small breasts to touch a pendant hanging from her necklace. The bodice of her garment has a border still tinged with red paint. The fabric is held in place by two rounded shoulder pads, which are attached with *fibulae* of a type found in graves throughout the sixth century BC. Aside from this and a few other funeral stelae, the only way to figure out how these people dressed is from the personal ornaments in their graves. The form of the vanished cloth, leather, and hair must be deduced from the placement of pins, buckles, beads, and all manner of jewelry. Here is a description by Nora Lucentini of the woman in grave #13 in a seventh to sixth century BC Piceno necropolis at Montedinove:

> The body is partially covered by a stole of leather or fabric embroidered with bronze rivets in angular patterns which could still be made out at the moment of excavation. The function of the stole, rectangular but with rounded ends, is not known; in other cases it was laid to the side of the body and thus did not seem directly to make a part of the clothing.

The face is framed by two bronze pendants that hang down from the temples, at the neck a delicate jewel of amber depends from the heavy necklace that covers the breast down to the waist, on the left shoulder a rich bundle of springwires fastened at the nape of the neck simulates a lustrous tail of bronze curls and ends with a cascade of small chains. On the breast is an ornament of concentric circles in iron and below, on the right, an exceptional *fibula* composed in part of amber, up to now without equal. The surprise, however, was in the fringe of amber and the trickle of tiny beads of bone, amber, and glass paste that issued from the cracks when an attempt was made to remove the grave in a block (N. Lucentini, *"I signori di Montedinove," Non Solo Frivolezze*, p. 71).

Unfortunately, the block of earth containing the woman's remains broke apart during this attempted removal, destroying most of the traces of beaded embroidered clothing, the possible net of amber beads…

Lucentini remarks that women's burials indicate both a strong local identity and the social organization of the clan. Certain styles of *fibulae* and other ornaments are unique to one area or even one necropolis. At Montedinove the women were arrayed in two distinct ways; it remains to be determined whether these two styles reflect the social class of the deceased, or, more likely, her social role, that is, single woman, wife, or mother.

The Queen of Numana was also buried with a *telaio a cintura*, or back strap loom, the first appearance of this device in a ritual deposit. This type of loom allows the weaver to maintain the tension of the warp threads by leaning back into a harness which is anchored at the other end to an upright support, like a tree. The looms are small, portable, but the width of the cloth is limited to the weaver's arm span. The more common vertical loom keeps the warp threads taut by hanging loom weights on their bottom ends. These free-standing structures, mentioned by Homer and depicted on ancient Greek vases, produce larger pieces of fabric, like the winding sheet Penelope was endlessly weaving. Loom weights appear as grave goods, and are a constant presence in sanctuary sites, reflecting perhaps the honored even sacred role of this female industry. They also turn up in more casual settings. Our cousin Anna Maria Ferri showed us a site in Monsampolo del Tronto, a classic hilltown fortress perched on the northern ridge of the Tronto River valley. The dig is on the outskirts, on a hillside where farmland is being converted into suburbs. Several already completed three-story apartment buildings surround it; this next foundation cannot be constructed until the archaeologists finish their work. What they have uncovered is, they think, a Piceno pottery workshop, with fire-darkened earth marking where the kilns were, basins indicating where the ceramics were set. The woman in charge hands us a clay loom weight that they had found that day; a slightly flattened orb the size of a small walnut, with a hole through the center, darker than the reddish dirt at our feet. It was fired, Anna instructs us, that's why it has lasted all these millennia. I hand it back to the supervisor, who seemed worried that I might not. The museums are full of these objects, but it is unusual to find one in a place that probably made them, a non-cemetery Piceno site. The scorched work area will be removed, stored where it can be examined later, and soon another apartment building will rise on this spot.

Men's Graves

The graves of Piceni men show a rather different assortment of objects. Instead of layers of jewelry and personal ornaments, they were buried with a panoply of weapons both functional and ceremonial. Perhaps no other region of Italy has yielded up such a rich and varied assortment from this time period. Some of these arms were clearly made for display, not use. The weapons may have indicated that the deceased was a warrior, perhaps a mercenary, or may have reflected his social status. The Piceni apparently had a warrior prince ruling class, but what was the proportion of warrior to prince? And perhaps the ruling class was based on the manufacture of and trade in weapons. Armed men protected shipments of goods, merchant caravans, and also extracted tolls and tribute from those who passed through their territory. Some of this activity may have been outright raiding and piracy. Piceni men were either buried wearing very little clothing, perhaps replicating the sparse garb worn in battle, or their garments were made of materials that completely disappeared over time; cloth, leather, fur, without the studs and beads that outline women's clothing.

A well-appointed example of a male Piceno burial was excavated near the mountainous inland town of Matelica, where a number of lavish circle tombs have been found. In 1998, while renovating the underground parking garage of a condominium building, workers found a trench burial within a circular ditch, once probably covered with a mound of pebbles. The grave dates to the end of the eighth and beginning of the seventh century BC.

The dead man had been buried lying on his back, with a rich array of bronze and iron weapons and a bronze helmet, equestrian gear, scepters and *fibulae*. Next to him were more than twenty ceramic vessels, presumably a funerary banquet service, and a heavily embossed bronze *situla*, a bucket-shaped container thought to be used for serving wine. A bronze bowl held more than 200 cultivated grape seeds, once bunches of grapes. This evidence of the cultivation of grapes, and by extension the making of wine, is the oldest testimony of this sort in Le Marche and some of the oldest and rarest in central Italy. On top of the ceramic vessels was the complete skeleton of a baby pig, showing no signs of having been cooked; next to it was an iron knife. This little piglet was perhaps sacrificed just before the tomb was closed. The presence of it and of the bowl of grapes suggests a codified funeral ritual (G. de Marinis; M. Silvestrini, *Eroi e Regine*, pp. 76–78).

Another nearby trench contained over two hundred ceramic vessels, a dozen bronze vessels, and banqueting equipment including a bronze grater. In "Nestor's Cup and the Etruscans," David Ridgeway has suggested that these bronze graters were introduced to the Etruscans by Euoboeans trading in the metal ores of Etruria, for use as part of the "heroic" drinking rituals practiced on the Greek island of Euoboea as early as the ninth century BC. In *The Iliad*, Hecamede, a woman captured and given to Nestor, prepares a restorative drink of "Pramnian wine, grating in goat's cheese with a grater of bronze" (Homer, *The Iliad*, p. 137). These graters are characteristic of Piceno grave goods. The smaller ones were perhaps used to grate spices to flavor wine; the larger ones for hard aged cheeses.

While these banqueting rituals and types of utensils may have been adopted from the Etruscans or, either through them or independently, from the Greeks, most of the goods found in Matelica were not imports. The warrior elite of this settlement supported skilled artisans who produced luxury items using all the latest styles and techniques. The craftsmen may have been native workers, or they may have been masters brought from other places. Designs and forms from all over southern Italy and Magna Graecia were seized upon and elaborated on in local workshops.

The Etruscans are often portrayed as being far in advance of their contemporary Italic neighbors. While Etruria and the Tyrrhenian coast were heavily involved in maritime trade with the cultures of the eastern Mediterranean, Picenum too had such contacts, comparable but distinct. This "orientalizing" influence of the eighth and seventh centuries BC appears to have come both over the Apennines and by way of the Adriatic, and was part of a broader network of elite classes. Small groups of people, families or clans, controlled the wealth of their individual regions, the agriculture and animal husbandry, the timber, the metals, the tolls extracted from those who came through by way of the mountain passes or valley roads. These elites were connected with their peers all around the Mediterranean, trading in goods, cultural styles and practices, probably even mates. The grand scale princely burial, with its chariots, its wealth of grave goods, its luxurious rituals of drinking wine and feasting on meat, was a tangible expression of an extensive international culture that was both commercial and aristocratic.

The Ancona Museum displays various examples of the *dischi-corazza* mentioned above. These round bronze breastplates were worn in pairs, the larger one on the chest, and the smaller on the back. They are very characteristic of the mid-Adriatic zone, and their presence marks the grave of a warrior chief, though they also appear in high-ranking women's graves. Some were decorated with engraved and embossed geometric patterns, others with stylized winged creatures and quadrupeds. One of the most frequently pictured sets, found in San Severino, is described as follows:

Breastplate / *Disco-corazza*
Museo Archeologico Nazionale delle Marche

On the larger disc the central area is decorated with a scene of two human figures and a monstrous fantastical animal, along with a small quadruped. More than an allusion to a fertility cult, the scene depicted has been interpreted as the expression of overpowering violence and arrogant aggression, with the humiliating submission, in a sexual context, of the defeated. In the presence of a male person [referred to elsewhere as the dead warrior], nude and with an erect phallus, standing in profile, a monster with a doubled horse's body sodomizes an enemy knocked upside down with legs stretched wide and arms open. On the smaller disc the center circle is decorated with a monstrous animal with a doubled horse's body, the two divergent heads turned towards the outer edge. Attributed to local Italian workers, the two discs are dated to the end of the seventh century BC (M. Landolfi, *Eroi e Regine*, p. 253).

There are two iconic representations of Piceni men. The first is the Head of a Warrior, found by chance near Numana at the end of the 1800s and on display at the Ancona Museum. Sculpted from local limestone, 45 cm/18 in high, this head was presumably once part of a larger-than-life-sized funerary statue dating from the end of the seventh century BC. It is described in *Eroi e Regine* as "the most ancient sculpture in stone of large dimensions in the entire circum-Adriatic region" (G. Baldelli,

Head of a Warrior-Numana
Museo Archeologico Nazionale delle
Marche

p. 240). The warrior has an oval face, a thick neck, and carefully sculpted ears. The large narrow nose is missing, as are the surface details of his lips. His eyes are small and round and his gaze a little off-kilter. Some red paint remains on his chin and cheeks. A delicate chinstrap, detailed to perhaps represent braided leather, passes in front of his ears up to his imposing helmet. This helmet can be identified as a specific type called the "Novilara," a style not found before the second half of the seventh century BC. The ridge of a double crest tops the smooth basin; the crest itself is gone.

The Piceni were known for their bronze helmets, and Picenum has been called the region richest in helmets in all Europe. The earliest helmets in Italy appeared in Etruscan burials from the ninth century BC; the oldest helmet in a Piceno tomb is an Etruscan one dating to the eighth century BC, found in the Villanovan outpost of Fermo. By the seventh century the Piceni were turning out their own helmets. They were a status symbol, buried with male members of the warrior ruling class. The evolution of forms helps date the burials, although some men may have been buried with heirloom items. The size of the brim, the lines of rivets, the crests, studs, spikes, the elaborately engraved decorations, are all markers of particular eras, particular places. Piceni helmets have been found throughout Italy, in Slovenia, the Balkans, southern France and northern Spain. A few Greek helmets, the Corinthian type with cheek and nose protection, have been found in Piceno; Piceni helmets for the most part left the face uncovered. Perhaps one of the most elaborate helmets on display here is from the mid-fourth century BC. Found in the Gallic cemetery in Fillotrano, it has a lofty iron trident on top to hold plumes, and a mixture of bronze and iron in the highly decorated headpiece and protective side flaps. It is attributed to a Celtic-Italian workshop. After the battle of Sentinum, when the Romans took control over much of Picenum, the 500-year-old Piceno custom of burying dead warriors with their helmets disappeared.

Bronze Piceno Helmet
Metropolitan Museum of Art, New York

The second example of a Piceno man is the *Guerriero di Capestrano*/Warrior of Capestrano. This funerary statue was found in pieces in 1934 by a farmer planting a vineyard near Capestrano in Abruzzo, on the southernmost edge of Piceno territory. Further archaeological excavations unearthed a seventh–sixth century BC necropolis, as well as the stone female torso mentioned above. The restored statue is now the star exhibit in the Chieti museum, a splendid 1830 villa surrounded by pine-shaded grounds in this provincial town.

The warrior stands over 2 m/6.5 ft tall, slightly larger than life size. Except for the headgear, the statue was carved out of a single block of local limestone. A bit flat front to back, the figure has broad shoulders, a narrow waist, and wide, rounded, hips; this last feature has led to numerous comments regarding his gender. He wears *dischi-corazza*/breastplates front and back, their still-red straps running over his shoulders and under his arms, of a type dated to the mid-fourth century BC. Both upper arms are encircled with bracelets, one with a fringe, and a *torque* or neckband with an amulet reaches partway around his neck. His mask-like face has the round inexpressive eyes, damaged nose and mouth, of the Numana warrior, and also the prominent ears. He gazes out from under a broad sombrero-style crested helmet, which might also serve as a shield. His arms are crossed one above the other over his torso in a gesture common to many archaic statues, signifying his high rank as well perhaps as beating his breast in grief. His right hand presses a delicate curved ax, an instrument of ceremonial sacrifices. The lower left hand lies across a short sheathed sword with a decorated and painted hilt. This type of sword was a more recent development, carefully strapped across the body so that it did not shift around or impede the horseman, and so that it could be easily drawn with his right hand. Mounted

Warrior of Capestrano
Museo Archeologico Nazionale di Abruzzo

on the face of the sword's sheath is a smaller separately sheathed dagger, ready for hand-to-hand combat. A pair of lances is carved onto the two supporting pillars.

On the front of the right pillar is an inscription that has been deciphered as identifying the figure as Nevio Pompuledio, *"Raki,"* or "King," a role that combined warrior chief, high priest, and administrator of justice. The inscription is written in South Picenean, one of the Oscan-Umbrian, or Sabellic, indo-european languages spoken in pre-Roman central and southern Italy. It uses an alphabet in which each letter relates to a sound; the Phoenicians invented this system of writing and it quickly spread to the Greeks, then to the Etruscans and the other Italic peoples. The South Piceno alphabet is based on the Etruscan, with variations reflecting local pronunciation. It is read right-to-left, then left-to-right, in alternating lines, "like an ox pulling a plow." There are only about twenty-three inscriptions in South Picenean, most of them carved in stone, mostly on stelae or, in the case of the Warrior of Capistrano, on a monumental stele-statue. The stelae date from the sixth to the fourth century BC; they are thought to be funeral monuments to eminent persons, often placed in cemeteries though not marking an individual tomb. The longest inscriptions are only a few lines, the shortest just a name. These inscriptions have been deciphered, in the sense that the letters and words can be identified, but the meaning is often unclear because we do not understand the vocabulary being used. By the third century BC, South Picenean had been supplanted by the Latin alphabet.

Stele di Novilara
Museo Archeologico Nazionale delle Marche

There is a second type of writing, called North Picenean; only fragmentary examples exist, containing about sixty words. The alphabet is based on northern Etruscan, as found around Bologna, but the meaning is unknown. This writing appears on the four so-called Novilara stelae, named after the site near Pesaro, but only one of the pieces can be directly linked to that site. The authenticity and provenance of the others is unclear. One fragment is in the Ancona Museum, two in the Pigorini Museum in Rome, and one in the Oliveriano Museum in Pesaro.

This last stele, which was indeed found near Pesaro in the 1860s and dates to the second half of the sixth century BC, shows a battle at sea carved into the sandstone. In the background is a large sailing vessel with fifteen oarsmen. In front are two smaller boats without sails, filled with men wielding lances and perhaps wearing helmets and carrying shields. All of the human figures are outlines lacking details. It is generally agreed that the stele honors a deceased prince or naval commander; the meaning of the scene is less clear. Lorenzo Braccesi (*Eroi e Regine,* pp. 33–34) proposes that the large ship is a Greek commercial craft; one of the smaller boats is that of attacking pirates, probably Illyrian (perhaps Liburni) from across the Adriatic, and the other is from Novilara, escorting and protecting the Greek merchants. The Italians are winning, the pirates' bodies are falling into the ocean. The stele may immortalize one memorable battle, or it may testify to the lifetime role of the deceased as protector of the sea trade. The various items depicted surrounding the boats can be interpreted as the goods involved in this trade, such as the wild and domesticated animals that were abundant in Piceno. A patterned rectangle with three human figures above it could represent a plowed and cultivated field, referring to the agricultural bounty of the region. Other paired human figures may be slaves, another type of commerce. The serpentine form at the top could be a river, the enlarged section signifying a port, an emporium along the inland river trade route. A final item may be a raft, necessary for hauling all this wealth.

Piracy was a big problem here. Elena Di Filippo Balestrazzi cites Diodorus of Sicily, who, writing in the first century BC, describes the Adriatic as historically being so infested with pirates that Greek merchants avoided it, preferring the Tyrhennian Sea for their trade routes (*La Pirateria nell'Adriatico Antico,* pp. 179–180). Various groups of pirates came from Illyria, the northwestern part of the Balkan peninsula. More specifically, the Liburni were based on the coast opposite Picenum, in what is now Croatia. Balestrazzi argues that this reputation for piracy could also be interpreted as a sign that the Adriatic was a zone of heavily laden merchant ships worth plundering, and of prosperous coastal towns worth raiding (Balestrazzi, p. 184).

The actual nature of this piracy is hard to define. Did the pirates attack all vessels, or only those with whom they were not allied? Did they protect some merchant ships from other pirates? To what extent were they themselves merchants? The bias towards the Etruscans as the source of all Greek and "orientalizing" goods favors the view of an Adriatic closed to direct trade with the East, but the exotic ivory, beads, graters, vases, etc. could have been imported into Picenum thanks in part to the pirates, not despite them. Specifically "piratical" objects do not exist to mark this industry. What can be traced is the diffusion of certain types of goods, such as the spiral *fibulae* characteristic of the Liburni, and the Daunian ceramics they brought from Apulia.

In the first century AD, Pliny refers to Truentum, at the mouth of the Tronto River, as the last remaining Liburni settlement in Italy (*Natural History III*, p. 110). Traces of the Liburni presence here and in the Tronto valley date from at least the ninth century BC and continue into the sixth century BC, when Daunian ceramics were abruptly replaced by Greek ones. Unlike the hilltop settlements overlooking the valley, defensible in the event of pirate raids, the port was easily accessible from the sea. Balestrazzi describes the site as a no-man's-land, an open trading post not controlled by any local territorial power. The presence of the Liburni faded as the Greeks came to dominate the sea.

The Handles of Luxury

In one of the large rooms of the Ancona Museum, in a glass case, sits the early fifth century BC *Dinos di Amandola*. This bronze vase, sitting on a tripod, was discovered by chance in 1890 on a farm near the rural hill town it is named for. From the highest piazza of Amandola, above the opera house La Fenice, you can see a spectacular panorama of the long ridge of the Sibillini Mountains. The Tenna River runs below the city, from its source in the mountains above the Gola del'Infernaccio to the Adriatic 60 km/37 mi away. A Roman antiquarian bought the *dinos* in 1891; he then donated it to the State in exchange for permission to export a group of illegally acquired 16th century marble statues. It was

Dinos di Amandola
Museo Archeologico Nazionale delle Marche

restored in Rome and in 1901 sent to the Ancona Museum. When the museum was bombed in WWII the *dinos* was badly damaged. It has been restored again but many pieces are missing.

The ovoid vase is made of molded and laminated bronze, with a small mouth and rounded bottom. It was probably used at banquets to mix wine and water. The low tripod that holds it has decorative spiral flourishes and palmettes and three little lion paws with jauntily bent ankles and sharp claws. On the rim of the vase are two handles in the form of crouching animals, a lioness and a bull—the bull is a copy of the lost original. There are empty spaces for two more handles. Over the years various scholars have attributed this work to Asia Minor, Magna Graecia, Peloponnesian Greece, or, perhaps most likely, to an Etruscan workshop. M. Landolfi notes that:

The presence at Amandola of this magnificent *dinos* proves to be of great interest. On the one hand, in fact, it attests to the formation *in loco* of an emerging aristocratic class that aimed to exhibit their well-being by way of adopting the practice of banqueting and the importation of precious vases used in this. On the other hand it documents the important role played by the Tenna valley in the process of acculturation of the Piceno population settled along the course of the river (M. Landolfi, *Museo Archeologico Nazionale delle Marche, Sezione Protostorica I Piceni*, p. 142).

When we were interviewing Nora Lucentini, at the time director of the State Archaeological Museum in Ascoli Piceno, she commented on where we live. "The Museum of Fine Arts [MFA] in Boston has two bronzes in its collection that may be the missing handles of the Amandola *dinos*. We have tried to arrange to borrow them, to see if they match. Perhaps, when you return home, you could make some inquiries...?"

So when we were back in the States Nathan called the MFA and was eventually able to talk with a curator in the appropriate department. "I know you think you're doing a good thing," she said, "But once the Italians get their hands on those things we'll never get them back."

These two bronzes, a lion and a boar, have been analyzed as coming from the same artisan, the same workshop, as the *dinos*. Books such as *Eroi e Regine* and *I Piceni* refer to them as probably being the missing handles. They were acquired in 1910 by the Boston MFA, bought from the collector E.P. Warren in a lot of seventy-one mixed objects for $4,000. Their listed provenances are "bought in Rome; said to come from the marshes (sic) of Ancona" and "said to come from the Marches of Ancona; bought in Rome." According to David Sox, in his group biography *Bachelors of Art*, E.P. Warren and his companion John Marshall, in a golden decade from 1892 to 1902, purchased a vast array of Italian and Greek antiquities which were subsequently sold to the MFA, the Metropolitan Museum in New York, and other museums. E.P. "Ned" Warren was the son of a Massachusetts paper manufacturer who had amassed a fortune after the Civil War with the new technology of making paper from wood pulp rather than from cloth and rags (including, during the war, the wrappings of mummies imported from Egypt.) Ned Warren grew up in Boston's elite Beacon Hill neighborhood; his older brother Sam took over the family business, and also eventually became the President of the Trustees of the MFA. This freed Ned to set up an expatriate life in England and Italy, in an enclave of scholars and art historians. Ned and John, acting as purchasing agents for the MFA, rounded up many of the masterpieces—and forgeries— that formed the basis of the fledgling museum's Classical Antiquity Greek and Roman collection. The business of collecting involved a certain amount of smuggling, of buying from tomb robbers and shady dealers, as Italian law forbade the exportation of works of art.

In the MFA's Greek gallery, we locate the two bronze handles. The label describes them as Greek, found near Ancona, Italy. The lion has plush cushioned paws, the curl of the boar's lip matches the lively curl of his tail. Like their counterparts in Ancona, the lioness and the bull, they crouch with their heads lowered, haunches raised; this sharp diagonal makes you question how well they would have functioned as handles.

Other ceremonial vessels found in Piceno have raised the same issue of utility. In the Ancona Museum is a pair of cast bronze handles from the Tomb of the Duke in Belmonte Piceno. Dated to the first half of the sixth century BC, they are attributed to artisans in contact with Greek workshops. The central figure of each, the so-called "Lord of the Horses," wears a Corinthian helmet covering his face and a short garment with breastplates incised into it. His hands are on the forelocks of two small horses. A beam across his shoulders supports a lion on each end. Two birds in flight bridge the gap between the lions and the horse, as do two serpents. Perhaps the most magnificent "Lord of the Horses" was found in Treia, in the Potenza River valley, now displayed in the Museo Oliveriano in Pesaro. The handle is still attached to a (damaged) bronze hydria, dating to the second quarter of the sixth century BC, from a workshop in Magna Graecia, perhaps Taranto. Compared to the handles from Belmonte Piceno, this warrior is less abstract, with more modeling of his face, body, even his toes. In each case, however, as the scholars point out, the rectangular form of the handle, the stacked figures of horses and lions and snakes surrounding their master, does not lend itself to actual use. They are for display—luxury goods for the banquets of the warrior class.

Lord of the Horses
Museo Archeologico Nazionale delle Marche

The Amber Trade

Judging from the abundance of foreign objects found in their tombs, the Piceni were well connected to the greater trade network of the eastern Mediterranean. What did they have to offer in this exchange? Agricultural products, livestock, timber, the jewelry, helmets and weapons they made from metal imported from elsewhere… and amber. From the ninth to the fourth century BC Picenum was a center of the amber trade and a major producer of amber objects.

Amber is the fossilized resin of extinct coniferous trees. The world's main source is the Baltic Sea, where for millennia collectors harvested remnants of vast submerged forests, which washed up on shore after storms. Many pieces have inclusions such as insects preserved within the hardened sap. Prized for ornamental and ritual uses because it is fragrant and easily worked, amber also has the property of producing static electricity when rubbed with a cloth; the word "electric" comes from the Greek "*elektron*," meaning "amber." A Greek myth describes the origin of amber, which was sacred to the Sun and used in funeral rites. When Phaeton, racing his father the Sun's chariot across the sky, lost control of the horses, Zeus killed him with a thunderbolt before he could destroy the world. His body fell into the mythical river Eridanus, sometimes identified with the Po. The gods transformed Phaeton's grieving sisters into poplar trees lining this river; the tears they shed turned into amber. (The seasonal clouds of poplar fluff that drift across the floor of the Torricella parking garage, on the Castellano River in Ascoli Piceno, show no signs of any such transformation.)

Even before the second millennium BC there was an established route bringing raw amber south. From the Baltic and North Seas, trade followed the Elbe and Moldau river valleys, crossed the Bohemian forest to the Danube, through the Alps by way of the Brenner pass to the Aldige River, to the Lago di

Garda, along the Mincio River to the Po Delta and into the Adriatic Sea. Later, probably by 1000 BC, the "Amber Road" was streamlined, following the Oder and Morava rivers and reaching the top of the Adriatic by way of the Isonzo. From here the route took to the seas, down the Adriatic to the Aegean and Mediterranean as far as Egypt.

In the Villanovan area north of Piceno are two later Bronze Age sites known for their amber workshops, Verucchio near San Marino and Frattesina (Fratta Polesine) in the Po Delta. From the middle of the 12th to the early ninth century BC they traded in Baltic amber ornaments, as well as producing glass beads of a type found all along the amber road. Ancona was a major port of call in this prehistoric amber trade.

For many years farmworkers, as they cultivated the hillsides near Belmonte Piceno, would discover human skeletons with iron weapons and ornamental objects made of bronze and amber. They sold these items to antiquarians in the surrounding towns such as Montegiorgio, Fermo, and Ancona. In 1909, the Ancona Museum, led by Soprintendente Innocenze Dall'Osso, acquired a small group of artifacts found on a particular property near the Lete River. The sharecropper who farmed this terrain was in the practice of selling the objects that he found in the course of his labors and also, he confessed, during the boredom of the winters he would dig ditches to find more. The property owner was happy to let him do so, attaching no importance to this old junk, and also calculating that the digging involved improved the soil.

In the fall of 1909, torrential rains flooded the lane that led to the farmer's house, and brought to light the upper part of an iron wheel. The Museum immediately excavated the spot and unearthed the first big tomb, which they called *Tomba del Duca*, Tomb of the Duke. Three years of further excavations followed, revealing more than 300 tombs and the traces of large huts. The area was already being used in the eighth century BC, and reached its peak in the sixth century BC; the quantity and luxuriousness of the grave goods surpassed all other Piceni necropoli.

The finds were taken to the Ancona Museum and displayed in a series of rooms, each dedicated to a particular site. In *The Illustrated Guide to the National Museum of Ancona*, published in 1915, Dall'Osso describes the contents of every display case, with photographs of many of the items. The objects from each tomb were kept together and displayed as they had been found. Dall'Osso remarks that rich and poor tombs were located side by side, not segregated into separate status-based zones. One photo shows the multitude of ornaments found in the tombs of two women, from their headpieces down to their feet. Because they were buried not only with jewelry but with weapons and chariots with iron rimmed wheels, they were named the Amazons. Whether they actually led warriors into battle or were buried with these as symbols of their social class cannot be proved. Dall'Osso describes at length the necklaces, armbands, bracelets, pettoralli, the great variety of pendants. In another tomb, a baby's skeleton was completely covered with a network of *fibulae*. This documentation is poignantly invaluable, as many of the artifacts were destroyed in the WWII bombing.

The amber objects can be roughly divided into two categories, figurative and geometric. One of the figurative pieces depicts a lion mounting a lioness. Made in the sixth century BC by an artisan of Magna Graecia, it is set up to be worn on a *fibula*. Dall'Osso mentions two amber pieces from the Tomb of the Amazons, one a lion devouring a goat, the other a lion biting an antelope. Other pieces included a crouching monkey, spheres carved with female and animal faces, a round pendant with a gorgon's mask in the center. Also from Belmonte Piceno, two winged ivory goddesses with (missing) amber face masks, a distinctively Piceno detail. Two sphynxes, one ivory and the other bone, with amber face masks, were found in a Celtic tomb near Stockholm; they are judged to be of Piceno production by Greek artisans. Nuccia Negroni-Catacchio describes "Afrodite and Adonis (or Anchise)," found at Falconara Marittima,

Aphrodite and Adonis
Metropolitan Museum of Art, New York

north of Ancona, and now in New York's Metropolitan Museum, as "the most beautiful figurative amber piece of Piceno and probably Italy" (*Eroi e Regine*, p. 103). From the sixth century BC, the 14 cm/5.5 in long carving depicts two reclining figures, perhaps Aphrodite making love to Adonis (or Anchise), perhaps an Etruscan couple at a banquet, like the sarcophaghi of Cervetri and Tarquinia that it resembles. Of Greek or Italian workmanship in an Etruscan setting, it was constructed to be mounted on a massive *fibula* Piceno-style, rather than hung as a necklace pendant.

These carved amber figures have been studied extensively. In most cases it is thought that they were the work of artisans from Magna Graecia or Etruria made to satisfy the particular tastes of Piceno clients. Less attention has been paid to the thousands of simpler geometric items. The most characteristic are the chunks of amber threaded onto massive *fibulae*. The Pigorini Museum in Rome has one such Piceno *fibula* on display; the thin bronze arc, almost 30 cm/1 ft wide, piercing the rough nut of dark amber, makes an intriguing combination of crude elegance. Some of these bronze or iron arcs are as long as 64 cm—more than two feet, and the amber can weigh as much as a kilo—more than two pounds. Typical of the region south of Numana, they would seem to be most suited for use in rituals. More common are amber discs of various sizes, with holes for mounting on *fibulae* or as charms hung on necklaces, bracelets, earrings, and *torques*. There are spheres and cylinders used as pendants or as spacers on *pettorali*, amber plaques set into ivory, bronze or silver, beads of all sizes. Because there are so many of these pieces, and because their form is so distinctive, it is thought that they were made in local Piceno workshops, from Baltic amber, during the ninth–fourth centuries BC. After that for unknown reasons the center of production shifted south, into the Pescara and L'Aquila regions of Abruzzo.

In Search of the Goddess Cupra

Belmonte Piceno perches on a hilltop between the Tenna and Ete Vivo Rivers, less than 16 km/10 mi inland from Fermo; the ridge is one of the characteristic teeth of the comb leading from the mountains to the sea. The honey-colored town you see today was mainly built in the 1700–1800s, on the footprint of a 12th century castle. We stop for coffee at a café set into the city wall, sitting outside in the sun. At a nearby table an expansive man is holding court, greeting everyone who passes, many of whom pause for news and commentary. So we ask him if he knows where the Piceni tombs were dug up. No, he doesn't, he admits, but here's someone who will. He calls over a young man who was just arriving. His name is Stefano, a student at the University of Macerata though he looks younger, and he does know where the sites were and will be happy to show us. Soon we are driving on a tree-lined road that runs along the knife-edge of the hill. Growing up here, Stefano says he learned a lot about the area's archaeology from the local priest who, as is so often the case, was a passionate scholar of regional history and pre-history. He directs us down a sharply angled side road that plunges into the valley through steep green fields. This was the area, he says, these hillsides were full of the Piceni, not just their bones but their stuff; "we only know about them because they were buried with so many things, metal and ceramics, that survived." The land is all being farmed now, but maybe there is more to be found. As we approach a tight curve Stefano points out a farm building. The owner of this, he says, wouldn't give permission to excavate, preferring to keep his barn intact; they say that another magnificent tomb lies beneath it.

Stefano generously expands the scope of our tour, directing us to the church Santa Maria in Muris, constructed by the Farfa monks in the 10th century on a Roman site, reusing a Roman stele at the entrance. The Lombard tower is pierced with narrow defensive peepholes, with views sweeping up and down the valley. Nearby, we hike up an overgrown path to a grove of trees on the top of a hillock in the middle of a field. In the shade of the low-hanging branches stand blocks of Roman concrete, called the *Morrecini*. The ruins of Augustan Era funeral monuments, their marble facings are gone and any epigraphs have disappeared; what remains are these massive hulks wrapped in briars, and underneath them suggestive crannies and crevasses. "The legend says that down there you can hear the sound of a golden loom weaving golden cloth," Stefano says laconically. "The local people think that maybe there's treasure buried here too."

A couple of years later, when we pass this way again, we try to locate the farm building he pointed out, the one sitting on top of the unexplored Piceno tomb. We find the side road, the remembered curve, but not the barn. When we get out of the car to peer this way and that, a woodpecker watches us from the telephone wire, his head cocked to one side… perhaps a message from Mars.

Judging from the large quantities of bronze figurines representing them, the people in this region worshipped a number of foreign gods. Mars was favored along the coast, Hercules in the mountain regions extending to the south. Cult sites dedicated to Diomedes were reported in the Greek colonies all around the Adriatic, including Ancona (A. Naso, *I Piceni*, pp. 236–7, 257). The Etruscan fertility goddess Ancaria is mentioned as a protector of the city of Ascoli and is remembered in the name of a town on the south side of the Tronto, Ancarano, where it is said a sanctuary devoted to her once stood.

Cupra is the uniquely local deity, her name found almost exclusively in Picenum and Umbria. She is generally seen as an Earth goddess, a goddess of fertility, a form of the Latin *Bona Dea*, the Great Mother. The Iguvine Tablets of Gubbio mention *Cubra Mater*. She was later linked to worship of the Greek goddess Hera and the Roman goddess Juno, and is sometimes accompanied by Jove. An alternate interpretation ties her to Venus or Aphrodite, goddesses of love, citing the Greek temple in Ancona as a superimposition on a site sacred to Cupra. No permanent structures such as temples have been definitively linked to her worship. Her cult sites, often identified by deposits of ceramic and metal votives, tend to be open air settings associated with water. Reflecting the non-urban nature of Piceno culture, these sites were generally located at mountain passes or ports, on frontiers or borders, serving also as trading posts or emporia. Fossato di Vico and Colfiorito, both near passes through the Apennines, have yielded up references to her. Cupramontana, a hilltop town halfway between Ancona and Fossato di Vico, bears her name, but no archaeological proof of the rumored temple dedicated to her.

At Colfiorito, fourth century BC inscriptions in Umbrian mentioning Cupra have been found, as well as a large number of votive bronze figurines, in an area that may have been an open-air sanctuary. A.L. Prosdocimi stresses that in that era there do not appear to have been any territorial, cultural, or ethnic distinctions between the Piceni and the Umbrians (*Eroi e Regine*, p. 86). The wide-open plain of Colfiorito was a borderland, a crossroads, a meeting place for exchanges between various groups on both sides of the mountains. No major city developed here; the settlements took root on the surrounding hills. Cupra's sanctuary was visited from at least the sixth century through the first century BC. When the Romans took over, they erected a monumental temple dedicated to her on the site where the Santa Maria di Plestia church now stands, built in the 11th century re-utilizing many Roman materials. True to its history, every year a livestock fair is held here (Naso, pp. 235–6, 244).

Cupra Marittima, on the Adriatic seacoast, is the other place most clearly tied to the goddess. Both Strabo and Silius Italicus refer to a sanctuary here devoted to Cupra; Strabo credits the Etruscans with founding it. The emperor Hadrian restored this temple in AD 127, according to a contemporary inscription. Hadrian may have undertaken this project because of family ties to Hadria / Atri to the south. The inscribed piece of stone, now in the church of San Martino in neighboring Grottammare, was found in the 1700s on the grounds of the *pieve* of San Basso in Cupra Marittima. The early Christian church may have been constructed on the site of the pagan sanctuary, a theory supported by the nearby *nymphaeum*, a spa where nymphs could gather around its freshwater spring.

The archeological exploration of Cupra Marittima has a long and confused history. Early finds were poorly documented and the objects ended up scattered far and wide, subject to an ongoing clandestine market. In the late 18th century, agents of the pope dug up the area identified as the Roman forum, looking for objects to enrich a papal museum. A marble head found here, said to be of Venus, is in the museum in Ripatransone; the body of the statue was apparently destroyed by a religious order because it was nude. Other marble statues from the site are now on display in Osimo. At the end of the 19th century, Concezio Rosa, the excavator of Ripoli, undertook a large project in the territory around Cupra Marittima which uncovered a number of Piceni burial sites. Most of his finds were sent to the Pigorini Museum in Rome. Systematic excavations of a Piceno settlement and related necropoli by Innocenzo Dall'Osso in 1911–1912 filled the display cases at the Ancona Museum. In a photograph taken then of the sixth century BC tomb of the "Queen of Cupra Marittima," the woman's body is virtually paved from head to toe with a mosaic of jewelry and ornaments, draped with swags of bronze pendants and chunks of amber. A massive *fibula* lies near her feet. Unfortunately, the "Queen of Cupra Marittima" was one of the victims of the 1944 bombs. Her grave goods were destroyed, or mixed with the other objects on display in the same room. A string of bronze seashell pendants has been identified as hers, as have some little bronze human figures that once hung from a large *fibula* attached on the right side of her breast.

Items closely identified with Cupra include the heavy bronze rings typical of women's tombs in the area of Cupra Marittima-Grottammare. These mysterious rings are found only in the Ascolani zone. One type has four or six lentil shaped nodes evenly spaced around the circle, the second has four or six round ones. While generally around 15 cm/6 in in diameter and weighing around 600 g/1.3 lb, some examples measure more than 20 cm/8 in and weigh 1880 g/4 lb. The function and significance of

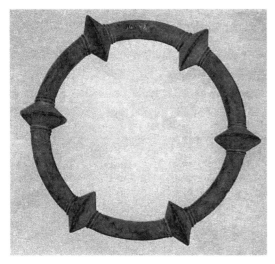

Bronze Ring
Museo Archeologico Nazionale delle Marche

these objects is unknown. They were placed either over the pelvis or by the (usually right) hand. The ring may have been a fertility symbol, or the regalia of a priestess of Cupra. In 1988, an archaeological dig in the Sant'Andrea district of Cupra Marittima unearthed around a thousand votives in the area between the Piceno settlement and its necropolis. Dating from the sixth into the fifth century BC the characteristic votives are miniature clay dishes and serving vessels which resemble nothing so much as crude dollhouse tea sets. Nothing explicitly marks these as related to Cupra, but this too has been suggested as the site of her temple (Naso, pp. 241–242).

A third possible location is the Roman forum itself. Our cousin Luana Lappa set up an appointment for us to tour this site with Andrea Morra, a surveyor with a passion for archeology. We drive down to the coast on a deserted road above the Tesino River. On this ridge a series of medieval hilltowns overlook the valley—Rotella, Montedinove, Castignano, Offida, Cossignano, Ripatransone—each with their own archaeological cache. The road itself is marked with signs reading *Crinale dei Piceni*, "Crest of the Piceni."

We wait for Andrea in the modern center of Cupra Marittima. The old town sits on the hill above us. Historically known as Marano, from the Roman era name *castrum marianum*, it is a rare instance where the medieval city was not built on top of the Roman town on top of the Piceno settlement. Each culture chose a different hill, in each case a highly defensible position that sheltered its inhabitants from attacks from the sea, whether Liburni or Saracen or Turks. Marano was primarily guarded by watchtower-houses (*case-torri*) until the end of the 12th century, when this function was taken over by an encircling stone wall. Since 1999, the town's archaeological museum has been housed in the Palazzo Cipolletti, a 10th century watchtower subsequently refashioned many times to serve a variety of purposes. The results of most excavations since the 1970s are on display here.

Behind us is the Adriatic. The congested seaside Rt. 16 follows what was in Roman times the coastline. Up until the mid-1800s this stretch was sparsely populated with small fishing settlements, the sailors pulled their boats up onto the beach where brightly painted wooden shacks stored their gear. Then in 1863, the Ancona–Pescara railway line was completed. By the end of the century the region was known for its summer resorts, frequented by foreign visitors. The new bourgeoisie built villas in the trendy Art Nouveau style (called *stile Liberty* in Italy, after the English textile firm whose designs exemplified the look). These villas, some lovingly restored and others not, still lend a turn of the last century charm amidst the sprawl of post-WWII development, block after block of multi-story apartment buildings used as vacation homes in July and August.

Andrea bounds down one of the two stone staircases, built in 1890, that frame the central square. He and Luana exchange a few pleasantries and then we are off. First stop is a Roman thermal spa, right along Rt. 16, next to a gas station. The bath tubs and frescoes are still here, a reminder that the Romans too appreciated a good summer resort. We wind up the hill above it and park the car, proceeding on foot. The path climbs through a terraced olive grove. Andrea explains that these terraces were created using the Roman walls of buildings now buried in the earth. Water still drains out of the Roman sewer pipes. Further along Andrea shows us the place where, some years back, the grave of a Roman soldier was discovered by a group of school children. The kids were in a European summer program, and had been set to dig in this spot because nothing was thought to be there.

The path leads upwards, skirting a vine-covered Roman wall, and then we reach a plateau with a wide view across the blue Adriatic. Those at sea, in turn, could have seen the temple which once stood here. The remains of an Augustan era structure have been partially excavated, and it resembles similar temples found at Ostia Antica and Pompeii. Two arches flank a set of stairs in reticulated stone which lead to a grassy field dominated by a centuries-old stone farmhouse. Perhaps Cupra's altar lies up there, Andrea says, or perhaps somewhere in the Roman forum, which contains the layout of another large building, maybe a basilica. As we wander around these blocks of stone Andrea gestures towards the hills behind us. "The Basile family still owns land here," he says, referring to the descendants of Lucius Minucius Basilus, one of the assassins of Julius Caesar and also perhaps the intended recipient of the Gilded Horses of Pergola.

On our way down we stop to talk with an old man whose garden abuts the archeological zone. His potted plants are set on pieces of sandstone columns and pediments, flowering orange trees and lilacs overhang an ancient stone trough still in use. When we get to the bottom a garden supply store is tucked under ruined stone walls, 12 m/40 ft high, probably some sort of warehouse from the late Republican era. The tile roof of a shed fits into one corner. The Roman port was right here, excavations along the state highway have revealed the ruins of stone piers and moorings.

And so we came to Cupra Marittima, looking for traces of the Piceno goddess, and mostly found a lot of Roman ruins. Because now the story of Picenum comes under the dominance of the Roman Empire.

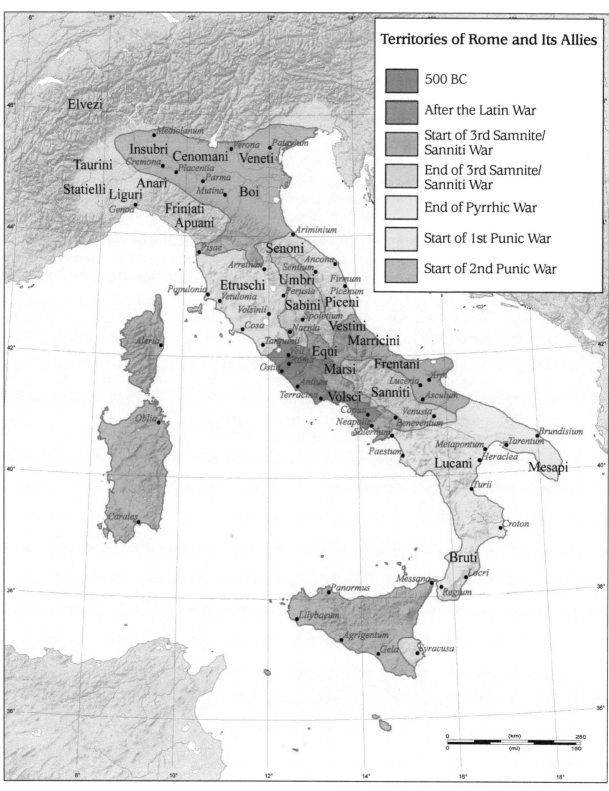

The Roman Conquest of Italy

Territories of Rome and Its Allies

- 500 BC
- After the Latin War
- Start of 3rd Samnite/ Sanniti War
- End of 3rd Samnite/ Sanniti War
- End of Pyrrhic War
- Start of 1st Punic War
- Start of 2nd Punic War

Elvezi

Taurini
Statielli Liguri
Anari
Friniati
Apuani

Insubri Cenomani Veneti
Cremona Placentia Parma
Mutina Boi
Mediolanum Verona Patavium
Genoa

Ariminium

Pisae
Populonia Arretium Senoni
Etruschi Vetulonia Perusia Sentium Ancona
Volsinii Umbri Firmum
Sabini Piceni Picenum
Cosa Spoletium
Narnia Vestini
Tarquinii Veii Equi Marricini
Roma Marsi Frentani
Ostia Antium Volsci Sanniti Luceria Arpi
Terracina Capua Venusia Asculum
Neapolis Beneventum
Salernum
Paestum Metapontum Tarentum Brundisium
Lucani Heraclea
Turii Mesapi
Croton
Bruti Locri
Messana Rhegium
Panormus
Lilybaeum
Agrigentum
Gela Syracusa

Aleria

Oblia

Carales

∽∽ 5 ∽∽

Picenum Under the Yoke — or the Picenean War

The Piceni entered written history at a peculiar moment in their social development—just as they were about to cease to exist as an independent entity. Livy, one of the earliest existing sources, says that they had completed a pact with Rome in 299 BC. "At Rome the rumor of a Gallic rising in addition to an Etruscan war caused alarm, and speeded up the conclusion of a treaty with the people of Picenum" (Livy, *Rome and Italy: The History of Rome from its Foundation*, p.302). An obscure reference, no doubt, but the background story is a recurring theme in world history.

The Piceni receive scant mention in the works of ancient writers. The Greek geographer Strabo (67 BC–AD 24) recounts the well-known fable told in every tourist guide about a group of Mars-worshipping Sabines following a woodpecker to a new land in the ritual of the Sacred Spring. Livy only gives them a few lines in Book X and in the summation of the lost Book XV. These lines refer to the Piceni's role in the buildup to the pivotal Samnite Wars. Livy was born in 64 or 59 BC, and his stories are based on writers who were themselves telling stories second or third hand. The noted ancient historian E.T. Salmon, in his book *Samnium and the Samnites,* gives a concise rendering of the situation:

> Whoever seeks to narrate the Second Samnite War is faced with the difficulty of describing a contest which, while in a sense within the full light of history, is remote enough to lack authentic primary sources. Details concerning the war have indeed survived, but from the pens of men who lived long after the events they recount and are often unreliable (p. 214).

Perhaps the most significant source was Fabius Pictor, born 254 BC, sometimes called the first Annalist. Annalists were early Roman historians who gave a year-by-year account of the most important events, recording for posterity the glories of Rome. He may have had an inside track; his great-uncle was Quintus Fabius Rullianus, leader of the Roman victory at the Battle of Sentinum. Unfortunately, his prose history of Rome is lost, known only through quotations and references by later authors.

By the fourth century BC, the Roman Republic had begun to extend its reach over the Italian peninsula. According to P. A. Brunt, the early Rome of 509 BC comprised only some 800 sq. km/300 sq. mi (Brunt, *Social Conflicts in the Roman Republic*, p. 1). The ongoing expansion of Rome doubtlessly induced some groups such as the Umbrians, Sabines, and Etruscans to fear for their independence and to make an alliance with the Samnites in an anti-Roman coalition. According to Livy the Samnites also invited the Piceni to join, who promptly informed the Romans, with whom they had already concluded a pact. The Romans thanked them.

Speculation about the reason for the Piceni's pact with Rome is easy. Scholars point out that with the Celts, or Gauls as the Romans called them, to the north, and the Piceni's cousins the Pretuzi to the south, the pact with the Romans offered ample protection. Maybe too ample? Perhaps the Piceni imagined that the Romans were a known quantity since they must have had dealings with them for centuries. Times had changed. The period of the Samnite Wars, 343–290 BC, saw an "unparalleled increase in the public and private wealth of Rome" (*Camb. Anc. His.*, VII, p. 403). The process of annexation undertaken by the Romans erupted in a series of wars, especially with Oscan speaking Samnites, throughout the second half of the fourth century BC into the third, and culminated in the decisive Battle of Sentinum in 295 BC, fought near today's Sassoferato in Le Marche.

The Romans and Samnites had also known each other for a long time. Sometimes fighting, sometimes allied, they competed for the extremely fertile Campania region south of the Liris River, once controlled by Greeks. The Samnites (also called Sanniti) are often described as coarse shepherds. But it is usually Romans doing the describing and some modern day historians seem content to pass that on, although it is hard to understand how such unsophisticates were able to learn Greek ways and teach the Romans a thing or two about warfare. They armed themselves with weapons to match the invaders even though their land was devoid of metal deposits. In fact, in the fourth century BC the people identified as the Samnites controlled more territory than the Romans. The Romans could never have commanded an army to enter and fight in Samnium without the hope of considerable war booty. It is important to remember that in the ancient army every man was an independent military contractor with his own armor and the right to his share of the loot. So different from modern empires where the legions fight for college tuition. Livy records how one Roman general convinced his men to sell off their booty to the buyers that followed military entourages so that they could travel lightly, pointing out that there was lots more ahead. The African-born Roman historian Florus (c. AD 74–130) describes the wealth of the Samnites "equipped with gold and silver armors, and with clothes of various colours even to ostentation" (Florus, *Epitome of Roman History, I*, pp. xi, 16).

The Piceni, Samnites, Etruscans, Umbrians, Latins, Frentani, Pretuzi, and so on were all groups inhabiting their respective regions of Italy. Some say that the still strong regional consciousness of Italians today dates this far back and further. Piceno and Le Marche correspond more than any other modern region of Italy when compared with its ancient counterpart. Until recent decades the tendency was to discount the significance of these "Italic tribes" as part of "pre-Roman" Italy, as if the Roman unification of Italy was preordained and the actions of the Italian peoples were only an opportunity for Rome to fulfill its grand destiny. And the word "tribe" is itself suspect because it brings to mind groups like the indigenous Americans, (another long-underestimated group) without international shipping and trade, metal working, or writing. Far from being Rome's primitive forbears, we know today that they were the fertile soil out of which the Roman Empire grew.

The "tribes" were in fact defined by the victors, the Romans. For them, the "Samnites" were the Oscan-speaking people of south-central Italy, comprised of the Carricini, Caudini, Hirpini, and Pentri, who presented an organized enemy. T. J. Cornell says that there is no direct evidence of any such permanent Samnite league or federation. Instead, clusters of small villages had united themselves under an elected local leader, and these groups banded together when militarily necessary, mostly to defend themselves from Roman aggression. In the same way, when ancient historians present the Etruscans as a single foe, they "hide the fact that the Etruscans were actually divided into politically independent city-states that rarely, if ever, acted together as a single confederation" (Cornell, "The 'Samnite Wars,' 343–290 BC," p. 2).

Before the fourth century BC, Rome was just another member of the "Italic tribes," the Latins. The other inhabitants of Italy would surely have been surprised to learn they were living in "pre-Roman Italy" since these groups had existed and prospered for centuries before their conquest by Rome. (On a related side-note: we are using the traditional dating system of BC/AD, because many of our sources do. This calendar was created in AD 525 but not widespread until after 800; obviously, for much of human history, people had no such conception of where they existed in time.) That the Italians would fall subject to the Roman Empire was never inevitable, the Roman drive to the domination of Italy could have fallen apart at many points. As Livy himself says, the battle of Sentinum was a key conflict that but for the engineered absence of the Etrurians and Umbrians, the Romans could have easily lost (Livy, p. 327).

Thirty years after the Celts sacked Rome following the battle of Allia (390 BC), the Romans and Samnites signed a treaty. Rome broke the treaty when they came to the defense of the Sidicini of northern Campania, then under attack by the Samnites—thus the First Samnite War, which ended with the Samnites' defeat and Rome taking a good bit of Campania. Hard on the heels of this victory, the Romans were able to annex a large portion of their neighbors' territory in Latinium, seizing the land of Latins who had risen up against the expansion of Roman power. These successes were the beginning of the less than hundred-year process in which Rome conquered the Italian peninsula, and served as important first lessons in the Roman imperial workbook.

As Livy implies, Rome could have dealt harshly with the Latins and ground them into dust; instead, a wiser path was chosen. Whatever alliances or deals that had existed between the Latins were dissolved and Rome dealt with the different Latin groups individually. Those who had remained loyal were granted full citizenship with rights to marry within the Latin community and make legally binding contracts. Others were granted partial citizenship (*civitas sine suffragio*) after the ringleaders were killed and Roman settlers moved in. Partial citizens could not vote, but had obligations, especially military service. They did receive rights to marriage and contracts but not to an independent foreign policy. The pattern of partial citizenship, allies, and the establishment of Roman colonies enabled Roman expansion throughout Italy, but not before scores were settled with other regional adversaries.

The Second Samnite War (326–304 BC) was the result of continued Roman and Samnite jockeying for dominance. The Romans set up a threatening colony here; the Samnites formed an alliance with perfidious Greeks there. Rome's annexation of Latium and the much-coveted coastal Campania with its agricultural wealth (three crops a year) guaranteed that Rome had the resources and manpower to take on the Samnites, even though Samnium was still larger in terms of land area. The war spanned some twenty-two years and included the resounding defeat of the Romans at the Caudine Forks, a humiliating disaster (perhaps fictionalized) reminiscent of the indigenous Americans tricking the US Calvary into a box canyon. Like the battle of Allia, it was an upset remembered for centuries. In what must have been an historic role reversal, this time the Roman prisoners were forced to pass under the ritual yoke of spears constructed to humiliate captives. Nevertheless, the Romans eventually won the war. The Samnites wanted peace, old treaties were renewed. But it did not last long.

According to Livy, representatives from Lucania came to the Roman consuls seeking help and protection from the Samnites who were waging war against them. Lucania was a region of southern Italy that bordered Campania, Samnium, and Apulia, i.e., today's Basilicata. The Romans and Lucanians signed a treaty. The Samnites rejected Rome's demands that they leave Lucanian territory, and the senate called for a war on the Samnites.

The Romans were already fighting multiple enemies in 298 BC when the Third Samnite War broke out. Conflicts with Etruria and Umbria had been underway for several years. Livy retells the next battle in Samnium as more flight than fight, since the Samnite army was unwilling to seriously engage anywhere and was ultimately forced to leave Samnium in retreat. They made their way to Etruria and met with Etruscan leaders hoping to forge an alliance. Meanwhile, the Roman army was rampaging across Samnium, burning and pillaging. As the Romans sacked cities and towns, the Samnites and Etruscans proposed a massive campaign—nearly all the Etruscans had agreed to war and the furor had also spread to their neighbors, the Umbrians.

Previously, when a huge army of hostile Celts had passed into Etruria, the Etruscans had hoped to convert the Celts to allies by offering to pay them to fight the Romans. The Celts took the money but refused to fight saying the payment was to prevent the Celts from destroying land and crops. "However they were willing to take up arms if the Etruscans really wanted them but only on condition that they were admitted to a share in Etruscan land where they could at last settle in some definite home" (Livy, pp. 301–302). The Etruscans declined, not so much because they could not spare the land, but because "everyone dreaded having men of so savage a race as his neighbors" (Livy, p. 302). The Celts went off with their huge cash settlement gotten with so little effort. The last line from this section of Livy bears repeating, "At Rome the rumor of a Gallic rising in addition to an Etruscan war caused much alarm and speeded up the conclusion of a treaty with the people of Picenum" (Livy, p. 302). Once again, the Etruscans decided to offer the Celts a high price to join up.

Some hundred years earlier, the Celts had settled in the north of Piceno, from Rimini to Ancona on the Adriatic and along the Esino River, supposedly having driven out the Umbrian inhabitants. A map at the archeological museum of Fabriano shows twenty-four Celtic settlements in northern and central Piceno. And these are only the settlements archeologists have found. Different groups of Celts, like the Boi, had been crossing the Alps from France into Italy for many years. These Senone Gauls, as they were called, had as their capital the coastal town now called Senigallia, between Rimini and Ancona. The Celts were, as Livy notes, formidable warriors, famous for going into battle painted and naked except for chain mail chest protection, fighting with total indifference to pain and danger. Speculation is unavoidable that the Piceni would see a pact with the Romans as a deterrent to the Celts (De Sanctis, *La conquista del primato in Italia*, p. 401). Maybe the Piceni hoped to regain ancestral lands that the Celts had since occupied (Cappelli, *ASKL*, p. 52). According to Livy, the Samnites sought out the Etruscans because "they knew them to be the richest people in Italy, in arms, men, and money, and they had for neighbors the Gauls, a race born to the clash of arms, fierce not only by nature, but also in their hatred of the people of Rome—of whose defeat and ransom for gold [the battle of Allia] they could tell, making no empty boast" (Livy, p. 310). Florus agrees, "The Galli Senones were a naturally wild race and quite uncivilized; moreover, by their vast stature and proportionally huge arms and all sorts of other circumstances, they inspired such terror that they seemed created for the destruction of human life and the ruin of cities" (Florus, *Epitome*, p. 301). At this point, Roman prejudice against their opponents has become evident. In his book *Celts and Romans,* Peter Ellis disputes the Roman account of Celtic civilization, pointing out that the Celts had metal working, carpentry, shipbuilding, tile and glass making. He quotes ancient historian Brunt:

> Polybius depicts the Celts as a relatively savage people, who lived in open villages with no permanent buildings, who followed no pursuits but war and agriculture and whose property consisted in cattle and gold. This picture is evidently exaggerated. Details of the wars show that they had fortified towns and stocks of grain. Livy refers to the 'vasa aenae Gallica' (bronze vases) and to other rich booty which Roman Generals secured, and archeological evidence too shows that Polybius is wrong in thinking that they had no arts or crafts (Ellis, p. 34).

The Romans could never admit to the Celts' contributions to central Italy, such as the coveted bronze vases, or the adoption of Celtic words such as "Apennine," or their expertise at chariot warfare.

The Battle of Sentinum

Rome's ongoing worry over war with Etruria was exacerbated by the knowledge received of the coalition forming of Etruscans, Samnites, Umbrians, and Gauls, "…the consuls set out for war with four legions [1 legion = approx. 4,500 men] and a strong contingent of Roman cavalry plus a thousand picked horsemen from Campania, dispatched for this campaign and an army of allies and Latins who outnumbered the Roman, but another two armies were stationed to bar the way from Ertruria…" (Livy, p. 326). No doubt Piceni numbered amongst the allies in this huge formation that Cornell estimates at 36,000, perhaps the largest army Rome had ever fielded. The Roman army and allies set up camp some four miles from Sentinum in the vicinity of the coalition forces.

Cornell and other historians locate Sentinum in Umbria, which is sort of true perhaps at one time, but not strictly true. Sentinum's geographical location merits closer investigation. The Apennine ridge constitutes a natural boundary and today marks the divide between Umbria and Le Marche. Sentinum, near Sassoferrato, lies just to the east on the Marchigiano side, close to the mountain pass of the future consular road the Via Flaminia, an old Etruscan way that connected Rome with the Adriatic. From here to the coast is about 60 km/35 mi. A branch of the road goes from Foligno in Umbria to Ancona passing in the vicinity of Sentinum. When Italy was divided into regions with set boundaries during the reign of Augustus, this northern part of Le Marche, where Piceni settlements have been found as far north as Pesaro, was designated as Umbria. Alberico Pagnani, a local scholar, places Sentinum in the *Ager Gallicus,* Celtic lands, at the time of the Third Samnite war. Celtic lands also became Umbrian. Indisputably, Sentinum lay at a crucial corner where Etrurian, Umbrian, Picenian, and Celtic lands intersected, in a time when boundaries were overshadowed by localities. It is not for nothing that ancient historians and archeologists Bradley, Isayev, and Riva gave their book, *Ancient Italy,* the subtitle "Regions without Boundaries."

The coalition forces had made a plan: the Celts and Samnites would attack the Romans head on while the Etruscans and Umbrians would attack their camp from the rear. But three deserters from the coalition told the Romans about these plans whereupon the Romans came up with a winning idea. They wrote to their armies held back in reserve to attack and destroy Etruscan and Umbrian lands "with utmost rigour" (Livy, p. 326). When the Etruscans and Umbrians heard about the devastation they withdrew to defend their home turf leaving the Samnites and Celts to face the Romans at Sentinum alone.

The Romans seized the opportunity and attempted to engage the enemy, but only a few skirmishes resulted. On the third day both sides drew up to battle. Here even Livy admits, "The first clash of arms showed both sides so equally matched that had the Etruscans and Umbrians been there, either in the battle or in the camp, wherever they had thrown their weight, the Romans would not have escaped disaster" (Livy, p. 327).

Rome's conquest of Italy was not inevitable; as with all great successes, luck—or the will of the gods—played a role. The omens were propitious; Livy deserves quoting in full:

> As they stood in battle formation a hind [female red deer] in flight from a wolf which had chased it down from the mountains ran across the plain between the two armies. Then the two animals turned in opposite directions, the hind towards Gauls and the wolf towards the Romans. The wolf was given a way through the ranks, but the hind was struck down by the Gauls. At this one of the soldiers from the Roman front ranks cried out 'That is how flight and bloodshed will go—you see the beast sacred to Diana lying dead, while here the wolf of Mars is the winner, unhurt and untouched, to remind us of the race of Mars and our Founder!' (Livy, p. 327).

The Roman consul Quintus Fabius Rullianus kept his forces on the defensive, hoping to wear out the enemy, but the other consul, Publius Decius Mus, became impatient and called for an aggressive cavalry attack. They forced the Celtic cavalry back but were soon surrounded by infantry. Decius's men were then thrown into a panicked retreat by a "new style of fighting; for the enemy, standing up and holding their weapons in wagons and chariots, bore down on them with a fearful noise of horses' hooves and wheels" (Livy, p. 328). Decius, witnessing the disarray of his troops, decided on a suicidal course of action just as his father had done before him against the Latins. He brazenly attacked the Gauls. He, too, was killed, but not without inspiring his men to counterattack and insuring himself a place in history. The tables were turned. The fighting was far from over, but the decisive blow was struck.

Livy records that 25,000 enemies were killed that day, including the Samnite commander Gellius Egnatius, and 8,000 taken prisoner. All told, the Romans lost 8,700. "Great is the fame of that day in which the battle was fought in the region of Sentinum" (Livy, p. 331). The battle here did not finish off the Samnites, Gauls, Etruscans, or Umbrians, but it left Rome in a position to deal with them one by one... which they did.

In 290 BC, the Samnites were encircled and peace made. They were granted the status of allies (socii) i.e., obligated to furnish men and arms, able to manage their own affairs, but without an independent policy with regard to other groups. Allies could not make alliances with other allies. After some struggle, by 264 BC the Etruscans and Umbrians were defeated and received a similar deal, but with time limits.

In 284 BC, the Celts were again on the warpath, handing the Romans a resounding defeat at Arretium (today's Arezzo). Roman ambassadors were sent to bargain for prisoners. Appian, the Greek historian of Rome, describes what happened:

Once a great number of the Senones, a Celtic tribe, aided the Etruscans in war against the Romans. The latter sent ambassadors to the towns of the Senones and complained that, while they were under treaty stipulations, they were furnishing mercenaries to fight against the Romans. Although they bore the *caduceus* [herald's staff] and wore garments of their office, Britomaris cut them in pieces and flung the parts away, alleging that his own father had been slain by the Romans while he was waging war in Etruria. The consul Publius Cornelius Dolabella, learning of this abominable deed while he was on the march, abandoned his campaign against the Etruscans, dashed with rapidity by way of the Sabine country and Picenum against the town of the Senones, and devastated them with fire and sword. He carried their women and children into slavery, and killed all the adult youth except a son of Britomaris, whom he reserved for awful torture, and led in his triumph.

When the Senones who were in Etruria heard of this calamity, they joined with the Etruscans and marched against Rome. After various mishaps these Senones, having no homes to return to, and being in a state of frenzy over their misfortunes fell upon consul Gnaeus Domitus Calvinus, by whom most of them were destroyed. The rest slew themselves in despair. Such was the punishment meted out to the Senones for their crime against the ambassadors (Appian, *History of Rome: Samnite Wars 2*, pp. 13, 14).

After what Carlo Cappelli calls Rome's "final solution" with respect to the Senone Celts, a Roman colony was planted at Senigallia, according to Polybius (203–120 BC), another Greek historian who had recounted the fate of the Senone Gauls (Polybius, *Histories*, II, p. 19). Livy says that a Roman colony was established in southern Piceno at Hatri, today's Atri, south of the Tronto River in Abruzzo (Summary Book XI). By 290 BC ,the Romans had already conquered the Sabines and Pretuzi, who were enrolled as citizens without votes. The Romans surrounded the Piceno district. What may have been ancestral Piceni lands taken by the Celts were distributed to Roman settlers. As Cappelli says, the Piceni could not have been happy about that. But the fact that Dolabella's route through Piceno must have gone down the Via Salaria and through Ascoli, no doubt receiving help from the Piceni, indicates a lack of animosity. Very little here is clear or simple. According to Pagnani, with the Celts killed and driven out, Sentinum for the first time became part of Piceno. But the archeological evidence shows Celtic settlements existing after the events of Sentinum, Rome's final solution, and the Picenean War. The Fabriano museum exhibit text notes that the Celts "probably" integrated with the local people, whose culture was already Etruscan-Italic with Greek influences.

The Greek cities that filled southern Italy and Sicily had managed to steer clear of the Romans up to this point. For centuries, Greeks had trading posts and colonies all over Italy, including Ancona in Piceno. Tarentum, the largest and safest seaport in Italy and the most important and powerful of the Greek cities in Italy, was situated on the instep of the foot of the Italian boot—the modern day Taranto. When the Greek city of Thurii, 145 km / 90 mi from Tarentum, asked Rome for protection from Lucanian and Bruttian attacks the Tarentines were alarmed. Rome had already established a colony in Venusia to divide Samnium from Lucania, which the Tarentines also perceived as a threat. A fleet of Roman warships in support of Thurii that appeared in Tarentine waters was attacked and destroyed, justly according to the Tarentines, because it broke a previous treaty between Rome and Tarentum banning Roman ships from those waters. The Romans counterattacked and drove the Tarentines behind their city walls; the Tarentines then appealed to King Pyrrhus of Epirus, a country straddling Greece and Albania, across the Adriatic from the heel of the Italian boot.

Ambitious and opportunistic, Pyrrhus came to the aid of Tarentum. He won two significant battles against the Romans in southern Italy, one at Heraclea and the other at Ausculum (not to be confused with Asculum Picenum). Both battles involved such large losses on Pyrrhus's part that he is said to have remarked, "One more such victory will undo me." With little success in Magna Graecia, he moved on to Sicily with even less luck. Another attempt on mainland Italy in 275 BC was defeated, and Pyrrhus went back to Greece, having bequeathed to the world the concept of a Pyrrhic victory.

After Pyrrhus left, the Romans attacked and subsumed all of Magna Graecia. Tarentum was taken in 272 BC. Pyrrhus's invasion had inspired revolt amongst the Samnites, Lucanians, and Bruttians, a ten-year war lasting from 282–272 BC but by 262 BC, Rome had conquered all of peninsular Italy.

The Picenian War

Doubtlessly, as Roman allies, the Piceni would have been required to supply troops for these campaigns. Writing in the time of Trajan and Hadrian, Florus notes that after the defeat of Tarentum, all Italy enjoyed peace, "except that the Romans thought proper, of their own accord, to pursue those who had joined the enemy. The people of Picenum were in consequence subdued, with Asculum, their metropolis, under the conduct of Sempronius; who, as there was a tremor of the earth during battle, appeased the goddess Earth by the promise of vowing a temple to her" (Florus, p. 311). Ancient sources (including Valerius Maximus and Dionysius of Halicarnassus) attest to this temple dedicated to the worship of Tellus on the Esquiline Hill. That the Romans conquered the Piceni under the leadership of consul P. Sempronius Sophus is officially documented in the Roman *Fasti Triumphalus*—or Register of Triumphs—for the year 268 BC. The story of how the Piceni came "under the yoke" of the Romans is a mosaic of brief mentions from diverse sources (Florus, Orosius, Eutropius, Strabo, Frontinus). Writing in the early 400s AD, some 600 years after the event, Orosius, the historian, theologian, and follower of St. Augustine recorded:

> In the year 477 [actually 485 by Roman dating, or 269 BC] happened many evil wonders; the first of which was, that thunder destroyed the house of the highest God, Jove and also threw down great part of the city wall. The second was that three wolves in the night brought a dead body into the city, and they would have torn the corpse into pieces, if the inhabitants had not awakened, and drove them away. In those days, like wise it happened that in a place near Rome, the earth opened and fire issued from it; on each side of this fire the land was burnt to ashes for the breadth of 5 acres.
>
> Soon after these prodigies, the consul Sempronius marched against the Picentines, a nation of Italy; and when they were prepared to engage, the earth shook so, that both armies conceived they should be swallowed up, after which they continued on the spot until their consternation was over. After this, a most desperate battle ensued, with an immense carnage on both sides, and though the Romans obtained victory, yet few of the conquerors survived. Thus was it seen, that this earthquake signified, they should have saved this profusion of blood (*King Alfred's Orosius*, pp. 132–3).

But had the Piceni really joined up with Pyrrhus or only failed to supply troops to the Romans, which the Romans saw as tantamount to aiding and abetting the enemy? Other sources such as Eutropius say the Piceni started the war. "In the consulate of Quintus Ogulnius and Caius Fabius Pictor, the Picenians commenced a war, and were conquered by the succeeding consuls, Publius Sempronius and Appius Claudius, and a triumph was celebrated over them. Two cities were founded by the Romans, Ariminum in Gaul and Beneventum in Samnium" (Eutropius, *Abridgement of Roman History,* II, 16). Eutropius was a eunuch historian writing in the late AD 300s in the service of the emperor. Modern historians such as De Sanctis and Scullard call the Picenean War a Piceni rebellion against their encirclement by the Romans, especially with the founding of another Roman colony at Rimini to the north of Piceno.

However, an earthquake may have been the decisive element in the defeat of the Piceni. Writing in the first century AD, Frontinus says, "When consul Tiberius Sempronius Gracchus was engaged in battle with the Picentines, a sudden earthquake threw both sides into panic. Thereupon Gracchus put new strength and courage into his men by urging them to attack the enemy while the latter were overwhelmed with superstitious awe. Thus he fell upon them and defeated them" (Frontinus, *Strategems,* I, XII, 3).

The Piceni must have been formidable fighters to have survived so many threats. The sheer amount of weapons found in their graves may be evidence for that, or maybe just evidence that they liked well made things, or that weapons were status symbols that because of the Piceni's unique geographical position and reputation were seldom necessary. Strabo took notice that "Asculum Picenum is a place that is well fortified by nature, not only where the wall is situated—but also the mountains that lie round it are impassable for armies" (Strabo, *Geography,* Book V, Chap. 4, p. 429). The Roman army under Sempronius must have come down the Via Salaria as Dolabella did in the campaign against the Celts. No one knows where in Picenum the battles during the two-year campaign were fought, although Carlo Cappelli guesses in the vicinity of Spinetoli, in the Tronto River valley. As Orosius noted, the conflict was won at considerable cost to the Romans. They deported some portion of the Piceni and confiscated their land. According to Strabo, "...on the Tyrrhenian Sea dwells the tribe of the Picentini, a small offshoot of the Picentini who dwell on the Adriatic, which has been transplanted by the Romans to the Poseidonian Gulf, this gulf is now called the Paestan Gulf" (Strabo V, p. 469). Other parts of Piceno were incorporated into Roman territory, and the inhabitants were granted citizenship without voting rights. Ascoli remained independent, an "ally." The Romans established a colony at Fermo, a thorn in Ascoli's side for centuries after Roman times, no doubt to keep an eye on the Ascolani. Speculation says that Ascoli was left alone for good reason; Rome knew better than to attack such a natural fortress. Ascoli stood as an ally and independent city for almost two more centuries before the Romans were constrained to subjugate the Ascolani.

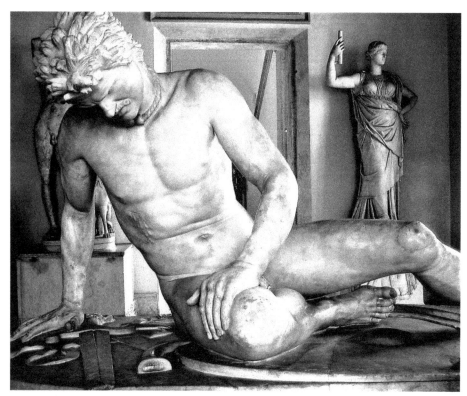

The Dying Gaul
Musei Capitolini, Rome

6

The Social War

"The event that more than any other helped to make Italy Roman was the Social War (91–87),
so-called, even by contemporaries, since it was a conflict between Rome and her *socii*"
(E.T. Salmon, *The Making of Roman Italy*, p. 128).

After the Picenian War the written record falls largely silent on the Piceni for almost two hundred years, though sources do acknowledge the essential role of the *socii* or allies in the projection of the Roman Empire throughout the Mediterranean.

Livy, recounting the Second Punic War, describes how the great Carthaginian general Hannibal, after his victory at Lake Trasimene in 217 BC "turned aside into the territory of Picenum, which abounded not only with every species of grain, but was stored with booty, which his rapacious and needy troops eagerly seized. There he continued encamped for several days, and his soldiers were re-freshed..." (Titus Livius, *The History of Rome* Book 22 Ch. IX, p. 775) before they laid waste to various lands on their way south. Some Piceni are mentioned as participants in the battle of Cannae in Apulia in 216 BC, on the losing Roman side. Livy considered the Battle of Metauro in 207 BC the turning point of this war. Hannibal's brother, Hasdrubal, had entered northern Picenum, with a large army including ten elephants. He intended to join up with his brother's forces, but the Romans got wind of the plan and in a brilliant lightning strike raced up from Apulia. Hasdrubal's army was wiped out on the southern bank of the Metauro River, inland from Fano. Hannibal only found out about this when the returning Romans flung his brother's head into the Carthaginian camp.

Livy relies on Polybius (200–118 BC), as everyone else does, as the main source for the Punic Wars. Polybius, born after the end of the Second Punic War (218–201 BC), relies on predecessors such as the Annalist Fabius. By the beginning of the first century BC the situation has changed, for now we are in the full light of written history with firsthand accounts written by contemporaries of the people and events they record.

The scene in Piceno circa 91 BC is dramatic enough to merit a Hollywood "Swords and Sandals" epic. In fact, Colleen McCullough's *The Grass Crown*, a historical novel, describes some of the events in gory detail, but predictably from a Roman perspective. In our epic, as told by the Greek historian Appian, the Ascolano native and Picenean general Vidalcilio returns with eight legions to Ascoli, then under siege by the Romans. He had sent a message ahead for the inhabitants to attack the besiegers so that they would have to fight on two fronts, but the Ascolani fail to comply. Vidalcilio and his troops break through the town walls anyway. Convinced there is no hope for saving Ascoli, Vidalcilio heaps scorn on the citizens for their cowardice and has his enemies, who out of jealousy had persuaded the people to disobey his message, put to death. "He built a funeral pyre in the Sanctuary and placed a couch on top of it; there he feasted beside it with his friends, and when the drinking was well under way took poison, laid himself down on the pyre, and ordered his friends to light it. Such was the end of Vidalcilio, who thought it honorable to die for his country" (Appian, *The Civil Wars*, p. 27). As the flames climb, the camera cuts to Rome some time before, with representatives from Piceno and other members of the Roman confederation presenting their grievances, and we learn in a flashback how things could have gone so far wrong.

Time was when any schoolchild would have been familiar with the background to this story: how the institutions that evolved from a small market town were ill adapted to deal with the administrative and military problems of controlling an empire—famous names such as the Gracchi brothers and Drusus, events like the destruction of Fregellae in 137 BC and, of course, the long running theme of agrarian reform. Once again, this is how the ancient writers described it and how it has come down to us through the centuries. Modern archeology has raised some objections (Dench, "From Barbarians to New Men," p. 95), but that is not the movie we are making.

Roman Politics and the Allies

Rome, despite its mining, trade, and manufacturing interests, was an agrarian society of peasant farmers as was the rest of Italy and much of the world. The Roman soldiers, both Romans and allies, were fathers and sons who owned their smaller farms and could afford the expense of weapons and armor. These men were the backbone of the forces that had conquered almost the entire Mediterranean basin by 140 BC. The system of peasant farmers was the basis of European society well into the 18th century and beyond in some places. In Roman society, the *paterfamilias* was the head of the household, which included not only immediate family members but also servants. Roman law divided his authority into three parts, "*potestas* or power over his children (including adoptees), his children's children and his slaves, *manus* or power over his wife and his sons' wives, and *dominium* or power over his possessions" (M.I. Finley, *The Ancient Economy*, p. 19).

By the latter part of the second century BC, the situation of the peasant farmer was changing drastically throughout Italy. The war with Hannibal had caused widespread destruction; some farms were abandoned, others destroyed. The wars of conquest had filled the pockets of wealthy senators and others who invested in land, creating vast absentee estates (sometimes called *latifundia*) manned largely by slaves, also acquired as war booty. The same wars had killed off high numbers of soldier/farmers. To the large tracts of land Rome annexed after conquering the allies were added punitive confiscations from people who had supported the Carthaginians. Estate owners bought up smaller farms and monopolized public land. Plutarch famously described the situation:

> Of the land which the Romans gained by conquest from their neighbors, part they sold publicly, and turned the remainder into common; this common land they assigned to such of the citizens as were poor and indigent, for which they were to pay only a small acknowledgment into the public treasury. But when the wealthy men began to offer large rents, and drive the poorer people out, it was enacted by law that no person whatever should enjoy more than five hundred acres of ground. This act for some time checked the avarice of the richer, and was of great assistance to the poorer people, who retained under it their respective proportions of ground, as they had been formerly

rented by them. Afterwards the rich men of the neighborhood contrived to get these lands again into their possession, under other people's names, and at last would not stick to claim most of them publicly in their own. The poor, who were thus deprived of their farms, were no longer either ready, as they had formerly been, to serve in war or careful in the education of their children; insomuch that in a short time there were comparatively few freemen remaining in all Italy, which swarmed with workhouses full of foreign-born slaves. These the rich men employed in cultivating their ground of which they dispossessed the citizens (Plutarch, *Lives*, Trans. by Dryden "Tiberius Gracchus," pp. 997–8).

These estates produced not only the traditional grains, but quantities of meats, olives, fruits, and vegetables, a system of agriculture requiring more working capital and larger expanses of fertile land than the small farms possessed. Peasant farmers gave up and moved into towns, becoming impoverished and ineligible to serve in the military. Small scale farming however survived and predominated, as it always had, in the Apennine highlands of Abruzzo and Piceno, terrain unsuited to large scale enterprise. The *latifundia* system had taken hold here to some extent, probably in the coastal lowlands of Piceno. Pompey Strabo, an important actor in the Social War and father of Pompey Magno (the Great), had extensive holdings in northern Picenum.

Whether for personal political ambition or farsighted altruism, some members of the Roman elite saw a need for reform, especially to supply the necessary manpower for their armies now that Rome was constantly at war. They could not have escaped noticing that some two-thirds of the Roman army consisted of non-Romans, i.e., allies. Other more grim factors were also in play. Slave uprisings frightened the masters, raising the specter of ruinous widespread rebellion. "The concentration in rural districts of desperate revengeful men, treated like cattle, imperiled the general peace, because if these men could combine against their masters, they could threaten the state with internecine warfare. And that is what they did" (Perowne, *Death of the Roman Republic*, p. 67).

Tiberius Gracchus proposed legislation that reasserted the ancient law limiting those holding state land, and formed a commission to survey and redistribute land to poor Romans. This legislation provoked violent opposition amongst aristocrats since some properties had been consolidated by large elite landowners or held by families for generations. Allies suspected the redistribution would lead to more Roman encroachment on their already precarious positions. Some allies had probably been clandestinely farming portions of these lands and feared their loss. In 133 BC, a crowd of senators and an ex-consul murdered Tiberius Gracchus and 300 of his followers, setting a dangerous precedent in Roman history.

After Gracchus's murder, sometimes called the first political assassination in Republican Rome in four centuries, the land commission he had set up continued to function. Naturally, there was continuing opposition, not only from senatorial oligarchs with large land holdings across Italy but also from wealthy Italians. Allied towns and individuals who held much of the public land saw the land commission actions as violations of treaties and their rights, but since they lacked citizenship, they had no legal right to appeal. The allies found a sympathizer in Scipio Aemilianus, the Gracchi's brother-in-law.

Scipio Aemilianus had returned from Spain after the sacking of Numantia in 133 BC. He was personally aware of the overworked condition of the Roman troops and the large role of the allies in winning Rome's empire, having also led the pillage and obliteration of Carthage in 146 BC. According to Appian, the allies asked Scipio Aemilianus to represent their cause before the senate, a clear instance of the allies' degrading need for patronage because of the lack of citizenship. "So he went to the senate, and although he did not openly attack Gracchus' law because of the common people, he examined its problems in detail and proposed that the legal actions should not be heard by the land commissioners, since they were regarded as prejudiced by the litigants, but by others" (Appian, *The Civil Wars*, p.11). The land dispute was handed over to Tuditanus, who, realizing the difficulties at hand, left for war in Illyria.

Apparently, Scipio was readying to propose legislation on behalf of the Italians when he was found dead, perhaps from natural causes or "perhaps Cornelius, mother of the Gracchi, killed him, to prevent repeal of Gracchus' law, assisted in the deed by her daughter Sempronia, who was married to Scipio but on account of her ugliness and childlessness neither was loved by, nor loved, him" (Appian, p. 12).

With Italian hopes dashed again, many were coming to Rome to lobby for their rights. A law was passed in 126 BC to prevent non-citizens from settling in Rome and expelling those who already had. The next year land commissioner Fulvius Flaccus became consul and proposed to enfranchise all the allies, or at least those who wanted it, and grant those who did not the right to appeal against Roman magistrates. Senatorial reactionaries responded by sending consul Flaccus to fight in Gaul. His proposal was dropped.

Fregellae, an ancient town on the Via Latina near the left bank of the Liris, revolted. The anonymous author of *De Viris Illustribus* states that Ascoli took part (section 65.1); scholars debate whether or not that was the case. Umberto Laffi, in his *Storia di Ascoli Piceno nell'Età Antica*, thinks there is as much reason to believe Ascoli participated in the revolt as not (Laffi, p. xviii). No one doubts however, that Fregellae was besieged, captured, and destroyed, and the remaining inhabitants deported. Romans still had no desire to share their privileges with their neighbors. As Appian says, "...but the senate resented the idea of giving their subjects political rights equal to their own, and so this attempt was abandoned and the populace, who had clung for so long to the hope of land, were in despair" (Appian, pp. 12–13).

In 123 BC, a new reformer stepped up to deal with the problem of agrarian reform. Gaius Gracchus, brother of Tiberius, was elected tribune. Gaius Gracchus was said to be a powerful orator whose speeches were recorded and preserved, but he found himself between the same rock and a hard place as his brother. If he helped the common Romans (whose votes he depended on) with agrarian reform, the Italian allies would worry about losing land. Helping the Italians by extending the vote would anger the Romans. Gaius overcame these difficulties by putting people to work building roads throughout Italy and by proposing the establishment of more colonies. All the Latins were to receive Roman citizenship with the rest of the allies receiving those rights in the future. According to Appian:

> The senate was particularly alarmed at this, and instructed the consuls to make a proclamation that no non-voter should stay in Rome or approach within five miles of the city during the periods when these laws were to be voted on. It prevailed on Livius Drusus, another one of the tribunes, to veto Gracchus' laws but not to tell the people his reasons (and there was no obligation for reasons to be given). The senators also authorized Drusus to conciliate the people by proposing twelve colonies, which so delighted them that they thought the laws put forward by Gracchus were contemptible (Appian, p. 14).

Then in a fit of magnanimity, Drusus and his senatorial backers proposed that Latins would be exempted from scourging, the whippings almost to death that were sometimes followed by crucifixion, as in the case of Jesus Christ. No Roman citizen could be scourged or executed, but allies could.

Gaius Gracchus's sympathy for the allies' situation is illustrated in some passages from the *Attic Nights* of Aulus Gellius, a Latin author and grammarian possibly of African parentage, born and brought up in Rome. *Attic Nights* is a compendium of his jottings about whatever interested him. In one section, Gellius compares Gaius Gracchus's speaking ability with Marcus Tullius aka Cicero, perhaps Rome's most renowned speaker. He quotes Gracchus as delivering the following speeches; these passages are often cited historically as prime examples of Roman arrogance and cruelty. The first event took place in Teanum Sidicinum, capital of the Oscan-speaking Sidicini tribe in today's province of Caserta:

> The consul lately came to Teanum Sidicinum. His wife said that she wished to bathe in the men's baths. Marcus Marius, the quaestor of Sidicinum, was instructed to send away the bathers from the baths. The wife tells her husband that the baths were not given up to her soon enough and that they were not sufficiently clean. Therefore, a stake was planted in the forum and Marcus Marius, the most illustrious man of his city was led to it. His clothing was stripped off, he was whipped with rods. The people of Cales, when they heard of this, passed a decree that no one should think of using the public baths when a Roman Magistrate was in town. At Ferentinum, for the same reason, our praetor ordered the quaestors arrested; one threw himself from the wall, the other was caught and beaten with rods…

> Gracchus also in another place speaks as follows: I will give you a single example of the lawlessness of our young men, and of their entire lack of self-control. Within the last few years a young man who had not yet held a magisterial office was sent as an envoy from Asia. He was carried in a litter. A herdsman, one of the peasants of Venusia, met him, and not knowing whom they were bearing, asked in jest if they were bearing a corpse. Upon hearing this, the young man ordered that the litter be set down and that the peasant be beaten to death with the thongs by which it was fastened (Gellius, Book 10).

The second occured in Venusia in Samnium, today's Venosa in Basilicata, which later joined the allies in the Social War.

Stories like these have a way of spreading, striking anger in some, fear in others—no other evil moves so quickly as rumors, says the Roman poet Virgil. The elder Drusus's successful co-optation of Gaius Gracchus and Gracchus's loss of popular support sent him and his friend Flaccus to Africa while the heat died down. Their mission was to investigate establishing a Roman colony near the former site of Carthage, but someone reported that wolves had torn up the surveying markers, a bad sign. Augurs (priests who interpreted the will of the gods by studying birds) declared that the settlement was ill omened. Up to this point the Romans had only set up colonies in Italy. In addition, other reforms Gracchus proposed had political implications that were anathema to senatorial reactionaries. As Roman historian Cyril Robinson explains, "The popular assembly, hitherto sovereign in theory alone, was henceforth to be sovereign in fact. To it the Senate would be strictly subordinate and the magistrates directly responsible" (Robinson, *History of Rome*, p. 126).

Gracchus's enemies were looking for any excuse when one of his followers provided one. A senatorial attendant, Quintus Antyllius, was killed by a Gracchus backer in response to jeers he uttered at an assembly, to Gaius Gracchus's consternation. The next day a big show was made of carrying Antyllius's body through the market place. Afterwards the Senate ordered that Opimius, the consul, should be granted special powers "to protect the commonwealth and suppress all tyrants" (Plutarch, p. 1,016). Gracchus tried to escape, but with his enemies following too close behind, he offered his throat to his servant, who killed Gracchus, then himself. Gracchus's friend Flaccus was also killed and both of their heads were presented to Opimius who had offered their weight in gold. Their bodies and those of 3,000 followers were dumped in the river. "…the inhabitants of Italy were still further provoked to anger; for they thought it wrong to be classed as subjects and not as partners, and wrong for Flaccus and Gracchus to have suffered this fate in a political struggle on their behalf" (Appian, p. 20).

The Gracchi brothers have been lauded through history as democrats, reformers, the first socialists. They have also been attacked as power hungry demagogues. Perhaps both versions are right. But what seems more certain is that they were true conservatives whose reforms were aimed at preserving their beloved republic, which had endured for hundreds of years and as it turned out had only a few left. Tiberius's projects to help the Roman poor were intended to strengthen the traditional Roman military. Gaius Gracchus saw "that the true basis of Rome's prosperity must rest on a prosperous and contented Italy" (Robinson, p. 127). Almost thirty years were needed before another reformer, Drusus, would take up the cause of the allies and their quest for citizenship and justice.

Drusus, son of the Drusus who had opposed Gaius Gracchus, was elected tribune in 91 BC. To have any influence on Roman politics, the Italians knew that they had to have Roman citizenship. According to Appian, "At the request of the Italians he [Drusus] promised once again to put forward legislation on the subject of citizenship, because this is what they most wanted, and they thought that by this single thing they would immediately become masters instead of subjects" (Appian, pp. 20–21). Four years earlier the consuls had passed a law aimed at investigating Italians who had illegally claimed citizenship and expelling them. According to P. A. Brunt, "Nothing, we are told, did so much to alienate the ruling class among the allied people and bring on the Social War" (Brunt, *Social Conflicts in the Roman Republic*, p. 101). The *socii* were already beyond fed up when Drusus took office.

Velleius Paterculus noted, "Livius Drusus entered on the office of Tribune; a man of the noblest birth, the greatest eloquence, and the strictest purity of life; but who, in all his undertaking, was more distinguished by ability and good intentions than by success" (Velleius Paterculus, *Compendium of Roman History,* II, XIII, p. 455). Drusus's attempts to ameliorate antagonisms between the senate and the equestrians/knights, soul of the business class of Rome, only angered both. In September 91 BC, Drusus was stabbed in the courtyard of his own house with a knife that was left sticking in his side. According to Velleius Paterculus, "while he was drawing almost his last breath, he uttered an expression, as he looked on the crowd standing round and lamenting over him, very consonant to his inward feelings. 'My relations and friends,' said he, 'will the Commonwealth ever again have a citizen like me?' Thus ended the life of an illustrious man" (Vellius Paterculus, p. 456).

The Italians had waged Rome's wars for centuries now, but always as underlings in the charge of Roman commanders. The Romans could treat the allies, who had no legal recourse, as badly as they liked. The *socii* had set out to get the vote but Drusus was their last hope, and when he was murdered the situation turned ugly. The arrogance, stubbornness, malfeasance, and callousness of the Roman elites would come back to haunt them.

Roman Theater Ascoli Piceno

The rulers should have known something was in the wind. Before Drusus was murdered, he had warned his rival, Phillipus, of a plot against him. Groups of Italians had been coming to Rome to lobby for change for some time. But Appian points out that the Romans were too preoccupied with internal strife within the city to take notice of organizational efforts that had been winding through the Italian peoples. By the fall of 91 BC, the Italians had formed a league and were exchanging hostages, a traditional sign of good faith. When some Romans began to suspect what was going on they sent agents out to take stock of the situation. One man witnessed the transfer of a hostage from Ascoli to another town (possibly Corfinium), and informed Servilius—the Roman proconsul, or governor, of the region.

Servilius went to Ascoli where a festival was being celebrated at the theater. This sacred place probably stood in the same place as the Augustan era theater whose ruins can be seen today in the heart of the city, edged by an auto repair shop. Servilius threatened and chided the Ascolani in an aggressive manner. As Diodorus puts it, he "did not speak with them as to free men and allies, but treated them despitefully as slaves, and by his threats of fearful punishments, spurred the allies to seek vengeance on him and the other Romans" (Diodorus, *Diodorus of Sicily*, p. 219). The Ascolani responded by killing Servilius and his deputy Fonteius, a senator who had been sent to accompany him. "Once these two had been killed, none of the other Romans was spared, the Asculans assaulted them, stabbed every one to death and looted their property" (Appian, p. 23). October 91 BC, and the Social War was under way.

But the Ascolani had jumped the gun; perhaps, Appian says, they believed their plans had already been detected. That coupled with all the social and economic woes the Romans had been heaping on them for a couple of centuries had resulted in an explosion of rage. B.G. Niebuhr, a 19th century ancient historian, called the Piceni "a cowardly and contemptible people" for what they did (Niebuhr, *Lectures on the History of Rome*, p. 355) on what Carlo Cappelli calls "that morning in Ascoli." Now the Romans would have the winter to prepare their response. The element of surprise, of catching the Romans with their pants down, was lost.

However, the Romans were still at a disadvantage. The allies made up the largest part of the Roman army; for years they had been providing soldiers so that Romans would not have to serve. Some two thirds of the Roman army was drawn from the twelve groups named by Appian that were attempting to secede from Rome's clutches: the Marsi, Paeligni, Vestini, Marrucini; followed by the Picentes, Frentani, Hirpini, the inhabitants of Pompeii and Venusia, the Iapyges, the Lucani, and the Samnites. All of them spoke Oscan or some related dialect of it, except the people of Venusia, and Venusia had a large Oscan population.

Ostensibly, the insurgents were not set on conquering Rome but only on separating from it. Academic scholars debate whether the allies were trying to forcefully obtain citizenship or form a new state. They had set up a counter government and army that obliged Rome, with its greatly weakened army of newly minted troops, to go on the offensive to restore order. The mountainous regions the twelve groups inhabited were favorable ground for defense. In the beginning, things went badly for Rome.

Salmon points out that the odds against the insurgents were formidable and that in the long run Rome was almost sure to win because of its extensive resources and remaining allies. The dissident allies, however, were looking at the short run and had probably decided to fight because they knew the troops they had ready at that moment were more than a match for Rome.

The war was prosecuted on two fronts: north and south, Marsic and Samnite. The conflict was variously called the Marsic War, the Italic War, and the Social War, which by the second century AD predominated. This war was "well named the Marsic War from that mountain folk whose gallant service under the Roman's eagle had given rise to the proverb that no triumph had been won without them, and whose leader, Q. Pompaedius Silo [friend of Drusus], is traditionally associated with the creation of the confederacy" (*Camb. Anc. Hist.*, IX, p. 185). The confederacy was headquartered in Corfinium (near modern Sulmona in Abruzzo) and named *Italia*, perhaps the first usage of this term, which was derived from an ancient Calabrian word for veal. Several coins issued by the insurgents survive; one shows the Roman wolf being gored by an Italian bull. Another coin bears the name Q. (Pompadeius) Silo and shows eight warriors swearing allegiance, probably representing the various groups constituting the confederacy.

The Roman troops were commanded by consuls P. Rutilius Lupus in the north and by L. Julius Caesar (Julius Caesar's great-uncle) in the south. The consuls were in turn assisted by deputies assigned to different sectors. The commander of the Roman troops operating in Piceno was Pompey Strabo, as noted before, father of Pompey the Great. The ancient sources do not relate how or why Pompey Strabo and his troops arrived at Monte Falerno, near today's Falerone, in the Tenna Valley. Pompey Strabo must have known Piceno well since he had substantial holdings there. He may have begun by attacking Ascoli (Orosius) but was repelled and fled north, pursued by the Piceni generals, T. Lafrenius, P. Ventidius, and C. Vidalcilio. Here he was defeated and sought refuge in nearby Fermo, a Roman colony on the Tenna River close to the coast. In the first months of 90 BC, while Lafrenius kept Fermo under siege, Vidalcilio and Ventidius set out for Apulia.

There Vidalcilio caused the Romans some serious trouble. The Paeligni handed the XIII Legion such a drubbing at Alba Fucens that Rutilius transferred its command from Gaius Perpenna to Marius, the man most responsible for the professionalization of the army. Roman losses continued to mount as the Marsi defeated the Romans at the Tolenus River. Consul Rutilius was killed in this battle, causing panic in Rome. Rutilius's command was divided between Marius and Caepio, who was also slain and his forces routed in the vicinity of Amniternum by a coalition of Vestini and Marsi led by Q. Pompadeius Silo.

Marius, the legendary Roman general and politician (and military reformer), was elected consul an unprecedented seven times. Realizing the Roman setbacks were largely caused by the lack of training, the break provided by the harvest season gave him an opportunity to drill the troops. Diodorus describes a moment when Marius's Romans and Silo's Marsi confronted each other:

> As the armies came close to one another their grim belligerency gave way to peaceful feelings. For as they reached the point where features could be distinguished, the soldiers on both sides detected many personal friends, refreshed their memory of not a few former comrades in arms, and identified numerous relatives and kinsmen, that is to say, men whom the law governing intermarriage had united in this kind of friendly tie. Since their common bonds compelled them to give voice to friendly greetings, they called one another by name and exchanged exhortations to abstain from murdering men bound to them by close ties. Laying aside their weapons, which had been placed in hostile poses of defense, they held out their hands in sign of friendly greeting. Seeing this Marius himself advanced from the battle line, and when Pompaedius had done the like they conversed with one another like kinsmen. When the commanders had discussed at the length the question of peace and the longed-for citizenship, in both armies a tide of joyous optimism surged up and the whole encounter lost its warlike air and took on a festive appearance. And inasmuch as the soldiers too had in private conversations been urging peace, they were all glad to be relieved of the necessity of mutual slaughter (Diodorus, p. 221).

Like the American Civil War, the Social War was a war of brother against brother and friend against friend. As a teenager Cicero served under Pompey Strabo in the Social War. Later in life he recounts how Publius Vettus Scato, general of the Marsi, came to a conference between the two camps. Pompey Strabo's brother Sextus, known to be a wise and learned man, had come from Rome to participate. "Scato, after saluting him [Sextus] said, 'What am I to call you? In will,' he said, 'a friend, by the imperious force of circumstance, an enemy.' That conference was marked by mutual generosity; no fear entered into it, no suspicion: even hatred only in a moderate degree" (Cicero, *The Fourteen Phillipic Orations*, No.12, p. 179).

The southern campaign began in 90 BC with various Roman defeats and setbacks, excepting their first real victory at Acerrae, won at the price of the losing the key city Aesernia (Isernia). Here the Roman hand was strengthened by the ongoing loyalty of Rome's Latin allies. Other Italian groups had not revolted either. Pompey Strabo probably had a legion of Piceni under his command (Salmon, p. 344). Notably, the Etruscans and Umbrians had not initially joined the rebellion, but later in the year demanded Roman citizenship and threatened military action. Now the Romans finally showed the pragmatism for which they had heretofore been famous. The consul L. Julius Caesar proposed, and the senate passed, a law that gave Roman citizenship to Latins and allied Italians who had not already joined the revolt. The Etruscans and Umbrians pulled back and accepted citizenship. Unaware of the Etruscan change of heart, rebels on the Adriatic side sent 15,000 men in the winter of 90–89 BC to fight alongside them. They were defeated by Pompey Strabo (now elected consul), who, according to Appian, killed 5,000. Many of the rest died in the frozen mountains, perhaps on Gran Sasso in Abruzzo, struggling to return home.

While Vidalcilio and Ventidius headed south for other theaters of operations, Lafrenius was able to keep Pompey Strabo under siege in Fermo, until the Romans sent reinforcements who attacked the Ascolani besiegers from the rear. Pompey Strabo, his troops freshly reorganized while under siege, broke out of the city and attacked the Ascolani troops from the front. Lafrenius was killed. When the reinforcements set fire to the Ascolani camp, the soldiers fled in disarray to Ascoli with the Romans in pursuit. In November 90 BC, Pompey Strabo set up the siege of Ascoli—which Vidalcilio desperately tried to break at the beginning of this chapter.

Archeological evidence in the form of lead sling bullets found around Ascoli Piceno lend a tangible physical connection to the story of the Social War in Piceno. Sling bullets have been recovered in the riverbed of the Castellano River, in the area of the Porta Romana and the Roman theater, and in the vicinity of today's train station, indicating the principal locations of the fighting. The almond-shaped bullets are usually inscribed with the name of the legion that threw them. Curses were also etched on many with such epithets as "runaway slave" or "hit the Picentes" or "hit Pompey," giving testimony to which side threw them (Mommsen, Vol 3, VII, p. 251). The evidence indicates that a number of Celts participated in the fighting.

After the self-immolation of Vidalcilius in December 90 BC, the siege of Ascoli continued for a year, until Pompey Strabo's troops broke through and sacked Ascoli. In Orosius's account, "Pompey entered Asculum and had the prefects, centurions, all the leading men beaten with rods and beheaded. He sold the slaves and all the booty at auction and ordered the remaining people to depart, free indeed, but stripped and destitute. Though the senate expected that the proceeds of the booty would somewhat increase the public income, Pompey did not contribute anything from it to the needy treasury" (Orosius, Book V, Chap. 18). On December 25, Pompey Strabo received a triumph in Rome for his victory over Ascoli. Amongst the captives marched through Rome in the celebratory procession were little Ventidius Basso and his mother, perhaps of the prestigious Ventidius family of Auximum/Osimo, according to Laffi. His father was likely the insurgent Ventidius, comrade of Vidalicilio and Lafrenius. Starting low down the rungs as a muleteer, young Ventidius Basso was to rise through the ranks of the Roman army ultimately winning fame as a general in Caesar's Gallic Wars. He achieved the level of consul and was famous in Roman history for defeating the Parthians (who left us the phrase "Parthian shot," which refers to their highly skilled equestrian technique of turning around in the saddle to shoot arrows at the pursuing enemy, aka "parting shot"). The child who had been paraded through Rome as a captive thus returned at the head of his own triumphal procession. In more recent times, he was represented as a character in Shakespeare's "Anthony and Cleopatra," and Ascoli Piceno's jewel box opera house is named for him.

Florus says that Pompey Strabo laid waste to the land, burning and killing, in revenge for the death and destruction the war had caused. The sack of Ascoli, the last outpost of Picenean independence, signaled the practical end of opposition in the north. Large-scale operations continued in the south, but the battles of 89 BC showed that the advantage had passed to the Romans. The citizenship laws had proven effective in keeping other groups from revolting and brought others back into the fold. By 88 BC, the Social War was largely over, although pockets of insurgents continued to fight for some time. As Salmon points out, their numbers were "by no means negligible for in addition to the Samnites and Lucani, there were the die-hard elements who had escaped from other war theaters, and also, so it is said, a mass of fugitive slaves" (Salmon, p. 370). Their resistance was eventually overcome.

Pompey Strabo and his Son, Pompey the Great

In the cast of characters associated with Piceno in ancient times, Pompey Strabo looms large. Even his name, *Strabo*—apparently what the Romans called a person with distorted or deformed eyes, also squinter or cross eyed, not to mention shifty—set him apart. Pompey Strabo was one of Roman society's New Men or *Novus Homo*, a man who was the first in his family to serve in the senate, from a family that had only in recent generations risen socially, upward mobility we would call it today. A large estate owner who worked his way up through the Roman *cursus honorum*, the requisite political job ladder, he was elected to Rome's highest office of consul, a remarkable feat for a provincial from northern Piceno. Consuls were commanders of multiple legions—whole armies were under their control as well as important provinces. Elected by their fellow senators and serving two at a time, consuls designed Rome's overarching policies, although their authority was limited by the senate, and by each other, since the consuls had to agree to enact a policy.

Pompey Strabo's legacy as a consul is documented by significant archeological evidence. The Capitoline Museum, with its piazza designed by Michelangelo, stands on the Capitoline Hill overlooking the ruins of the Roman forum. Almost every tourist passes through or past this place with its famous statue of Marcus Aurelius. In one of the rooms of the museum there is a bronze tablet, dated November 89 BC, which once had been nailed to the wall of a public building in ancient Rome. The tablet commemorates thirty Spanish cavalrymen granted citizenship in the vicinity of Ascoli by Pompey Strabo for valor in the siege of Asculum Picenum. Another fifty-nine names listed were members of his advisory council (*consilium*); senators, a magistrate, military tribunes, and centurions. Also included were thirty-three *tirones*, young apprentices in the army, one of them his son, the 17-year-old Gnaeus Pompeius, not yet "the Great." The list shows that he had a substantial pack of *clientelae*, a formal roll call of the inside track, people who had served a purpose, pecuniary or military, that needed rewarding.

The bronze tablet came to light in 1909 when Prof. Giuseppe Gatti, director of the city archeological commission of Rome, published an article on it in the commission's bulletin. The tablet was probably discovered by a laborer during excavations at the foot of the Rupe Tarpea, at the front of today's Piazza della Consolazione on the south side of the Campidoglio. With the helpful mediation of a friend who suspected the importance of the piece, Gatti was able to see a large fragment, which was held in private by someone who did not comprehend its enormous historical significance and would let it go for a low price. Funding to purchase the bronze was immediately arranged, and not long after Gatti was able to purchase another large fragment of the bronze held by another private collector.

The Cambridge Ancient History calls Pompey Strabo's enfranchisment of the thirty Spanish cavalrymen a landmark in the history of Western Civilization because, for the first time, Roman citizenship was given to people from outside Italy (*CAH, IX*, p. 198). But not all of Pompey Strabo's legacy is so glorious. As previously noted, after the sack of Ascoli, he had all the Ascolani officers scourged and beheaded. In Orosius's account the slaves and booty were auctioned off and the proceeds went into Pompey Strabo's pocket. Orosius records that Rome was really broke from the Social War and now it had gotten so bad that they were selling off ancient possessions under the "pressure of Necessity" (Book V, Chap. 18). Pompey Strabo's failure to remit the proceeds of the auction to the Roman treasury may help explain why he was so disliked, but there is also his reputation for double-dealing. It should come as no surprise that a power struggle erupted after the Social War for, as E. Badian puts it, "The Social War, as might be expected, does not mark the end of the Italian problem but only the beginning of its solution" (Badian, *Foreign Clientelae*, p. 226). There is little doubt that Pompey Strabo wanted another consulship, but the office went to others as did coveted generalships. At one point Sulla tried to relieve him of his command and sent a replacement out to Piceno to take over his army, but Pompey Strabo's loyal soldiers assassinated the newcomer.

The bronze tablet, and Pompey Strabo's *Lex Pompeia*, which gave voting rights to the communities between the Alps and the Po during his consulship, are evidence that he was a supporter of voting rights, but the issue had not been definitively resolved. In 87 BC, when consul Cinna tried to revive citizenship legislation, he was violently opposed by the still recalcitrant senatorial oligarchs. Cinna was stripped of his citizenship, his consulship, and was sent into exile, but he returned with an army to march on Rome. Pompey Strabo was recalled from Picenum with his troops and placed in the dire position of combatting a force that likely included many friends, who were fighting on behalf of a cause that he had evidently supported. The clash was calamitous; Cinna's army was not destroyed and, according to Vellieus Paterculus, both sides were struck by a plague. Pompey Strabo died.

Both Velleius Paterculus and Plutarch agree that Pompey Strabo was disliked and feared. Velleius Paterculus says that he was disillusioned when he did not get a second consulship, and after that, everything he did was with an eye to his own advantage, looking for "the opportunity of turning himself and his army to one side or the other wherever the greater prospect of Power for himself should appear... but the joy felt at his death was in great measure counterbalanced by sorrow for the loss of so many citizens, cut off by sword or sickness. The Roman people vented on his corpse the resentment which they owed him when alive" (Velleius Paterculus, pp. 461–462).

Plutarch says that the Romans never hated a general so much as Pompey Strabo, "but they feared his talent as a soldier, for he was a very war-like man." Plutarch tells it that Pompey Strabo was killed by a thunderbolt and that while his "body was on its way to the funeral pyre, they dragged it from its bier and heaped insults on it" (Plutarch, *Life of Pompey*, Waterfield trans., p. 223). *The Cambridge Ancient History* alleges that this mention of a thunderbolt may just be a mistranslation of a phrase meaning struck by a disease. (*CAH, IX*, p. 264). We can breathe a sigh of relief that the story of Pompey Strabo is not some moralizing tale about the cosmic consequences of treachery and greed. As everyone knows, treachery and greed often do very well for themselves with seemingly little Karmic retribution. Besides, all the negativity aimed at Pompey Strabo may have just been the slander of his enemies.

Plutarch contrasts the father with the son regarding their popularity among Romans, quoting what Aeschylus has Prometheus say to Hercules, "I hate the sire but dearly love this child of his." He then goes on, "And although there was only the one reason why they hated the father—namely, his insatiable appetite for money—there were many reasons for their affection for the son: the modesty of his lifestyle, his honed military skills, the persuasiveness of his public speaking, his trustworthiness, and his easy manner with acquaintances..." (Plutarch, p. 222). Nevertheless, few seem to think that the boy had not learned anything from the father.

Moreover, shortly after the death of Pompey Strabo, magistrates indicted his son for the theft of public property. Pompey must have been all of nineteen years old. He was accused of receiving stolen goods, specifically, some hunting tackle and books from the booty taken in the sack of Asculum, which he had received from his father. Pompey admitted having had these things but professed they were lost when Cinna's guards broke into his house and ransacked it. Pompey so impressed the judge with his reasoning and comportment that the judge offered his daughter's hand in marriage. More important from our perspective and the perspective of scholars such as Laffi and Cappelli, the existence of these books in Asculum points to the existence of a higher intellectual culture and perhaps, the existence of a public library.

Pompey had received a substantial inheritance from his father, not just in land and money, but especially influence. Pompey Strabo had quite a list of *clientelae*. The bronze tablet indicates moreover that he was able to spread his sphere of influence into Spain and northern Italy— a useful patrimony for a young man starting out. Around this time, according to Plutarch, "Pompey was in Italy, in Picenum, partly because he had estates there, but mainly because he was happy in the Picenan communities, which made him feel at home and treated him as a friend ever since the time of his father" (Plutarch, p. 226). Young Pompey had grown up in Picenum and been educated there; and a privileged education it was. Early on, he was taught by Aristodemus of Nysa, an accomplished grammarian and rhetorician. Nysa was an ancient Greek city—an important learning center—in what is now Turkey. He was also a pupil of L.Voltacilius Pilutus, a rhetorician later famous as the first freedman to write history, including the stories of both Pompeys (Leach, p. 22). The subsequent exploits and triumphs of Pompey the Great are well known. His boast that all he had to do was stamp his foot to raise an army no doubt referred to Piceno and his extensive power there (Plutarch, p. 781), (Rostovzeff, *The Social and Economic History of The Roman Empire*, pp. 30, 31).

Although the rebels lost the Social War, they also won because ultimately all the insurgent troops obtained citizenship. This citizenship was obtained at a terrible cost. Asculum was sacked. Many high-ranking officers on both sides, including Q. Poppaedius Silo and Publius Vettius Scato, died in battle. Diodorus calls the Social War the greatest in recorded history, surpassing all others in "valorous exhibits of its leaders and in the magnitude of its operations" (Diodorus, p. 183). Florus asks, "what could be sadder, what more disastrous than this calamity?" And he goes on to add that the devastation wrought by Hannibal and Pyrrhus was less serious (Florus, II, pp. 6, 11). According to Mommsen, the Social War "was the most fearful civil war that has ever desolated the fair land of Italy" (Mommsen, p. 251). If something of all this has a familiar ring Stuart Perowne, in his *Death of the Roman Republic*, has this explanation:

> At this point it may be observed that the sequence of events, of ignorance, lack of sympathy, obstinacy, the preference of privilege to principle, leading to disaster, and the final victory of the nationalist cause, the determination of the colonial government "not to yield to violence," its ultimately yielding to nothing less than violence—this whole process was to be repeated over and over again in the history of later European empires. That Rome's Social War is the first recorded example of the sad syndrome is not the least of the reasons which make it of such interest to us today. For, of course, in the end the allies won; they were bound to, if Rome was itself to survive (Perowne, p. 93).

The Gilded Bronzes of Cartoceto di Pergola

7

The Romanization of Piceno

"Ascoli era Ascoli quando Roma era pascoli / Ascoli was Ascoli when Rome was pastures"
—Local Ascolano saying

"Romanization" is the word scholars have traditionally used to describe the process whereby the various Italian peoples lost their particular cultural identities and took on Rome's. As E.T. Salmon writes, "Yet by AD 14, when Rome's first emperor died, Italy was not only politically united, but also to a great extent culturally homogenous; and this was true of upper Italy as well as of the peninsula proper. As the emperor Claudius noted in AD 48, Italy had been pushed forward as far as the Alps and its regions, tribes and individual inhabitants fashioned into a single nation" (Salmon, *The Making of Roman Italy*, pp. I–2). More recently, scholars have seen that as oversimplified and foreshortened, a top-down account that obliterates variations in the application of Roman power. And for our money, it recapitulates the seeming inevitability of Romanization. After all, would not the different pre-Roman groups with their diverse cultures have reacted differently to Roman influence? Besides, Rome was itself a carrier of Greek culture. Romanization was also Hellenization and as we have seen, the Greek influence on the Italian peninsula started long before the rise of Rome. Patrick Geary points out in his book, *The Myth of Nations*:

> The Empire had been, since its inception, a network of cities (and their surrounding territories), bound by specific treaties to the city of Rome. Many local notables were descendants of regional elites whose families had dominated local society from before the arrival of the Roman Empire. As much as possible, Roman imperial expansion had always drawn pre-existing local powers into the Roman orbit. In the pluralistic religious and cultural tradition of Rome, the central state had never demanded exclusive adherence to Roman values: whenever possible, local tradition was assimilated into or equated with that of Rome. Thus, becoming Roman didn't mean abandoning old ways for new; rather, it meant discovering the old in the new (Geary, p. 67).

Provincial elites could proudly hold onto their own customs, and non-Roman families like that of Pompey the Great could rise to the heights of power.

Rome's dominion in Piceno predates the Social War by many years, about 177 to be exact. By 232 BC, the *Lex Flaminia* had already divided off the northern part of Umbro/Piceno, which had pre-existing Roman settlements, and encouraged more Roman settlers. Only Ascoli and Ancona had remained as independent entities after the Picenean War. But as Geary implies, the Romans could also be seen as reluctant imperialists. Maybe because, as Mary Beard points out, "The Romans had neither the manpower nor the will to impose the kind of direct control and cultural uniformity…" of an all-out takeover (Beard, *Confronting the Classics*, p. 278). Many of the *socii* such as Ascoli had been allowed to retain their own laws, leaders, and culture in a complex network of treaties and rights that had been incorporated into Rome's political and administrative edifice. Andrew Wallace-Hadrill says, "The Social War destroyed the basis of the dialectic, between Roman and non-Roman that had characterized Italy for at least two centuries, a dialectic which presupposed, and thereby promoted, a separation of identities" (Wallace-Hadrill, *Rome's Cultural Revolution*, p. 81). But no one seems to be able to answer the question, "What of Piceno culture survived or informed some 700 years of Roman control and domination?"

Romanization was seeded through the implantation of colonies in conquered territories. According to Appian, "As they subdued successive parts of Italy by war, the Romans confiscated a portion of the land and founded towns, or chose settlers from their own people to go to existing towns—this being the alternative they devised to garrisons" (Appian, *The Civil Wars*, p. 4). Rome established colonies in Picenum at Hadria/Atri (282 BC), Firmum/Fermo (264 BC) and Auximum/Osimo (128 BC). Roman author Aulus Gellius writes in AD 169 that the colonies "have the appearance of miniatures, and are reproductions of Rome herself," and Salmon, quoting him, affirms that this was largely true in the Republican era as well (Salmon, *Roman Colonization under the Republic*, p. 15). We do not have to go that far, but the towns were laid out on the Roman urban model, with its grid of east-west *decumanus* and north-south *cardo* streets intersecting at right angles, with similar sets of public buildings and infrastructure, surrounded by defensive walls. Parts of these walls are still visible in Osimo, as well as many other places. Latin became the language of government.

A lot of scholarly debate swirls around Rome's policies, programs, aims, and plans for Romanization and colonization, with the young Turks of today setting the old fuddy-duddies of previous generations in their place. But here we are struck with the same uncertainties regarding the lack of pre-Roman evidence, the rigidity of classical authors' pro-Roman perspectives, and the historical tendency of some scholars to take those authors at face value. The diffuse and unclear relationships between the heterogeneous group called the Piceni and their neighbors and amongst themselves is sufficiently opaque and undocumented as to guarantee work for academic archeologists and ancient historians for generations to come. What seems certain, however, is that Rome had a policy and a program for aggression and larceny. Romanization and colonization were the tools Rome used for taking, settling, and organizing large amounts of land seized from conquered people. The main effect of which was the growth of urban environments.

In Picenum after the conquests, the cities were small, without the full complement

Via Flaminia (purple) and its branches (red and orange)

of public buildings found in other Roman cities, but there were lots of them, often erected on the sites of pre-existing settlements (Vermeulen, pp. 141–3). In 220 BC, the Via Flaminia was constructed. The consular road no doubt followed previous roadways, from Rome over the Apennines through the Scheggia pass to Fano and up the coast to Rimini. Another branch of this road crossed the mountains at Colfiorito through Camerino then along the Potenza River valley to Ancona. In 232 BC, despite senatorial opposition, consul Gaius Flaminius was able to pass the *Lex Flaminia*. This law facili-

Porta Gemina / Romana, where the Via Salaria enters Ascoli

tated the growth of colonial towns by allowing for lands confiscated from the Gauls south of Rimini to be divided into smaller portions of property to be awarded to citizens. Here a series of cities were established over the years by grants to military veterans and others, enabled by the improved road network of the Romans.

Vermeulen points out that there was a "dense urban network" in Picenum and the adjoining Umbrian area with an average distance between towns of 13.5 km / 8 mi (Vermeulen, p. 147):

> The growing wealth of the Picene elite and the gradual emergence of the towns as significant centers ensured the almost unbroken prosperity of municipal life during the first and large part of the 2nd c. AD. From Augustan times onwards the towns in Picenum, colonies and *municipia* alike, were embellished with theaters, amphitheaters, *Capitolia* and other temples, *basilicae*, aqueducts, sewerage systems, cisterns, public baths and monumental gates. Originally created as rudimentary administrative centers, they grew into flourishing centers of population, and hence of marketing and exchange (Vermeulen, p. 156).

As any decent tourist guide will attest, the land of Piceno is littered with the remnants and detritus of the Roman Empire: bridges over the Tronto, thermal baths at Cupra Marittima, the archaeological park of Suasa, the city of Urbs Salvia destroyed by Alaric, a huge lump of Roman concrete on a hillside overlooking Belmonte Piceno. The ground is layered with Roman graves, milestones and paving stones, the tracks of sewer systems. Arched stone vaults line the path up to the Chiesa dell'Annunziata above Ascoli, perhaps the remains of a Roman sanctuary. Fermo sits atop a vast system of cisterns, thirty chambers built in the first century AD of Roman cement, fed by pipes to keep the city supplied with water. A look at just a few of the salient Roman events and artifacts that involve Piceno follows.

Julius Caesar in Picenum

"Let the die be cast." Everybody knows that Julius Caesar "crossed the Rubicon"—a phrase that came to mean there is no going back—but few know that he then passed through Picenum. Caesar's legions were not the first to march on Rome. That distinction goes to Sulla, who took Rome in 88 BC, marking the beginning of a series of civil wars. In 72 BC, somewhere in northern Piceno, Spartacus defeated two Roman legions sent out to halt his army of 100,000 rebellious slaves. Despite this victory, the heroic ex-slave-gladiator decided not to advance on Rome after all, returning instead to southern Italy and death.

The Rubicon was the boundary between Cisalpine Gaul (Gaul south of the Alps) and Italy proper. The river flowed into the Adriatic somewhere just to the north of Rimini, above the upper edge of today's Le Marche. Its exact location is not known since storms, tides, and droughts have changed the riverbed. Caesar's crossing of the Rubicon with his legions was an act of war, forbidden by Roman laws.

Caesar and Pompey the Great had been close allies—relatives, in fact, since Pompey was married to Caesar's daughter Julia until she died in childbirth in 54 BC. But now they were political enemies, and Caesar's advance threatened Pompey's power in Rome. Caesar had assembled his forces near Rimini and in January 49 BC he took the fateful step. His legions quickly occupied Pesaro, Fano, and Ancona. The townspeople of Osimo welcomed him, Cingoli offered its support. The Roman consul fled Ascoli and his troops deserted. Pompey had considered confronting Caesar in Picenum; it was after all his home turf. But, as John Leach writes in his *Pompey the Great*:

> For all their supposed loyalty to Pompey the Picentines were not prepared to risk their farms and their homes to support him and the Optimates, who had done so little to help them in the past, in a private quarrel with Caesar. Whatever force the defense of the constitution had as a rallying cry among the members of the senatorial class it failed dismally among the hill farmers of north Italy. When personal livelihood was at stake the bonds of patronage and 'patriotism' were just too weak (Leach, *Pompey the Great*, p. 178).

Caesar forged on south to Sulmona and Corfinium. Pompey retreated to Brindisi, sailing from there and leaving Italy to Caesar. The two continued their war in the eastern Mediterranean. After losing a series of battles, Pompey sailed to Egypt to seek protection under King Ptolemy XIII. A welcoming committee came out to escort him ashore but killed him just before he set foot on land. His severed head was presented to a horrified Caesar when he arrived in Alexandria. On the Ides of March in 44 BC, the Dictator Caesar was fatally stabbed twenty-three times by a crowd of senators in the Theater of Pompey in Rome, his blood splashing the base of a statue of Pompey the Great.

The assassination of Caesar culminated in the destruction of the Roman Republic and the rise to power of Octavian, who ruled as the first emperor, Augustus. During Augustus's reign Piceno became Picenum, a defined legal entity with set boundaries administrated by Rome as Region V. The consular road, the Via Salaria, was extended all the way to the Adriatic.

By the time Caesar crossed the Rubicon an era had passed:

> Once there had been free cities dotted throughout the Mediterranean. In the Greek world and Italy, too, these cities had been inhabited by men who identified themselves not as subjects of a pharaoh,

or a king of kings, but as citizens, and who proudly boasted the values that distinguished them from slaves—free speech, private property, rights before the law… By the first century, only one free city was left and that was Rome. And Caesar crossed the Rubicon, the Republic imploded, and none was left at all" (Holland, *Rubicon*, p. xv).

Disputed Art Treasures

Crowning the roof of the Ancona Museum are four figures, two men on horseback and two women on foot. They are idealized, fully reconstructed copies of the Gilded Bronzes of Pergola, "the only group of gilded bronzes dating from Ancient Rome still in existence," according to museum publications.

Nereo Alfieri, a leading expert in ancient topography, recounts that in 1946 he was working at the Ancona Museum, attempting to retrieve what remained of the archeological collection from the bombed ruins of its former site. On the morning of July 9, he got a phone call from Msg. Giovanni Vernarecci, the archaelogical inspector in Fossombrone. Rumors had reached him of an extraordinary find of "golden horses" in the Cartoceto section of Pergola, a hill town a short distance inland of Ancona. Alfieri set out at once, and the two men went to the farm where the horses were said to have been found. The owner of the land, at first reluctant, took them to the chicken coop housing the many fragments that had been collected, including a horse's head. The story was that a farm worker digging a trench to drain a pool of water had struck a metal surface. Thinking that it might be a container full of the "treasure" that local legend assigned to the area, the worker broke through the metal but found nothing inside. This was, in fact, the belly of a life-size statue of a horse. He soon found horse's hooves and other pieces of horses and humans, all bronze covered with gold leaf. At first the farm workers hid these but over a few days word spread throughout the countryside, until it reached the ear of Vernarecci. The owners of the farm ultimately turned over 318 fragments to Alfieri, who brought the hoard back to the Ancona Museum (Nereo Alfieri, *"Il trovamento e il ricupero dei 'Bronzi di Cartoceto di Pergola,'"* *La Civiltà Picena nelle Marche*, pp. 521–525).

Between 1949 and 1987, decades that included the disruption of the 1972 earthquake, the pieces were reconstructed into four figures. The most complete is an older woman; her hairstyle dates the work to later than the second half of the first century BC. One of the horsemen, mostly complete, is a middle-aged military man with one arm raised in a gesture of peace. Very little remains of the second horseman: his legs set in the stirrups. The two horses have their heads and enough other pieces to add up to a general presentation of the animals. The fourth figure, a woman, consists only of her draped garments from the waist down.

Various identities have been assigned to these four people, who are clearly of high rank. One theory is that they represent Livia, mother of the Emperor Tiberius, Agrippina the wife of his nephew Germanicus, and her sons Nero Caesar and Drusus III, and that they were destroyed on the orders of Tiberius in the first century AD as an act of *damnatio memoriae*. Another theory suggests that they were members of a local legate's family. Several families have been suggested, including that of Lucius Minucius Basilus of Cupra Marittima, who was involved in the assassination of Julius Caesar in 44 BC.

Why were these gilded statues buried here? Cartoceto di Pergola lies not far from the intersection of the Via Flaminia and a branch of the Via Salaria, the Via Salaria Gallica, which leads south through the mountains to Ascoli Piceno. They may have been made in the metal foundry at Sentinum, and on their way to Cupra Marittima, homeland of the Basilus family. A similar gilded bronze horse's head was found on the site of the nearby Roman outpost of Suasa. Perhaps they were deliberately destroyed by enemies of the persons depicted, or hijacked and hidden by brigands in the Roman era, or looted during the Byzantine Wars.

In 1988, when their restoration had been completed, the Ancona Museum loaned the statues to the town museum in Pergola. At the end of this temporary exhibit the people of Pergola refused to return them, blocking the way first with their bodies and then with a brick wall. Legal proceedings ensued. Delia Lollini, Soprintendente ai Beni Archeologici from 1979 to 1991, led the fight to get the bronzes back to Ancona. In 2008, the courts gave legal custody to Pergola, where they are displayed at the museum constructed for them. Ancona contested this in 2009. In a compromise, an exact copy of the group has been made and the Ancona Museum has had to settle for them; technically, the originals and copies are supposed to exchange places, switching between Ancona and Pergola. At stake are not only the archaeological heritage and local history and pride of each community, but also the tourist money attracted by these art treasures.

Italian law rules that Piceni *fibulae* found by farm workers do not belong to the finders or to the landowners, to keep or sell as they wish, but to the Italian State. But which museum should display finds such as the Roman-era Bronzes of Cartoceto di Pergola; the national museum in Rome, the regional museum in Ancona, or the museum closest to where they were found? If brigands waylaid these artworks as they traveled down the Via Flaminia, at some time many centuries ago, does that mean they belong to the village where the robbers hid them, rather than to the hometown of the personages depicted, where they were perhaps headed?

Giacomo Medici, a notorious dealer in antiquities, and his organization supplied the J. Paul Getty Museum in Los Angeles with looted art, so much so that the Getty was known as "The Museum of the *Tombaroli* (Grave robbers)." In 2004, Medici was sent to Italian prison for ten years and fined ten million euros for this dirty business. The next year Marion True, the Getty's curator of antiquities, went on trial in Italy, charged with conspiracy to traffic in illicit antiquities. The case was dismissed in 2010 because the statute of limitations had run out. Forty of the smuggled items have been returned to Italy. But the Getty still owns a masterpiece of ancient art with connections to Le Marche.

In August 1964 the crew of a fishing boat operating out of Fano, a port between Pesaro and Ancona, pulled a life-size bronze statue out of the Adriatic Sea. Their net was tangled with the arm of the young man; his feet were missing, probably left behind embedded in the ocean floor. The fishermen took the statue back to Fano where it was hidden first in a cabbage field and later, after being sold to an antiques dealer from Gubbio, in a priest's house. The priest's housekeeper reported the presence of the object to the *carabinieri*, the state police. The fishermen and others were tried on charges of concealing the find from the Italian State, which claimed ownership of the statue. They were acquitted because it could not be proved that the statue had been found in Italian, as opposed to international, waters. Here the ownership and whereabouts of the statue become murky, until 1977 when it was bought by the Getty Museum for almost four million dollars. It is now a star attraction at the Getty Villa in Malibu, California.

The "Victorious Youth/*Atleta vittorioso*," also known as *"L'atleta di Fano"* and the Getty Bronze, is an extremely rare Greek statue from the fourth century BC, said to be the work of Lysippos, Alexander the Great's personal sculptor. The bronze statue was made using the "lost wax" method of casting. The beautiful young athlete is nude, with copper nipples, and his missing eyes were probably ivory. With one hand he reaches upwards to place a victory wreath on his own head. The theory is that the statue was being transported from Greece to Ancona, perhaps as war booty by Roman troops, when the ship sank.

In 2010, a judge in Pesaro ruled that the statue must be returned to Italy, on grounds that it was found by a boat flying an Italian flag, and that once it was on Italian soil it was exported without the proper licenses. The Getty Museum has appealed, arguing again that the statue was found in international waters, and was therefore never the property of Italy, and that even if it was illegally exported that does not justify its seizure now.

The Athlete of Fano, made in Greece, was probably being transported from Greece (does it belong to the Greek State?) by a Roman ship, perhaps as war loot (does it belong to the Roman State / Italian national museum?) but it sank in the Adriatic Sea. If it was in international waters, is it up for grabs? Does it belong to the Italian fishermen who found it, or to the Italian State because they landed their boat on Italian soil? If the Roman ship was headed for Ancona, does the Ancona Museum have a claim? Or, does the statue rightfully belong to the Getty Museum because they paid all that money for it?

The international debate rages on the ownership of the archaeological art work of the world. Around the Mediterranean, in Greece, Turkey, Egypt, Italy, battles involve such masterpieces as the Elgin Marbles from the Parthenon, the Euphronius Krater, the bust of Nefertiti, the Lydian Hoard of gold jewelry. Is there a role for international museums that display cultural treasures from all parts of the world, making them available to the largest number of people, with the highest level of security? Or should such things stay where they are found? And what about places like Italy, so rich in ancient objects but lacking the financial wherewithal to excavate, examine, display, and protect them all?

Luca Speranza is an archeologist who has worked on a number of sites in Picenum, including one at Colli del Tronto, where a sixth century BC Piceno warrior was unearthed at a construction site. Or at least the lower half of a warrior; the rest had already been destroyed. Luca is small and muscular, boyishly angular but with graying hair. He and his team are called in when something is found in the course of digging a foundation or laying underground utility services, as required by law. We dropped by one such location in the industrial zone along the Tronto River, where a utility trench had run across a Roman burial. Luca showed us the first century AD skeleton still lying in the grave, headless. "The skull is over here," he says, lifting a tray of coffee cups off of the crate that held the cranium. A volunteer crewmember had just found a bronze ring by the side of the highway, across from the big box shopping centers. Luca holds it out on a paper towel, the center hole still packed with dirt; a year later we see it cleaned up and on display in the Ascoli Museum.

The problem, Luca says later, is that Italy is so full of archaeological sites, one on top of the other, but there's neither the money nor the will on the part of the government to support archaeological research. What money and attention there is gets focused on the most famous places, like Pompeii, that attract lots of tourists. At the next level, there are so many sites in competition that nothing gets funded. This is the paradox—so much potential work in his field, so much that could be done, but in fact jobs are insecure and underfunded. Warehouses are packed with containers of ceramic potshards yet to be examined and catalogued. It takes years to line up the permits and funds for a particular site, and by the time the archaeologists get to work the site may already be irreparably damaged. Grave robbers swoop in as soon as word gets out of a discovery, sometimes that same night. They usually take only the most obvious treasures, the jewelry and weapons, perhaps leaving behind jars buried at the feet of the corpse, but the grave has been despoiled and disrupted.

Our conversation with Luca Speranza took place in an art gallery in Castel di Lama, at the opening of an exhibit of the works of the local contemporary artist Vittorio Amadio. In the group are our cousins the Lappa sisters. Luana has worked with Luca; Maria Grazia writes for the newspaper *Il Resto del Carlino*. Maria Grazia points out another problem with this abundance of sites. She describes a local farmer, digging postholes in his vineyard, who brought to light something unusual. He immediately filled the hole back up, not wanting the required archaeological examination to get in the way of his agricultural schedule. And, she says, some places you just know there's something. The sisters exchange a glance and one says, yes, near their house there's a spot with all the characteristics of places that the Piceni chose for their necropoli: the orientation on the hillside, the stand of oaks… The two nod. Yes, if they could ever get the state to fund a dig…

Christianity Enters Picenum

Picenum may have been "Romanized," but another culture would take hold; in the first century of the new millennium, Christianity made its way across the land. The new religion entered the region from two directions; from the east by way of Ancona and other ports, and from the west, from Rome, along the consular roads. The oldest mention of Christianity in Piceno comes from St. Augustine. In a sermon in 425, he spoke of a place in Ancona which contained a relic of St. Stephen, known as the first martyr, who was stoned to death near Jeruselam in 31 or 32. Apparently the future St. Paul was there, and so was a Jewish/Christian merchant. A stone bounced off Stephen's elbow and landed at this trader's feet. He picked it up and sailed to Ancona, where he was inspired to leave it. The site (perhaps under the church of Santa Maria della Piazza) became a pilgrimage destination for those seeking miraculous cures. St. Augustine muses on the rightness of this location, since *ankon* means "elbow" in Greek. Indeed, Ancona was a logical entry point. As a major port, there was long-established contact with the Middle East. As a Greek colony, it shared the language used by the early Christians. And there were Jews there, which was the community where the new sect sought its first converts (Santarelli, *Le Origini del Cristianesimo nelle Marche*, pp. 29–30, 189).

The second, later, means of diffusion was along the consular roads radiating out of Rome, as marked by the tombs of martyrs that line them, including the Via Flaminia and the Via Salaria. Such was the fate of St. Mauro, or Marone, Piceno's first evangelist and first martyr, sometime around the year 100. He was perhaps a disciple of St. Peter, though all of the historical details are murky. He was one of several Christians accused of converting Flavia, the niece of the Emperor Domitian, to their religion, which included a vow of chastity. Flavia's would-be husband, son of a Roman consul, was furious and had the missionaries exiled, enslaved and killed. One of them was St. Vittorino of Cotilla, whose death suspended over the sulpherous thermal springs on the Via Salaria was described earlier. Mauro was sent to labor at a place located at the 130th (Roman) mile on the Via Salaria, and then sentenced to death for

The Beheading of St. Emidio, *Tempietto di Sant'Emidio Rosso*, Ascoli Piceno

continuing to proselytize. The plan was to crush him with a giant stone, so huge it took seventy men using a pulley to load it onto his back. But he carried it as if it was straw, walking two miles to the place where he usually prayed. The Romans killed him anyway, and Mauro's followers buried him within the massive boulder. Given the distance listed, this place would have been somewhere between Ascoli and the Adriatic, maybe where a no longer existing monastery in his name was built near Stella di Monsampolo, where a medieval Chiesa San Mauro still stands. On the coast at Porto Civitanova, an ancient sanctuary was devoted to him; perhaps his remains were transferred here (Santarelli, pp. 35–56).

By 250 or so, around 100 Christian districts, administered by bishops, had been established in Italy, including ones in Ancona, Ascoli, Fermo, Fano, Rimini, and maybe Camerino and Pesaro. The Emperor Diocletian (ruled 284–305) set off the Great Persecution which lasted from from circa 303–311, a period which included the martyrdom of St. Emidio, the three martyrs of Osimo, and many many others. He also divided the Roman Empire into two geographical realms, the Western and Eastern. In 313 during the reign of Constantine the Great (306–337), the Edict of Milan gave legal status to the religion. Constantine, who died a Christian, moved the capital from Rome to the city of Byzantium, later called Constantinople. In 380, the Edict of Thessalonica, issued by the three Roman Emperors Theodosius I, Gratian, and Valentinian II, made Christianity the official religion of the entire state; Theodosius I was the last emperor to rule both halves of the Roman Empire. A new bureaucracy grew up alongside the weakening, divided, Roman administration, a far-reaching, powerful, and very expensive network—the Christian church—which made its way down the furthest paths of Picenum.

Byzantine Mosaics, Basilica San Vitale, Ravenna

Emperor Justinian, probably Belisarius on his right, Narses on his left

Empress Theodora, probably Antonina on her left

8

Piceno and Her Invaders

Thomas Hodgkin, Quaker banker turned historian, also nephew and namesake of the man for whom Hodgkin's disease is named, authored eight volumes entitled *Italy and Her Invaders* (published 1880–1899). That most of the invaders passed through Piceno should come as no surprise. Piceno had a ringside seat at the decline and fall of the Roman Empire, which generations of children were taught led to the Dark Ages. Poet, scholar, and humanist Petrarch (1304–1374, born in Arezzo) is usually credited with inventing the phrase. He had in mind the long period of time up to his own in which the light of Roman literary and cultural genius had been extinguished. Over the centuries the duration of the "Dark Ages" has changed from the thousand-plus years of 476 to 1500 to the shorter 476 to 1000. More recently the phrase has fallen into disuse as wildly inaccurate and ideological. In his essay "Petrarch's Conception of the Dark Ages," (1942) Theodor Ernst Mommsen (grandson of Nobel Prize winner Theodor Mommsen, whose magisterial *A History of Rome* was published in the 1850s) says that the phrase gained widest use during the Enlightenment. "…the expression was never primarily a scientific term, but rather a battle cry, 'a denunciation of the medieval conception of the world, of the medieval attitude toward life, and the culture of the Middle Ages.'" Mommsen the Younger also asserts, "It would seem that the notion of the medieval period as 'The Dark Ages,' is now destined to pass away for good" (Mommsen, pp. 226–227). Some people stubbornly continue to use "the Dark Ages" to signify the lack of information about those times as compared with classical antiquity. The old meaning of decline into backwardness, barbaric cruelty, and ignorance that lasted a millenium is probably just another case of buying into a Roman version of history.

Theories abound as to why the Roman Empire declined and fell, including that it never did. Rome is still there—represented by its most stable creation, the Roman Catholic Church, official state religion of the late empire. The barbarian invasions (or migration period, as our contemporaries call it) are often blamed, although some would argue that they were not the cause but the effect. All jokes about bone spurs aside, if Roman elites had taken an interest in their own defense, the Western Empire might have lasted longer. But as it was, the easy path of using mercenaries proved disastrous. AD 476 is the year usually given for the end of the Roman Empire. That was when Odoacer, chieftain of the Germanic mercenaries they had hired, took over Ravenna, the capital at that point of the Western Empire and on the northern-most edge of Piceno. Pieces of the Roman Empire in Britain and North Africa had already started to break off, leaving Italy as the last remnant of the Western Empire. And Alaric, king of the Visigoths, had sacked Rome in 410, for the first time in 800 years. As previously noted, he and his forces stormed through Piceno but bypassed Ascoli, frightened by the sight of the headless St. Emidio walking the city walls.

Alaric invaded Italy three times before finally over-running Rome on the third attempt. During one of those invasions the Roman city of Urbs Salvia in Piceno was destroyed. Founded by the Romans during the Republican period, Urbs Salvia became a colony during Augustus's reign. The Roman origins of the town are confirmed by the archeological record, since Piceni remains have been found in neighboring areas but none on the actual site of the town. Urbs Salvia's location at the intersection of two important roads, one from Firmum (Fermo) to Septempeda (San Severino Marche), the other from Asculum (Ascoli) to Auximum (Osimo), spurred its founding but may have also assured its destruction since it was in the path of Alaric's incursions. A visitor to the archeological site, one of Le Marche's most extensive, will likely witness ribbons of school children walking single file past the huge Roman walls, more than 5 m/15 ft high, and the second-century AD theater. The grand opening was celebrated in ancient times with a spectacle of forty pairs of gladiators fighting; today classic dramas are performed here. Significantly, after the destruction of Urbs Salvia, the survivors moved to the nearby hilltop where today's Urbisaglia stands, returning to pre-Roman patterns when the Roman Empire could no longer provide its far-reaching security.

After the death of Theodosius I in 395, the empire had split in two for good, with the western capital moving to Trier, Milan and finally, in 402, to the more defendable Ravenna on the Adriatic coast. At this point Ravenna was actually a part of Piceno, *Flaminia et Picenum Annonarium* to be precise, following reforms begun by Emperor Diocletian and revisited in the fifth century. The Eastern, or Byzantine Empire as it came to be called long after it disappeared, ruled for another thousand years with Constantinople as its capital. The Western Empire did not disappear overnight; the Roman Senate lasted well into the sixth century. The "barbarian invaders" were admirers of the empire; they just wanted to take it over, not destroy it, but in doing so great changes occurred in spite and because of them.

The Romans had provided security, infrastructure, and wealth on a grand scale. But according to Chris Wickham, the archeological record from this point forward shows a progressive simplification. Large villas were subdivided or abandoned, artisan production was less skillful and more limited, and fewer exchanges took place between former provinces of the Empire. Literacy plummeted. The formula for Roman cement, more durable than its modern counterpart, was lost. The large urban expanses of ancient times were replaced with medieval cities, tightly walled and smaller. Rome at its peak had a population of a million people; Wickham thinks that by the mid-fifth century the population had already dropped drastically, and by the next century it had shrunk more than 80 percent (Wickham, *The Inheritance of Rome*, p. 78). According to Carlo M. Cipolla, "Towns had prospered and proliferated in the Greco-Roman world, but the decline of the Empire brought with it their ruin. In a letter dated A.D., 381 Ambrose, bishop of Milan, described the towns of central Italy as 'semirutarum urbium cadavera'—remains of half-ruined cities. If some urban centers survived, their role was simply that of headquarters of religious and military administration. In the primitive world of the Dark Ages, the city was an anachronism" (Cipolla, *Before the Industrial Revolution*, p. 143).

The Gothic Wars

When Odoacer, a man of uncertain Germanic origins, became king of Italy by deposing the last Western Roman Emperor, he kept the existing Roman political system of laws, taxes, and senate, which won him some popularity with Italians. His rule was recognized by the Eastern Emperor Zeno, who raised Odoacer to the rank of patrician. But ongoing friction between the two leaders, and Odoacer's spreading power, caused Zeno to offer Italy to the Ostrogoths and their leader, Theodoric. By sending the Germanic Ostrogoths, who had recently settled in the Western Balkans, into Italy, Zeno also distanced them from Constantinople. Theodoric himself was well educated in the ways of Constantinople; born in the Roman province of Pannonia (today's southwest Hungary and assorted neighboring areas), he had spent ten years in the Byzantine capitol as a political hostage. The Goths invaded Italy in 489 and quickly took over most of the peninsula. Odoacer barricaded himself in his capital, Ravenna, and protected by the extensive marshes that rose and fell with the tides, withstood Theodoric's siege for three years. Eventually the two sides agreed on a compromise; Odoacer and Theodoric would both occupy Ravenna "on terms of complete equality" (Procopius, *The History of the Wars (Gothic Wars)*, Vol. V, p. 11), which they did for some time. But then Theodoric, suspecting that Odoacer was plotting against him, invited his adversary to a banquet. J.B. Bury's edition of Gibbon's *Decline and Fall of the Roman Empire* gives an account of this incident in a footnote taken from a fragment of John of Antioch—it bears an ancient flavor:

> Theodoric invited Odoacer (then sixty years old) to a feast in the Palace of the Consul of the southeast corner of Ravenna on March 15. As Odoacer sat at a table, two men knelt before him with a petition and clasped his hands. The soldiers, who were hidden in recesses on either side of the hall rushed out, but for some cause they could not bring themselves to strike the king. Theodoric himself stepped forward and raised his sword. 'Where is God?' cried Odoacer. 'This dist thou to my friends,' said Theodoric, and clave him from the collarbone to the loin. Surprised at his own stroke, he exclaimed, 'The wretch can have had no bones in his body' (Gibbon, *The History of the Decline and Fall of the Roman Empire*, Vol. IV, note 29, p. 180).

Procopius of Caesarea praises Theodoric, "for he was exceedingly careful to observe justice, he preserved the laws on a sure basis, he protected the land and kept it safe from barbarians dwelling round about, and attained the highest possible degree of wisdom and manliness" (Procopius, Vol V, p. 11). Procopius, a scholar from Palestine, spent twelve to fifteen years as councilor and secretary to Belisarius, the Byzantine commander-in-chief under Emperor Justinian, who ruled the Eastern Empire from 527–565. Procopius's *Gothic Wars* is the classic history and eyewitness account of these events, many of which he had experienced at the side of Belisarius.

According to Procopius, "Theodoric reigned for thirty-seven years and when he died, he had not only made himself an object of terror to all his enemies, but he also left to his subjects a keen sense of bereavement at his loss" (Procopius, Vol. V, p. 13). However, Theodoric's long reign was marred by a great crime against Philosophy, perhaps on a scale of the Athenians against Socrates. Boethius, born in Rome, was a member of Theodoric's court in Ravenna. Procopius records that:

> Symmachus and his son-in-law Boethius were men of noble and ancient lineage, and both had been leading men in the Roman Senate and had been consuls. But because they practiced philosophy and were mindful of justice in a manner surpassed by no other men, relieving the destitution of both citizens and stranger by generous gifts of money, they attained great fame and thus led men of the basest sort to envy them (Procopius, Vol. V, p. 13).

These lowlifes reported to Theodoric that Boethius and his father-in-law were planning a revolt.

Their properties were confiscated and the two men were condemned to die. In prison, Boethius wrote his masterwork, *The Consolation of Philosophy*; he was executed for treason in 524, Symmachus in 525. Theodoric did not get off lightly.

> And a few days later, while he was dining, the servers set before him the head of a great fish. This seemed to Theodoric to be the head of Symmachus newly slain. Indeed, with its teeth set in its lower lip and eyes looking at him with a grim and insane stare, it did resemble exceedingly a person threatening him. And becoming greatly frightened at the extraordinary prodigy and shivering excessively, he retired running to his own chamber, and bidding them place many covers upon him, remained quiet. But afterwards he disclosed to his physician Elpidius all that had happened and wept for the wrong he had done Symmachus and Boethius. Then having lamented and grieved exceedingly over the unfortunate occurrence, he died not long afterward (Procopius, Vol. V, p. 15).

Since Theodoric the Great died in August 526 without a male heir, his grandson Athalaric succeeded him with defacto power lying in the regency of his mother, Amalasuntha. While Procopius praises her character, noting that she returned the estates of Boethius and Symmachus to their families, Amalasuntha's emulation of Roman ways did not endear her to some of her fellow Goths. They particularly objected to the classical education of Athalaric, saying it made him a sissy and not a warrior. When Amalasuntha became aware of a plot against her, she sent three of the most active conspirators on military missions to the north, with a secret plan to have them killed there. As a back-up, she wrote the Emperor Justinian asking him for sanctuary in case she needed it. Justinian agreed, and she packed up a ship with all her belongings and a stash of gold to wait for her off the Albanian coast. When Amalasuntha learned that the murders had been carried out successfully, she decided to stay on in Ravenna, and recalled the boat.

But her son Athalaric was not growing up in a mode suitable for a king. He chose bad companions and led a life of dissipation, dying of a "wasting disease" in 534. Amalasuntha offered the kingship to her cousin Theodahad on the condition that the reins of government remain in her hands, disregarding the fact that she had already severely punished him for his treatment of his Roman subjects in Tuscany. Theodahad accepted the position but wasted little time in betraying his cousin, imprisoning her on an island in Lake Bolsena. There, she was strangled in her bath by relatives of the plotters she had assassinated.

If Amalasuntha's travails seem worthy of opera or tragedy, they were. Carlo Goldoni (1707–1793) wrote a play, "Amalasuntha," which was such a critical and financial failure that he burned the manuscript. A fitting result perhaps, paralleling as it does the circumstances that developed after Amalasuntha's death, events of immense and tragic proportions.

Justinian had tried to protect Amalasuntha, but to no avail. Now he decided to reclaim his power over the parts of the empire that had been lost to the "barbarians." According to Procopius, "…the Emperor, upon learning what had befallen Amalasuntha, immediately entered upon the war, being in the ninth year of his reign" (Procopius, V, p. 43). The builder of the Hagia Sophia also sought to crush the threat to Catholicism posed by their Arianism. Having already triumphed in Persia and North Africa, he sent Belisarius, sometimes called the last Roman general, to wrest Italy from the Goths.

Emperor Justinian, Empress Theodora, Belisarius and his wife Antonina, Narses—some of the main characters in this military drama—are all depicted in the Basilica San Vitale's famed Byzantine mosaics. (Despite their Arian religious beliefs, the Goths under Amalasuntha had allowed construction of this important church in Ravenna.) While the *Gothic Wars* gives a straightforward history of these events, Procopius saved the real dirt for his *Anecdota/Secret History*. In it he tells another story behind Amalasuntha's death; the scandalously low-born Empress Theodora did not want the beautiful, clever, aristocratic queen taking refuge in her husband's court, so she sent a secret message to Theodahad that induced him to eliminate his cousin (Procopius, *Anecdota*, p. 189).

When Theodahad had revealed himself to be a cowardly incompetent, the Goths chose a new king, a military man named Witigis. On his orders Theodahad was slaughtered as he made a run for Ravenna. Witigis married Amalasuntha's young daughter Matasuntha against her will, hoping to cement his place in the Gothic dynasty. He wrote Justinian offering peace, but Belisarius and his men had already conquered Sicily, won their siege of Naples and were heading towards Rome. The Romans invited Belisarius in, not realizing that the general was preparing to fight it out in their city. Witigis, when he heard that Belisarius was holding Rome with only a small force, decided to leave Ravenna and attack with his full army; Belisarius, in a letter to Justinian, said that it was 5,000 vs. 150,000 (Procopius, V, p. 229), perhaps an exaggeration. In the early spring of 538, the Goths descended on Rome by way of the Via Salaria, and after a skirmish at the Salarian Gate, the siege of Rome began.

The Byzantines and Romans held out for a year and nine days. The Goths failed to completely encircle them and over time Belisarius was able to resupply the city and call for reinforcements. When the sick and starving Goths heard of these approaching troops they sent an envoy requesting a truce. A three-month armistice was agreed to while Justinian decided on the final terms of the treaty.

Belisarius instructed John, known as "the Bloodthirsty," nephew of the famous general Vitalian, to pass the winter near Alba in Picenum with 2,000 horsemen. According to Procopius:

> He gave John instructions that as long as he saw the enemy was keeping the agreement made between them, he should remain quiet; but whenever he found that the armistice had been violated by them, he should do as follows: With his whole force he was to make a sudden raid and overrun the land of Picenum, visiting all the districts of that region and reaching each one before the report of his coming. For in this whole land there was virtually not a single man left, since all, as it appeared, had marched against Rome, but everywhere there were women and children of the enemy and money. He was instructed, therefore, to enslave or plunder whatever he found, taking care never to injure any of the Romans living there (Procopius, VI. p. 355).

After several attempts by the Goths to sneak into Rome, Belisarius judged the truce violated and sent John the Bloodthirsty on a course of pillaging, plundering, and enslaving women and children throughout Piceno. These were the families of the Gothic soldiers, who had settled in the fertile countryside, with the booty their menfolk had accumulated. The Gothic army had an outpost in the region, but they were no match for the Byzantines/Romans. According to J. B. Bury, the battle between the two armies must have been fought somewhere in the southern part of Piceno, because from there the victors headed north towards Osimo (Bury, *History of the Later Roman Empire*, Vol. II, p. 193). John decided to bypass this hilltop fortress town, occupied by the Goths, because of the natural defenses of the place. He bypassed Urbino for the same reasons, in both cases a violation of his orders to either attack or stay put so as not to leave his rear undefended, and continued on to Rimini. There, the frightened Goths fled to Ravenna, a day's march away, and the citizens of Rimini invited the Byzantine army in. Matasun-tha, the unwilling wife of Witigis, initiated a secret correspondence with John, proposing that she betray Ravenna and marry him.

Procopius describes John as carried away by "unreasoning boldness," but John was right about one thing. When the Goths learned that he was so close to Ravenna, they abandoned Rome, in mid-March 538. Belisarius inflicted heavy casualties on the retreating forces as they crossed the Tiber, and Witigis headed east with what was left of his army. On the way he deployed troops in strategic places, mostly in Tuscany on the western side of the Apennines but including Petra Pertusa in Piceno, about 40 km/ 25 mi inland from the Adriatic. Procopius describes this as a natural fortress, where the Via Flaminia passes through a narrow pass with sheer rock on one side and an unfordable river on the other. In AD 76, Emperor Vespasian had a tunnel excavated through the rock, with gates at either end (today's road still uses this tunnel, known as the Furlo Pass).

Hoping to outrun Witigis, Belisarius sent 1,000 horsemen commanded by Martin and Ildiger carrying orders for John and his cavalry to withdraw from Rimini, to be replaced with a small infantry force from Ancona. They cleverly overcame the obstruction at Petra Pertusa by climbing nearby cliffs and toppling a shower of huge boulders on the Gothic garrison there, until the terrified gatekeepers surrendered. By speeding along the Via Flaminia, the most direct route, Martin and Ildiger reached the Adriatic ahead of the Goths. From Fano they headed south to pick up the infantrymen at Ancona, then retraced their steps north to deliver Belisarius's orders to John. The idea was that the Goths, hurrying towards Ravenna, would not bother with an undefended Rimini, and John's forces could be better used elsewhere. But John disagreed and chose to stay. Leaving the infantrymen behind, Martin and Ildiger went back to tell their general about John's insubordination.

Once Witigis and his army made their way across the Apennines, they attacked Rimini and laid siege in April 538.

In the meantime, Belisarius had been marching toward Piceno, taking over the Gothic fortresses at Chiusi and Todi. His next target was Orvieto but he changed course when news reached him that Justinian had sent reinforcements. An army of 7000 men, most of them under the command of Narses, had landed, presumably at Ancona which had recently repelled a Gothic attack from their stronghold in Osimo. Narses, an Armenian eunuch, had served Justinian and Theodora for many years, ultimately as Grand Chamberlain of the Court. Not a military man, or young, but undeniably loyal, he was probably sent by the emperor to counterbalance the growing power of Belisarius (Duckett, *The Gateway to the Middle Ages: Italy*, p. 26). The two generals met in Fermo to plan the next action. Belisarius wanted to attack the Goths at Osimo, and was very reluctant to commit his forces to Rimini while turning his back on the enemy. The majority of the army commanders felt that John had brought the trouble on himself and were unwilling to risk their troops to save him. However, Narses, a close friend of John's, argued that it would not only be cruel, but a shameful waste of men and material to abandon him; he could be punished for his disobedience later. Ultimately, when a message arrived from John that he and his starving soldiers were on the verge of surrender, Belisarius suppressed his doubts and decided to do everything he could to free Rimini. He sent Ildiger by sea with a fleet of ships, Martin along the coastal road, and led his own forces up through the mountains, by way of Urbisaglia and probably part of the Via Flaminia, to strike from the northwest. He instructed Martin to hold back until the navy was in place, and to light a disproportionate number of campfires at night, to give the impression that his army was much larger than it was. Scared by the exaggerated strength of the three-pronged threat, the Goths panicked and retreated in disorder to Ravenna without a fight. Procopius thought the war might have ended there if John had pursued and attacked them, but John's forces were too debilitated from the siege.

Procopius records much horrendous slaughter and calamitous starvation in his _Gothic Wars_. By 539, there had been four years of conflict in central Italy. Years of poor crops due to the disruption of rampaging troops caused starvation and disease in Liguria, Emilia, Etruria, Umbria, and Piceno. According to him, at least 50,000 Roman farmers died in Piceno due to the famine. Those fleeing inland Emilia to Piceno and hoping to find seafood instead found more desolation. Unburied corpses lining the roads, bodies so emaciated that there was nothing for the vultures to eat, people scrabbling to devour grass and acorns, fill the pages of Procopius's history. A particularly sordid story relates:

> And it is said that two women in a certain place in the country above the city of Ariminum ate seventeen men; for these women, as it happened, were the only inhabitants of the place who survived, and consequently it came about that strangers traveling that way lodged in the little house where these women lived; so they would kill these strangers while they slept and eat them (Procopius, VI, p. 43).

The eighteenth traveler awoke just as they were about to make a meal of him and killed them both.

Procopius also describes an amusing incident he witnessed firsthand, which took place near Urbisaglia. In the general confusion of war, a new-born infant had been abandoned by his mother, who was captured or had escaped without her baby. When a goat heard the infant's cries, she felt pity and suckled him; this went on "for a very long time." Later, when the local people realized that the Byzantine army was only after the Goths and meant the Romans / Italians no harm, they returned home and to their great amazement found the goat and child. When some of the women tried to breastfeed the baby, he refused to drink human milk and the goat insisted on keeping the baby for herself. Procopius wrote that when he was staying in the area, they took him to see the infant, whom they had named Aegisthus, which means "goat." Someone deliberately hurt the child to make him cry out, and the mother goat came to the baby's defense. "Such then is the story of Aegisthus" (Procopius, VI, p. 13–15).

After the Byzantines took control of Rome, they had occupied Milan, but the Goths laid siege to their small force there, with help from their allies the Burgundians. Conflicts between Belisarius and Narses led to a series of delays in any relief being sent. Finally, the Byzantines surrendered and the Goths destroyed the city, taking the soldiers captive and brutally slaughtering some 300,000 male inhabitants; the women were given to the Burgundians as slaves. Justinian, when he heard this outcome of the divided authority he had created, recalled Narses to Constantinople.

Having successfully besieged Urbino and Orvieto, the Byzantine forces moved against Osimo. Interestingly, Procopius describes Osimo, not Ascoli, as "…the first of the cities in Picenum, being the metropolis, as the Romans are accustomed to call it… And it is situated upon a very high hill having no approach at all upon the level ground, and for this it is entirely inaccessible for an enemy" (Procopius, VI, p. 65). Witigis had stationed some of his best troops there, figuring that any attack on Ravenna would have to pass this way. Since he could not take Osimo by force of arms, Belisarius set up a siege in April 539.

Urbino had fallen because its water supply failed; Belisarius now poisoned Osimo's main water source, a cistern outside the city walls, with toxic herbs, quicklime, and dead animals. Luckily for the Goths, there was another small well inside the city, but food was running out. The besieged commander sent a plea to Ravenna, describing their plight; Witigis wrote back that he would arrive soon with his entire army, but did nothing. Belisarius tightened the guard so that no more messengers could evade it. The Goths, however, were able to bribe a Roman soldier to carry another message, which said they would have to capitulate in five days if no help was forthcoming. In his reply, Witigis repeated his promises, encouraging the trapped and starving men to resist. In the meantime, Belisarius had offered the Goths a surrender on attractive terms, which they refused. Suspecting something was up, Belisarius arranged for the capture of a Goth who had slipped out to forage for grass. The prisoner revealed the treachery of the Roman, who was then handed over to his fellow soldiers for judgement. They burned him alive just outside the city walls. Witigis never did send any reinforcements, keeping them for his own protection. Osimo held out for a total of six months, but finally capitulated when emaciated fellow Goths captured at Fiesole were marched in full view below them. The Goths accepted that surrender was their best option; they gave up half their possessions and passed into the service of the empire in October or November 539.

Now it was Ravenna's turn. The Byzantines took control of the Po River and the Adriatic coast so the Goth capitol could not be restocked with provisions. At the same time, a warehouse holding a large amount of the city's precious grain burned. Whether the fire was started by someone Belisarius had bribed, by the orders of Matasuntha, or even by lightning, is unknown, but the net effect was to inspire Witigis and the Goths to believe, "that war was being waged against them by God Himself" (Procopius VI, p. 121). After first considering a pact with their longtime allies / enemies the Franks, who as always were hovering on the northern borders, Witigis and his advisors opted instead to negotiate a peace with the Emperor Justinian.

Justinian, taking into account the immense cost of the ongoing wars in Italy and Persia, made them a generous offer that divided Italy in two, with the lands north of the Po going to the Goths and those south of it to the Romans, and the royal treasury split between them. Belisarius balked at this since a total victory over the Goths seemed so close. He refused to sign, and the Goths had no faith in a treaty that did not include him. Instead, they made a secret proposal to Belisarius to crown him the Emperor of the West, because they respected him so highly. Playing a double game, Belisarius feigned acceptance and agreed to all terms proposed, but said he would only take possession of the throne in the presence of Witigis himself. He then asked his officers and the envoys from Justinian's court if they would go along with his unspecified plan that would capture the Goths, their wealth, and all of Italy. This sounded good to them. Thus, Belisarius and his army entered Ravenna in May 540, cheered by all. But instead of taking the crown from Witigis, he placed the king under guard. Most remaining Gothic garrisons, except Verona and Pavia, surrendered to the man they thought was their new emperor. Belisarius forbade any plundering and encouraged the Goths who lived south of the Po to return home. But, honoring his vows to serve Justinian, if not the promises he had made to Witigis, he did not actually become their ruler.

Justinian, hearing the gossip and perhaps doubting Belisarius's loyalty, called him back to Constantinople to take charge of the Persian War. The general took Witigis, Matasuntha, and the Gothic royal treasury with him, which must have pleased the emperor. According to Bury:

"If Belisarius had not been recalled, he would probably have completed the conquest of the peninsula within a few months. This, which would have been the best solution, was defeated by the jealousy of Justinian; and the peace proposed by the Emperor, which was the next best course, was defeated by the disobedience of his general. Between them they bear the responsibility of inflicting upon Italy twelve more years of war" (Bury, *History of the Later Roman Empire*, Ch. XIX, p. 226).

The power vacuum created by Justinian allowed the Goths to retrench and reorganize. After the brief failed reigns of Ildibad and Eraric, both murdered by their own subjects, the charismatic and able Totila was elected king in 541. By 543, he had recovered almost all of the territory the Goths had lost to the Byzantine Romans. Justinian recognized that he had to send Belisarius back to Italy.

In the meantime, an even more treacherous invader found its way into Italy; the bubonic plague, carried by fleas on rats. Procopius says, "During these times there was a pestilence, by which the whole human race came near to being annihilated" (Procopius, *History of the Wars*, II, p. 451). Estimates ran as high as twenty-five million deaths across Europe and Asia, caused by what was later called the Plague of Justinian (Rosen, *Justinian's Flea*, p. 3). Procopius reports that at its peak 10,000 a day were dying in Constantinople. Justinian himself contracted the disease; while it did not kill him, witnesses say he was never his old self again.

There is no concrete evidence of the effects of the plague upon Piceno, although it seems likely that the bacteria passed through the Adriatic port of Ancona. As Procopius says, "And this disease always took its start from the coast, and from there went up to the interior" (Procopius, *History of the Wars*, II, p. 455). Recently, a mass grave of its victims was found south of Rome, more than 48 km / 30 mi inland. Less extreme, localized outbreaks of the plague continued until the eighth century, and it reappeared in the 14th century as the infamous Black Death. This much may be surmised: the plague considerably weakened the Byzantine Romans and facilitated the Goths' reoccupation of the region. By 545, Ascoli and Fermo had surrendered to Totila, and according to Laffi, were sacked (Laffi, *Storia del Ascoli nell' Età Antica*, p. xlviii). Rome was besieged three times and only a touching letter from Belisarius telling Totila what bad manners it would be to utterly destroy the ancient city stopped him from doing so.

Belisarius, woefully underfunded and undermanned, was not able to accomplish much during his five years in Italy. Procopius says that the general and his army were too scared to take on the Goths, and instead just sailed from port to port, only touching land at secure fortresses (*Anecdota*, p. 55). Justinian recalled him again, perhaps at the urging of Belisarius's wife Antonina, and sent Narses.

In 551, before Narses arrived, a major blow was delivered to the Goths. They had surrounded the strategically vital port of Ancona, blockading it by land and sea. The Byzantine commander at Ravenna wrote to John the Bloodthirsty, asking for his help in lifting the lengthy siege. John, again disobeying Justinian's orders, assembled a large fleet. The two commanders joined their naval forces on the Dalmatian coast and sailed across the Adriatic to confront the enemy off the coast of Senigallia, some 30 km / 19 mi north of Ancona. While the two fleets were of nearly equal size, the more skillful Roman mariners won the Battle of Sena Gallica, wiping out the disorganized Goth navy. The Goths retreated back to Osimo—and Ancona was freed.

Narses had collected a substantial force of about 25,000 men, including Longobardi (aka Lombards) and Heruls, at Salona, a Byzantine port near today's Split, Croatia. They marched up the Adriatic but were forced to leave the coastal road for the actual seacoast at Venice, held at that time by the Franks. Since the Franks and the Longobardi were bitter enemies, the Franks refused passage through their territory. The Byzantine army successfully made their way around them.

On his arrival in Ravenna, Narses wasted little time pushing forward to confront Totila and his army. Totila was in Rome, so Narses set out in that direction, rejoining the Via Flaminia after Petra Pertusa, which was again held by the Goths. When Totila heard of this, he headed for the Apennines, also by way of the Via Flaminia, and camped at a village called Taginae to the north of today's Gualdo Taldino in Umbria. Narses and his army stopped just west of Fabriano, not far south of the site of the Battle of Sentinum, at Busta Gallorum; the Celtic presence in this part of Piceno is reflected in this name, which means "Tomb of the Gauls." Historians alternate between calling this seminal event the Battle of Busta Gallorum and the Battle of Taginae.

Totila sent word to Teias, one of his best commanders, to join him in battle, but Totila's forces would be outnumbered even with the addition of Teias's 2,000 cavalrymen. Narses sent a message to Totila advising him to either retire in the face of a greater army, or to name his day of battle. Although Totila made an appointment for eight days hence, Narses knew better. The next morning, when Totila's forces were revealed at daybreak to be two bow shots away, Narses's army had already taken a strong defensive position awaiting their attack.

Totila began delaying tactics in anticipation of Teias's arrival. With the two armies facing off against one another, a certain Coccas, a highly reputed fighter and deserter from the Roman army, rode out from amongst the Goths and challenged anyone to single combat. An Armenian spearman named Anzalas rose to the challenge. Coccas charged with his spear but Anzalas turned his horse aside and thrust his spear into Coccas's side. Coccas fell dead. Not a good omen for the Goths.

Now Totila got word that his reinforcements were approaching so he entered the space between the two armies to buy some more time. He was riding an enormous steed, wearing gold plated armor with purple adornments Procopius describes as "befitting a king, marvelous in their abundance." He commenced showing off his skills, hurling his javelin in the air and catching it, all the while maneuvering his horse skillfully, "…he gloried in his practice in such matters, falling back on his shoulders, spreading his legs and leaning from side to side, like one who has been instructed with precision in the art of dancing from childhood. By these tactics he wore away the whole early part of the day" (Procopius, VIII, p. 375).

Totila then sent word that he wanted to negotiate but Narses knew he was just stalling. When Totila got back to his camp, he found that Teias had arrived. He ordered everyone to eat lunch and prepare for battle, hoping to catch Narses unaware, but again Narses, who had developed into a very astute military leader, was ready for him. His men had eaten standing in their positions.

Here Procopius notes that Totila had given a strange command: that the entire Gothic army should use only spears and not bows or any other weapons. "Consequently it came about that Totila was out-generalled by his own folly" (Procopius, VIII, p. 377). The Goths suffered a crushing defeat; according to Procopius more than 6,000 lost their lives that day.

In one version, Totila fled with five men, they were overtaken, and Totila was killed; a cowardly end. Procopius relates an alternative in which Totila, dressed like every other soldier and fighting side by side with them, was struck by a random arrow. Mortally injured, he was carried away from the fight and buried in a nearby village. Regardless of how Totila died, Narses was overjoyed at the outcome of the battle. He was especially glad to take leave of his allies the Longobardi and their "outrageous behavior… for, in addition to the general lawlessness of their conduct, they kept setting fire to whatever buildings they chanced upon, and violating by force the women who had taken refuge in the sanctuaries" (Procopius, VIII, p. 389). The Longobardi left carrying large sacks of money, a gift—or rather a bribe—from Narses.

The Battle of Busta Gallorum was not the end of Gothic efforts in Italy, but their hold on Italy was essentially broken. Narses went on to recapture Rome and then defeat the Goths at the Battle of Mons Lacterius (aka the Battle of Vesuvius) in 552 or 553. Here, Teius died a hero's death and the Ostrogoths were largely eliminated from the scene, though Narses still had various mopping-up operations to complete. Surviving Goth soldiers were allowed to leave Italy on the condition of never returning or making war against the empire. Italy, at least temporarily, became part of the Byzantine/Roman Empire again.

In his tell-all *Anecdota*, Procopius lets us in on the fates of four main characters. The book was written in 550 and never published in the author's lifetime, for obvious reasons. In the section titled by one translator, "Everyone and Everything Sacrificed to the Emperor's Greed," Procopius details the many ways Justinian plundered countries and people; "…nor did any consideration weigh with him other than simply and solely the snatching of all the money there was in the world" (*Anecdota*, p. 319). Procopius piles on the insults, but perhaps Justinian's major sin was that he allowed his wife to push him around. According to Procopius, Theodora was born into a family of circus performers and at an early age became a prostitute. His descriptions of her sexual behavior are such that some editions preferred not to translate the Greek. Justinian, a humbly born Goth adopted by his uncle, the Emperor Justin, fell madly in love with her and had the laws barring marriages between patricians and prostitutes voided so that they could wed. Apparently, she then gave up her lascivious ways, but Procopius could not forgive her for assuming powers unbecoming a woman. One example contradicts what he wrote in his published work *Buildings*. Therein he says that Justinian and Theodora, "who always shared a common piety in all that they did," had established and funded a convent in a former palace on the Bosphorus, as "a refuge for women who repented of their past lives" (*The Buildings of Procopius*, Book I, p. 77). His alternate version: Theodora rounded up more than 500 "harlots" and "confined them in the Convent of Repentance, as it is called, trying there to compel them to adopt a new manner of life. And some of them threw themselves down from a height at night and thus escaped the unwelcome transformation" (*Anecdota*, p. 199). Bury gives a more positive take, describing Theodora as a savior of child sex slaves (such as she herself may have been), who sponsored laws that banned the trafficking in girls, and who bought their freedom with her own money (Bury, p. 32).

Antonina, a similarly disgraceful female in Procopius's eyes, was the daughter of a charioteer and a performer/prostitute. Using sinister magical arts, she captured the heart and soul of Belisarius, when he was a rising young military man and she a promiscuous older woman. As his wife, she accompanied the general on many of his campaigns, playing an active role as his military aide, but broke his heart by carrying on a torrid affair with their adopted son. Procopius scorns his one-time commander for being so weak, undercutting much of the praise he had lavished upon him in *The History of the Wars*. Procopius also details a number of cases where Theodora and Antonina, often in cahoots, carried out plots behind their husbands' backs, wreaking disgrace and death on their personal and political enemies. Belisarius himself, accused late in life of treason, was ruined and then redeemed through the palace intrigues of the other three characters. Donizetti wrote an opera, "Belisario," in 1820, inspired by the fallen hero. Robert Graves's historical novel *Count Belisarius* relies heavily on Procopius in his detailed account of battles and strategies, with a healthy dollop of scandal (he gives Antonina a lot more credit than Procopius did). Belisarius, Justinian, and, probably, Procopius, all died in 565. Theodora had already died of cancer in 548; Antonina survived her husband.

The end of the Gothic Wars did not eliminate the Gothic presence in Italy; some Goths were able to remain in Italy, continuing to live on their land and gradually integrate themselves into local society. There were two Arian churches in Rome until the end of the sixth century. The Goths had settled around Milan and Pavia, Ravenna, and in the central Apennines—Picenum. While the first two areas were urban centers, the last was a crucial border zone with small agricultural settlements and military garrisons. The Goths had stationed troops along the Via Salaria to repel Byzantine attacks from the south and the east, as well as from the sea.

What the Goths Left Behind

An area notably rich in Gothic archaeological finds spreads across today's provinces of Ascoli Piceno, Teramo, and Chieti; on the mountain ridges between the Tronto and Tordino river valleys; in the lower valley at Colli del Tronto; and on the coast at Cupra Marittima / Grottammare. One of the most notable sites is at Cagnano, above the Tronto at Aquasanta Terme, on a rock spur with a view of the Via Salaria. In 1952, workers were constructing a playing field next to a building that had originally served as a tuberculosis sanitarium for children (the spot no doubt chosen because it was so isolated). They uncovered three graves, two female and one male, with personal belongings that were gathered up haphazardly. Subsequent archeological excavations found four more bodies with no grave goods. None of the skeletons were analyzed or preserved. The women had been buried with the jewelry they wore: a silver necklace with amber and glass beads, a gold ring, and characteristic gold-plated silver belt buckles where the tongue ends in a snake's head. Also, a bronze ring carrying an array of toiletry utensils, and maybe a bronze needle; a dark red cloisonné belt buckle is thought to have belonged to the man. The Goths, no fools they, did not bury weapons with the dead. The only Gothic dress helmets found in Italy come from this zone, discovered in storage sites, not graves. On the opposite side of the Tronto, Gothic jewelry and belt buckles were found at Forcella, known for its waterfall and part of the township of Roccafluvione. One set of earrings is particularly charming: gold hoops with airy little boxes holding blue glass beads. Two *fibulae* are almost identical to a pair found at Colli del Tronto: gold-plated silver with an arched top and a decorated shaft that ends with an animal's head (Maria Cecilia Profumo, "I Goti nelle Marche," *La Necropoli Altomedievale di Castel Trosino*).

In *Ascoli nel Piceno*, Secondo Balena retells the following story, found in the work of local historian Padre Luigi Pastori. After the Goths were defeated and most had left Italy, a large Gothic colony remained in Ascoli. Perhaps hoping to hold on to their lands and plunder, they began to make efforts to fraternize with the Ascolani. But according to Balena, by 554 the locals must have been champing at the bit to settle scores. A banquet was organized to which members of the Ascolani and Gothic nobility were invited. During the entertainment two women, an Ascolana and a Goth, started a discussion about religion, with the Ascolana defending the Catholic Church and the popes while the other supported the

Looking across Piceno from Ripatransone toward Gran Sasso, Abruzzo

Arian version of Christianity. The discussion soon came to a boil. Perhaps having exhausted her argu-ments, in frustration the Gothic woman threw a cushion at the Ascolana, who grabbed a knife from the table and planted it in the Gothic woman's breast. The killer was immediately transported to prison.

According to Balena, we do not know if the Ascolana noblewoman was condemned to death, but she was granted a special request to have dinner with her husband and younger brother in prison. After dinner, the brother slipped on her clothes while the woman, dressed as a man, fled with her husband. When the switch was discovered, the brother was brought in front of the governor, who Balena says must have been a Byzantine. Showing much admiration for the brother's courage and spirit of sacrifice, and possibly desiring to stay on the native Ascolanis' good side, the governor was inclined to let him go and to pardon the noblewoman. This angered the Goths, who pressed him to make an example of the two; their daring escape was an insult to all the Goths. While the governor tried to buy time, the Ascol-ani took matters into their own hands. In no time the streets were full of people armed in the strangest ways and led by representatives of the noble class. They attacked the governor's palace, freed the young brother, and assaulted the Goths. Seeing the combat going in their favor, they liberated the entire city. The Goths who were not killed fled Ascoli. Shouting the praises of their independence, the Ascolani people returned to self-government (Balena, *Ascoli nel Piceno*, pp. 152–3).

The reassertion of Ascoli's independence did not signal a return to prosperity. New outbreaks of the plague, in addition to the damage caused by twenty years of the Gothic Wars, left not just Piceno but all of Italy in a reduced state, much of it devastated and depopulated. In 568, the Longobardi entered Italy, and nobody could stop them.

Lombard Church of Sant'Angelo in Montespino

9

The Longbeards in Piceno

The Byzantine attempt to revive imperial power in Italy had succeeded at an enormous cost. The Goths were routed, but much of Italy, especially Piceno, lay in ruins. Narses stayed in Italy for thirteen years as an administrator and overseer of reconstruction, trying to bring Italy back to its role as the westernmost province of the empire, also in decline after years of war and plague. However, according to Paul the Deacon (c. 720–c. 799), a Lombard, Benedictine monk, and the main historical source for this era, Narses had provoked considerable rancor amongst the native Romans by amassing personal wealth at their expense.

The Romans complained to the new Emperor Justinian II and his wife Sophia, asking to be freed from Narses's grasp and threatening that they would otherwise hand themselves over to the barbarians. When Narses heard this he responded brusquely, "If I have acted badly with the Romans it will go hard with me." The emperor was so enraged by Narses's remark that he sent Longinus to replace him. Narses did not go back to Constantinople, fearing Sofia's anger above all. Reportedly, the empress had told him that since he was a eunuch he would end up in the women's quarters helping the girls untangle yarn. Narses replied: "…that he would begin to weave her such a web as she could not lay down as long as she lived." In his *Historia Langobardorum*, Paul the Deacon says:

> Therefore, greatly racked by hate and fear, he withdrew to Neapolis (Naples) a city of Campania, and soon sent messengers to the nation of the Langobards, urging them to abandon the barren fields of Pannonia and come take possession of Italy, teeming with every sort of riches… The Langobards receive joyfully the glad tidings which they themselves had also been desiring, and they form high expectations of future advantages. In Italy terrible signs were continually seen at night, that is, fiery swords appeared in Heaven, gleaming with that blood which was afterwards shed (Paul the Deacon, pp. 59–60).

Scholars dispute Paul the Deacon's account, arguing that the Lombards had already been in Italy serving as mercenaries to the Byzantine Empire. They surely knew about Italy's bounty and how to go about getting it; an invitation from Narses was unnecessary. Rather, the Longobardi saw their chance to take over regions decimated by the Gothic-Byzantine wars. The Byzantines, overstretched in the east, were unable to stop them. They did manage to hang on to Ravenna, the Duchy of Rome, the Duchy of Naples, some small portions of southern Italy, and most important here, the Pentapolis—the five coastal cities (Ancona, Senigallia, Fano, Pesaro, Rimini), which today, stopping short of Rimini, constitute the northern ports of Le Marche. In the late sixth century, the Byzantines established the office of the exarch, the agent of the emperor, and Ravenna became the Exarchate of Ravenna.

The name Lombard or Langobard or Longobardi (in Italian) is generaly translated as "long beards." A Latin manuscript dated to the second half of the seventh century, "*Origo gentis Langobardorum*," contains the first written version of their oral origin myth, which Paul the Deacon retells. According to the saga, a people in a region now thought to be southern Sweden appealed to their war god Odin/Wotan for support in an upcoming battle. To help them, the god's wife Frea/Freya suggested a tactic to make their forces more impressive—the women should appear on the battlefield with their hair combed down the sides of their faces, like beards, to look like warriors. Odin/Wotan, on seeing this army, asked, "Who are these long beards?" and granted them the victory. The group took on the name, and the men kept the hairstyle.

Over the centuries, the Lombards made their way into the Roman Empire, through Germany, Bohemia, Czechoslovakia, entering the Roman province of Pannonia fifty years before reaching Italy. They travelled in caravans with their families and livestock, hunting wild game and searching for fresh pastures. From the nomads of Asia, they acquired the technique of fighting on horseback. They were not farmers. Nor were they a homogenous group; other people joined them as they passed through. About 100,000 entered Italy in 568, establishing the capital of their kingdom in Pavia, and were in power until 774, taking over most of modern Lombardy and parts of Venetia, Liguria, and Tuscany. Scholars debate whether the Lombards, when they arrived in Italy, were pagans or followers of the Arian sect, a heresy that asserted that Christ was not a divinity on the same level with God (Fanning, "Lombard Arianism Reconsidered"). By 680, they had officially converted to Roman Catholicism (Geary, p. 125).

After taking over the Padana region of Italy, the Lombards descended into Piceno "as if by gravity" (C. Cappelli, *I Barbari*, p. 116). Not a sea-faring people, they left the coastal regions, the Pentapolis, to the maritime empire and chose to dominate the inland areas, establishing the two powerful Duchies of Spoleto and Benevento. They captured the Via Flaminia in hopes of interrupting traffic between Rome and Ravenna, but the Romans and Byzantines found alternate routes. According to local lore, as the Duchy of Spoleto expanded toward the Adriatic coast, Ascoli was destroyed in 578 and Fermo taken in 580. No archeological evidence has been discovered to support the destruction of Ascoli, and the city still has two Roman temples that live on as Christian churches (San Gregorio Magno and San Venanzio). The Lombard's urban pattern was to build heavily fortified, family-based compounds within the city walls. These newcomers lacked an urban tradition and its bureaucratic apparatus; unlike the Goths, they had not co-existed with the Romans. There is in fact very little documentation of the two centuries of Lombard rule here, but the Lombards did leave a treasure trove of archeological evidence in the form of Castel Trosino and its necropolis, which lie only 4 km/2.5 mi from Ascoli.

Castel Trosino

The medieval town of Castel Trosino sits on an ideally defensible spit of travertine high above the Castellano River, just upstream from where it joins the Tronto River to create the site of Ascoli Piceno. Like the Goths before them, this was the kind of place the Lombards preferred, at least in the beginning; not a big city but a sort of military camp controlling access to a big city. From these heights, the inhabitants could monitor traffic along the river and the path it cut through the mountains. Traces of a Piceno settlement have been found here, followed by the Romans. A Byzantine castle became the Lombard outpost. In the Middle Ages, it housed a Benedictine monastery owned by the powerful Abbey of Farfa, later turned over to the local diocese. One arched gateway allows access to the town, a single street of

Castel Trosino

picturesque stone buildings which ascends to the church of San Lorenzo, rebuilt in 1855.

In 1893, the parish priest of this church approached Guilio Gabrielle, the director of the library and civic museum in Ascoli Piceno, to show him objects that had been found by a farmer on church land in the San Stefano district. There were already records of such finds in this area; various "barbarian" objects had turned up over the centuries. In 1872, the tomb of a cavalier, perhaps the first Lombard leader of Castel Trosino, had been unearthed in the nearby Pedata district. Those rich funeral goods were quickly dispersed, sold to private dealers, and eventually ended up in museums in New York and Paris.

Gabrielle immediately recognized the importance of the priest's collection. He bought the first batch of finds for the museum with his own money, and then set about organizing a systematic scientific excavation. However, Raniero Mengarelli, from the Museo delle Terme in Rome, was assigned the job of leading the project. The priest and his workers had already dug up some fifty graves, mixing the objects together. Gabrielli was determined to document the dig, and his careful notebooks and sketches of the site can be seen today in the Pinacoteca Civica of Ascoli Piceno. More than 200 tombs dating from the end of the sixth century through the seventh century were quickly excavated, as well as the ruins of the church of San Stefano.

In the end, Gabrielle faced the bitter day when all the grave goods were loaded onto a train and taken to Rome for further study. Despite promises that they would be returned to Ascoli, only a small portion made it back. The bulk were displayed at the Museo delle Terme, and after 1967, at the Museo Nazionale dell'Alto Medioevo, in the EUR district of Rome.

We went to this Fascist-era complex, the only visitors aside from another foreign couple, to see the gold, the treasure, of the Longobardi of Castel Trosino. One case displays the objects found in Tomb 119, labeled as the richest trove of Lombard warrior equipment found in Italy to date, giving the most complete picture of the horseman and his gear. Sword, scramasax, spear, shield, helmet, arrows and quiver, and other weapons in gold, silver, and bronze. Highly decorative belt buckles and cintures for the straps that held all these arms, and simple gold crosses meant to be stitched onto clothing. Spurs and bits, harnesses and saddles, with buckles, belt tips, and plaques in incised gold and silver. Banqueting utensils including a drinking horn.

The richest women's graves contained gold rings, pins, and

Lombard Gold Pin, British Museum, London

earrings, including a uniquely magnificent pair with golden triangular plaques, pearls, and amethyst pendants. Necklaces of glass beads, silver pins in the shape of animals. Certain distinctive round golden pins, decorated with filigree, are unique to Castel Trosino, probably the work of Byzantine artists based there or in a nearby center of production.

Studies have shown that this was not a strictly "Lombard" cemetery. While the style of some of the items show a Germanic influence, for the most part they are the work of Italo-Byzantine artisans. Some incorporate carved stones from the Roman era. Forty-six percent of the graves contained no burial goods, reflecting Late Roman customs. The dead buried here seem to have been Roman and Byzantine inhabitants of Castel Trosino, Germanic Longobards, local people, and even one African (Lidia Paroli, "*La necropolis di Castel Trosino: un riesame critico,*" La Necropoli Altomedievale di Castel Trosino, p. 199).

At the EUR entrance, various tempting books were on display, including one we had been searching for, the exhibit catalogue *La Necropoli Altomedievale di Castel Trosino: Bizantini e Longobardi nelle Marche.* But when we asked the attendant about buying it, he said they were out of stock, maybe we could contact the publishing house… Before leaving the complex we checked out the Neanderthal skulls found in the Aniene River, a Paleolithic Venus figurine, and the Praeneste *Fibula,* a gold pin found in Palestrina which is engraved with the earliest known Latin inscription (verified as authentic in 2011). Then we got a couple of cappuccinos at the on-site café, the only place that was lively and bustling, full of workers from the surrounding offices.

After the interest aroused by the publication of Gabrielle and Mengarelli's findings died down, the archeological site of San Stefano slid into oblivion. Used for a variety of agricultural purposes, in the 1970s it was planted with a stand of pine trees intended to halt soil erosion. The earthmoving and subsequent intrusion of tree roots further damaged the site. In 1995, the exhibit whose catalogue is mentioned above was mounted in Ascoli, in conjunction with a convention on the Lombard era in northern central Italy. After a hundred years, the precious finds were returned for a temporary display at the archaeological museum in the Palazzo Panichi. When visiting experts went to Castel Trosino, they were appalled by the total neglect of the important site—unmarked, overgrown, and inaccessible. This disgrace spurred the communal government of Ascoli to buy the area from the church and to develop it as an archaeological and environmental park (2001–2002).

The drive is less than fifteen minutes from Ascoli to Castel Trosino. Approaching it you can fully appreciate the magnificent position high above the road and the river. Sulphur springs at the base of the cliffs were prized through the millennia. For centuries laundry was brought here from Ascoli to be washed. The Romans built an aquaduct to carry the medicinal waters to a thermal spa located at the site of the Forte Malatesta in Ascoli; the arched stone entrance to an access tunnel is still visible in the riverbed. The ruined Monastero di San Giorgio high on the opposite cliffside started out as a leper colony in 1343; sulphur water was seen as a treatment for leprosy. The town itself is preserved as a medieval tourist attraction with costumed festivals, though only two of its buildings are verifiably of that era. One of them is said to have housed Manfredi, illegitimate son of Federico II, or at least the woman he loved. His ruined castle, Castel Manfrino, is just a few hours horseback ride away, further up the Valle Castellana in the Monti della Laga.

Outside the walled town a path climbs the hillside, lined with wooden railings installed by the park. A surreal group of statues, straight out of a children's book, depicting the burial of a Lombard warrior, welcomes you to the archeological site. Further along, still shaded by the pine trees that were planted on top of them, is a replica of an excavated tomb, and the outline of the church of San Stefano.

This church was built in the later years of the Lombard era, mid-seventh century. The area was already a burial place and the private family chapel was built on top of earlier graves. By the beginning of the eighth century, the cemetery was no longer in use. Parts of the church were still standing when Gabrielli and Mengarelli did their excavations, and they documented two high-status tombs within and adjoining it. In 2001, the ruins, in much worse shape, were located again. As part of the archaeological park, the foundation was reconstructed so you can see the outline of the church and of the two tombs. During this project a gold ring, mounted with a repurposed Roman stone or seal inscribed with two oxen, and still encircling a male fingerbone, was unearthed in one of the tombs inside the church. Somehow, it had been missed by the earlier diggers.

The few objects that were returned to Ascoli, and others found separately, were displayed for many years in the Museo Archeologico Statale in Piazza Arringo. In 2014, the collection was moved to the recently renovated Forte Malatesta, which stands guard on the eastern edge of Ascoli where the Ponte di Cecco crosses the Castellano River. The Piceni apparently had defensive works here; the Romans had their thermal spa. The Lombards destroyed a pre-existing fortress in 578; it has since been rebuilt several times. Federico II knocked it down in 1242. Galeotto Malatesta of Rimini set up headquarters here in 1349, but when he was ousted in 1356, the Ascolani tore down his fort as well. The present building was designed and constructed by Antonio da Sangallo il Giovane in 1543, and incorporates an earlier tower and the deconsecrated church of Santa Maria del Lago. It has been used as an army barracks and as a convent, and in 1828 became the town prison. The last prisoners were moved out in 1982 when the new maximum-security prison in Marino del Tronto opened. An exhibit of black and white photos shows the grim conditions, the meager mattresses, and the graffiti scratched into the walls. Echoes of the Count of Monte Cristo follow you as you wander through the labyrinth of passageways. Odd little rooms, built into acute angles of the massive walls, were once those miserable cells. Here they stand, clean and empty, the windows still barred. (Francesco Eleuteri makes full use of this setting for a climactic scene in his murder mystery, *Il Sangue dei Sibillini / The Blood of the Sibillini.*) The Museo dell'Alto Medioevo is on the light and spacious top floor. The contents of two rich tombs, one male, one female, are on display, as well as the more recent finds from Castel Trosino. They are ready to receive the rest of the stuff—if and when Rome sends it back.

The Lombards never succeeded in taking over all of Italy; at most, they were able to control about three-quarters, and that only for a time. Supposedly all the duchies were ruled by the king in Pavia, but the reality was that Spoleto, Benevento, and the others exercised considerable autonomy. From the distance of the present, the Lombards' main accomplishment was to create a major break in Italian history, since after their appearance in 568 it would be another fourteen centuries before Italy became a unified country again.

In spite of the Lombard invasions, the exarchate retained important parts of coastal and central Italy. Exarchate rule, especially its merciless system of taxation, continued to rankle native Italians. In fact, Geary suggests that for the local population that was not killed off, life under the Lombards may have been better than under the Byzantines (Geary, p. 122). The Pentapolis, one of the most commercially active parts of Italy, was continually trying to reduce or challenge the exarchate's authority, while

Byzantine Italy underwent a general decentralization. "By the end of the seventh century Italy was led politically, socially, and economically by men whose careers, families, and fortunes were increasingly tied to particular communities" (Noble, p. 9).

The two-hundred-plus years of Lombard rule, however, were marked by recurring warfare and jockeying for turf. When the pope came into conflict with the exarch and Byzantium over the iconoclastic controversy about religious imagery, the Lombards in 571 took advantage of the situation to seize Ravenna and the Pentapolis, following decades of attack, occupation, and retreat. In 754, fearing the ongoing menace of the Lombards, Pope Stephen II called in Pippin, King of the Franks, who drove them from Ravenna. Pippin donated the lands he conquered, including the Pentapolis, Osimo, and Numana, to the church.

When the Lombard King Desiderius started up hostilities again, Pope Hadrian turned to Pippin's son Charlemagne, who defeated Desiderius and his armies in 774. Charlemagne conquered the Duchy of Spoleto two years later but, to Pope Hadrian's chagrin, he maintained control over it, keeping it as a part of the Holy Roman Empire, of which he became emperor in 800. Charlemagne did confirm the donations of his father Pippin.

The disruption caused by the Gothic Wars, the Lombard invasions, and ineffective Byzantine administration meant that the church had to step up not only as a defender of widows, orphans, and minors, but also took over responsibility for public spectacles, infrastructure such as water supplies and sanitation, hospitals, and prisons. Ecclesiastical courts settled internal disputes and civil cases involving laymen and clerics. These worldly duties combined with the enormous land holdings or patrimonies of the church were attendant on the church's increasing temporal power. That these powers created friction was inevitable. "Most of the revenue generated by the patrimonies flowed into Rome and were spent there for the immediate advantage of the Roman populace. While papal charity and largesse were appreciated in Rome, they may have been somewhat less highly esteemed in the dozens of rural communities whose local exertions paid for them" (Noble, p. 11). A papal record shows the church receiving a payment from Picenum in 560 (Moorhead, *The Pope and the Church in Late Antiquity*, p. 254). Much of church revenue was collected through rents, creating strong ties to the church, not only with those who received charity, but also with the great number of people who lived on and worked church lands.

The Roman Emperor Constantine the Great had already recognized the church as a property-owning organization in the early fourth century. Most of the land came to the church via donations by patrons, although some was bought or traded. The majority of these properties were in central and southern Italy. Kristin Sessa, in her book *The Formation of Papal Authority in Late Antique Italy*, says that these regions, including Picenum, were the most prosperous in Italy during the sixth century. She goes on to add that, although some territory was lost during the Lombard invasions, "the Roman church remained a large-scale transregional property owner during the late period" (Sessa, p. 117).

Sometime in the late 700s, the apocryphal Donation of Constantine came to light. In it, the Emperor Constantine declares "…we hand over and relinquish our palace, the city of Rome, and all the provinces, places and cities of Italy and the western region, to the most blessed Pontiff and universal Pope, Silvester; and we order by our pragmatic constitution that they shall be governed by him and his successors…" Nobody knows who authored it; maybe it came from deep in the church bureaucracy. Hodgkin, in his *Italy and Her Invaders*, prefaces his remarks on the Donation with the following observation:

> It is one of the commonplaces of history, that in considering the causes which have produced any given event, we have often to deal not only with that which is True and can be proved, but also with that which though False is yet believed (Hodgkin, Vol. VII, p. 135).

The Donation provided apt ideological justification for the church's ever-expanding temporal powers. Some scholars like Noble argue that the Papal States had their origins in these times, though centuries were to pass before the Land of Piceno was fully incorporated into the *Stato della Chiesa*.

The Lombard King Liutprand had already broken off the Duchy of Fermo, with its four subdivisions, Fermo, Camerino, Ascoli, and Abruzzo, from the Duchy of Spoleto in 727. With the advent of the Frankish takeover, Charlemagne installed various Frankish counts to oversee these territories. At some undetermined point, the Duchy was changed to a March—the March of Fermo, which stretched from the Musone River below Ancona to the Valle del Sangro in Abruzzo. (Some commentators call this a downgrade but neglect to explain how a duke is different from a marquis.)

The Lombards themselves stayed on, by now part of the Italian population. Their presence is seen in place names such as Fara Sabina, *fara* meaning a military group, and Gualdo Tadino, *gualdo* from the Germanic *wald*, or "wood." Another important legacy was the amount of land that the foreign conquerers bequeathed to the church, especially to the Benedictine orders, including the Abbey of Farfa. Aside from the spiritual rewards of these donations, there were practical benefits. The Lombards had seized more property than they cared to manage themselves, and the local populace needed to eat.

The Works of Saint Benedict

St. Benedict, or *San Benedetto*, was born on the Umbrian side of the Apennines, in Norcia, probably in 480. He is one of the patron saints of Europe, and also of speleologists and spelunkers, amongst many others. The future saint studied in Rome and then turned to the hermetic life, eventually establishing a cluster of twelve monasteries on Mt. Subiaco in Lazio and then his order's headquarters at Montecassino, between Naples and Rome. Totila visited him there just before Benedict's death in 543. This monastery, built on top of a temple of Apollo, was razed by the Lombards in 570, rebuilt, sacked by the Saracens in 883, destroyed by an earthquake in 1349, rebuilt. That monumental edifice was bombed by the Allies in WWII, and is now once again restored. In Norcia, the basilica that was erected on the site where St. Benedict and his twin sister St. Scholastica were born was badly damaged by the 2016–17 earthquakes.

The Benedictine order was based the principle *"Ora e labora/*Pray and work." The monasteries promoted not simply religious life but also the life of manual labor. The monks worked to improve the land through agriculture, to create self-sustaining communities of farmers and artisans of all types. They not only did this work themselves but contracted it out to the local people in a form of *mezzadria/*sharecropping. The standard agreement lasted for three generations. From 700–1300, the Benedictines provided an organizational network at a time when there was no powerful central government.

In 890, Saracen forces began a seven-year siege of the Abbazia di Farfa, in Fara Sabina near Rieti. When the Benedictine monks finally abandoned their monastery, the abbot Pietro and a group of followers fled with the church treasures to an Apennine crest between the Tenna and Aso Rivers, where they built their highly fortified center in San Vittoria in Matenano in 934.

Many churches in this area were originally built in the Lombard era. St. Michael the Archangel was a favorite of the Longobardi, who credited him with their victory over the Greek Neapolitans at Sipontum/Manfredonia on May 8, 663. He is the patron saint of warriors and knights, and also of healers; many of his shrines are associated with natural springs and thermal waters. The Sanctuary of Monte Sant'Angelo on the Gargano peninsula was built around a cave where believers had seen visions of the Angel, the oldest shrine dedicated to him in Western Europe. Legend has it that St. Francis came here but felt too unworthy to enter. (Nearby is San Giovanni Rotondo, the modern pilgrimage site of Padre Pio whose image graces the walls in every local nook and cranny.) Closer to home, we find the already mentioned Grotta Sant'Angelo in the Monte dei Fiori. Downtown Ascoli has the Chiesa Sant' Angelo Magno, founded in the ninth century with a convent whose first abbess was a Lombard noblewoman. The institutions set up on property donated by the Lombards often provided nice positions for their family members. Sant'Angelo in Montespina, perched on an isolated hilltop between Montemonaco and Montefortino, was built by the Lombards reusing Roman architectural elements. It was the central church in a rural district called a *pieve*, based on earlier Roman divisions. The word is derived from the Latin *plebs*, "commoner," which with the rise of Christianity had come to mean a community of baptized people. While some say it goes back to the sixth or seventh century, the first documented mention of the site, as a *pieve*, appears in 977; the main altar was consecrated in 1064. In Piceno, most of these country parishes were administered by the Benedictine Abby of Farfa. Montegallo was under their control from 1039–1572; the church of Santa Maria in Lapide has its origins in the eighth/ninth century. The structure you see today is what remains of a larger church built in the 15th century (Rossi-Brunori, *Memorie di Montegallo*, pp. 13–15).

An historic exception is the church of San Mauro, also known as *San Benedetto in Trunto*. It has been speculated that this may have been the location of the martyrdom of St. Mauro, said to have taken place 130 (Roman) miles along the Via Salaria from Rome, but there is no actual evidence to prove that. Driving down the *autostrada* curving above the Tronto River from Ascoli to the coast, you can catch a glimpse of the church just below you on the right at Stella di Monsampolo. The exterior is nondescript, renovated at various times over the centuries, and hung with strings of festival lights. Inside, the crypt dates back to the early Middle Ages, a rare example of the era, like the exterior walls of San Stefano in Castel Trosino and (probably) the crypt of SS. Ruffino e Vitale in Amandola. The first mention is in 989, as an already existing monastery under the jurisdiction of the Benedictine Abbey of Montecassino, in the Duchy of Benevento. This affiliation underlines the borderland aspect of the Tronto valley, a patchwork of settlements whose allegiances fluctuated between the various powers, north and south. One example is the Castello di Ottavo, at Colli del Tronto, which was donated to Montecassino in 1045, transferred to the abbot of Farfa in 1050, and ultimately conceded to the bishop of Ascoli in 1052 (Furio Cappelli, *San Benedetto in Trunto, Frammento dell'Alto Medioevo Piceno*, p. 20).

The Normans expelled the Saracens, and in 1080 united southern Italy under the Regno di Sicilia, which pushed the southern border of the March of Fermo up to the Tronto. In 1055, the Holy Roman

Emperor had signed over the Duchy of Spoleto and the March of Fermo to the pope, which limited how far north the Normans could expand. The southern border of the Papal States wove in and out below the Tronto, with still visible stone markers and frontline military outposts like Ascoli's at Castel Manfrino.

As Mariolina Massignani explained to us over coffee one day, in the south the foreign, often absentee, Norman landlords established a system of *latifundia*, large tracts of land worked by serfs, overseen by an isolated fortified castle. In central Italy, a different system took hold, with smaller localized holdings, many owned by the church. Papal control ebbed and flowed in the ongoing struggles between papacy and empire, the Guelphs and the Ghibillines, but ultimately, the real power was local. From this context of numerous neighboring city states, each with its own collection of competing classes, arose the communes.

Santa Maria in Lapide–Montegallo

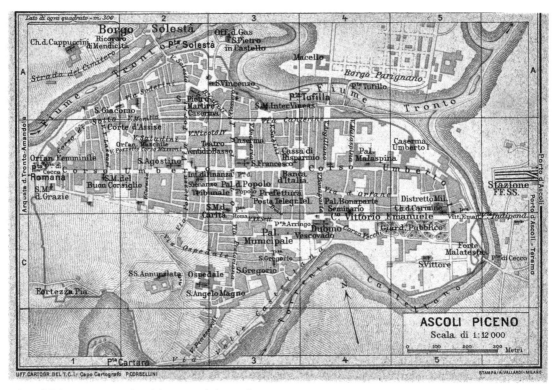

Ascoli Piceno 1924 Italian Touring Club Guide

Cecco's Bridge and the Malatesta Fortress

ᏯᎧ 10 ᏯᎧ

91 Towers

Piazza Arringo 1860s Ascoli Piceno

Piazza del Popolo 1900 Ascoli Piceno

When tourist boosters call Le Marche "undiscovered Italy," we ask, undiscovered by whom? Fault our educational system if any college-educated person who knows about Etruria has never heard of Picenum. In fact, a steady stream of travelers has been coming through here for decades and centuries, indeed millennia, just not the mobs of tourists descending on Rome, Florence, and Venice. Numerous visiting luminaries have remarked on Ascoli's beauty and its human scale. Perhaps most insightful was Renaissance humanist Flavio Biondo—but more about him later. Jean Paul Sartre and Simone de Beauvoir, Ernest Hemingway, and Andre Gide passed through. A 1961 *New York Times* travel article captured Ascoli charmingly—*Ascoli com'era*—Ascoli as it was. *"I Delfini*/The Dauphins,"* featuring international star Claudia Cardinale, was filmed in Ascoli in 1960. Dustin Hoffman starred with Stefania Sandrelli in *"Alfredo, Alfredo"* (1972) shot here by the master filmmaker Pietro Germi.

An often-quoted line from the local tourist literature has Sartre saying, "A walk through the streets of Ascoli Piceno, through its lanes divided between sun and shade, is like browsing at random a volume of the history of art and being lucky enough to meet the most representative illustrations of the various periods of Italian art." Perhaps Sartre thought it too obvious to remark that the urban texture of old Ascoli, from churches to government buildings to piazzas, signals a unique time in Italian history—the time of medieval communes and city-states.

The names of Ascoli's two main piazzas, the Piazza Arringo and the Piazza del Popolo, refer specifically to the communal political structure. *Arringo*, also *Arengo*, was the popular assembly; the word is related to the English "harangue." *Popolo* here means something more restricted than "the people." The

125

popolo were those citizens who had political rights—at first nobles and wealthy merchants, later artisans were included, but the *popolo* was never as all-inclusive as contemporary voter rights purport to be.

In the 11th century, a form of government began to spread across central and northern Italy based on the association of free men who had taken an oath to defend their rights. J.C.L. de Sismondi, writing in the first decades of the 1800s, was one of the earliest commentators on the Italian communes, "the science of governing men for their advantage, of developing their individual faculties, intellectual and moral, for their greater happiness—that political philosophy, began in modern Europe only with the Italian republics of the middle ages, and from them diffused itself over other nations" (Sismondi, *A History of the Italian Republics*, p. 1). Economic historian Carlo Cipolla wrote in his *Before the Industrial Revolution*:

> One of the fundamental characteristics of the urban societies of pre-industrial Europe was the tendency toward association, which manifested itself increasingly from the end of the 12th century. If in the preceding centuries men had sought protection and the safe guards of their own interests in a relationship of subordination to the powerful (feudalism), with the emergence of urban societies the safeguard of personal interests was sought mainly in association among equals. This was the essence of the urban revolution. The common was initially nothing more that the sworn association of citizens—the super association, above and beyond the particular associations which took the name of Arti, guilds, companies, confraternities, societies, or universities (Cipolla, p. 95).

The origins of the communes are obscure, rooted in the vast changes that occurred across Italy in the early Middle Ages; ruralization, localization, castleization, demographic decline, and contraction. "A few of the larger cities, among them Rome itself, and Milan, survived as important centers of population, but most of the ancient municipalities must have declined into a sordid if picturesque decay, villages in a setting of classical ruins" (Waley, *The Italian City-Republics*, p. 4).

The Saracen (Arab, or more generally, Muslim) and Magyar/Hungarian invasions played no small part in the move toward concentrated and walled settlements. At one point, the Saracens controlled the whole western Mediterranean basin, including Sicily with a colony in Provence. Vulnerable coastal settlements were abandoned in favor of hilltops and fortifiable positions. In 839, the Saracens were tempted by Ascoli because of its reputed riches, but their advance scouts warned against it because Ascoli was too well protected. Instead, under the leadership of one of the Frankish counts that Charlemagne had installed all over his part of Italy, the Ascolani attacked the Saracens and drove them off. The Saracens did sack Ancona in 848. In 1025, Pisa and Genoa together defeated the Saracens off Sardinia, and the Normans took Palermo from them in 1063. By the early 1100s, the Saracens were ousted from their last toehold in the Balearics, and the western Mediterranean was again in the Christian orbit. Their presence had been felt for some two hundred years. The removal of the Arabs was accompanied by a renewal of trade, industry, and international commerce in general, as well as the growth of towns. The population of northern and central Italy has been estimated to have doubled in the 11th and 12th centuries.

The decline of the Holy Roman Empire after the death of Charlemagne, coupled with corruption in the church, were some of the pre-conditions for the rise of the communes. The counts whom the emperor had assigned to the various towns were able to make their positions hereditary with all the feudal rights, becoming local magnates. Preoccupied with their own squabbles, the organization of defense against invaders had passed to local people and their church. When Otto the Great became emperor, intent on restoring the Holy Roman Empire to its former glory, he encouraged the transfer of power to the bishops. By the end of the 10th century, the citizens of northern Italy were ruled by the so-called *conti/vescovi*, counts/bishops, who played a secular as well as a religious role in the regions they oversaw. Their rule was weakened by church crises concerning the marriage of priests (banned by the church since the fourth century), simony (the purchase of church offices), and investiture (the appointment of bishops and church officials by emperors and kings).

The communes arose out of the conflicts between emperor and pope, the decline of feudal arrangements, and the economic growth of cities and towns. The feudal system, essentially a Germanic phenomenon, never had the tight grip on Italy that existed in more northern parts of Europe. In Italy, feudalism took hold later and fell apart sooner. The communes were a definitive challenge to the feudal status quo, even though early on nobles were often essential to their growth (Hyde, *Society and Politics in Medieval Italy*, p. 2). Many historians maintain that the communes began in the conflict between social classes. Machiavelli says, "The grave and natural enmity which arises between the common people and the nobility, because the latter wish to rule and the former shun obedience, are the source of the instability and conflict in the cities" (Machiavelli, *History of Florence*, Book III, Chapter I, p. 82).

Ascoli was a relative latecomer to the communal political arrangement. Legend says the Ascoli Commune was founded in 1183; no existing document supports that, but a letter from Pope Celestino III of 1197 is addressed to the bishop as well as the consuls and people. The oldest reference to the Palazzo Communale in the Piazzo Arringo goes back to 1254. The Palazzo Communale that we see today underwent a total renovation which was completed in 1745, but the baptistery and cathedral that line the east side of the piazza are much as they were in communal times.

Piazza Arringo

When we first started visiting Ascoli in 1989, traffic ran through the Piazza Arringo with an awkward turn around the baptistery. The piazza contained a major bus stop and a parking lot; the repointing and cleaning of the soot-blackened travertine had not yet been undertaken. This busy urban street was later blocked off and turned into a public space for pedestrians. Cafes and shops, and the 15th century Palazzo Panichi, which houses the archeological museum, line the north side. On the south side is the bishop's residence—or Palazzo Roverella—and the Palazzo Communale, now known as the Palazzo dell'Arringo. The array of buildings ringing the square gives testimony to the historical public, religious, and civil life of communal Ascoli. In medieval times, there was a huge elm in the Piazza Arringo that was replaced every time it died. Under its shade, officials came together to discuss politics; in the mid-1100s, a stone stand was erected to accommodate orators. Here, St. Francis spoke in 1215, recruiting thirty new friars. Today there are two fountains (1882), where passers-by drink water spouting from the mouths of bronze seahorses. In the nearby church of San Gregorio Magno, which incorporates walls and columns of a previous Roman temple, a 13th century fresco of St. Frances preaching to the birds is one of the earliest depictions of the saint.

The Romanesque baptistery and cathedral add considerable gravitas to the piazza, harkening back to ancient times; the communes were consciously modelling themselves on Roman republicanism. The baptistery sits on the foundation of an older Christian baptistery of the same dimensions. The count/bishop Presbitero (1126–1165), in later years named a prince, commissioned its rebuilding, honoring the traditions and rituals of the early Christians (even though the practice of baptism had changed). A rock incised with an epigraph conserved at the Palazzo Communale says, "Presbitero governs the town as the light governs the stars."

The sixth century Cathedral of St. Emidio, honoring Ascoli's patron saint and Christian martyr, was itself built over Roman structures and used Roman materials. Construction on the building that we see today began in 1060, although renovations and adaptations stretch from the seventh to the 16th century. The façade was created by Cola dell'Amatrice in 1529–30. In the crypt, a Roman sarcophagus contains the bones of St. Emidio, who according to tradition was the first bishop of Ascoli. Born in Trier towards the end of the third century, the young convert made his way down through Italy, preaching the Word and performing medical miracles. Supposedly, on his arrival in Ascoli an earthquake destroyed every pagan temple. As bishop, he baptized Polisia, the daughter of Ascoli's Roman prefect, for which he was executed in 303 or 309. The martyr's remains were transferred to the cathedral around 1000. The cave where he had originally been buried was transformed into the Tempietto di Sant'Emidio alle Grotte by Giuseppe Giosafatti between 1717 and 1721, after a devastating earthquake in 1703 spared Ascoli. Ascolanis spread his cult throughout southern Italy in seismic zones where his protection in case of earthquakes was highly valued.

The Duomo di Sant'Emidio displays a prized work by the Renaissance painter Carlo Crivelli in one of its chapels. Crivelli was born in Venice between 1430 and 1435, but was exiled in 1457 after being convicted of adultery. After working in Padua and Dalmatia, he appeared in the March of Ancona, near Fermo, where he painted an altarpiece for a church in Massa Fermana sometime around 1468. He moved to Ascoli in 1472 or '73. His younger brother Vittorio, also a painter, followed him. Carlo died, probably in Ascoli, around 1495. His style, which straddles the Gothic and the Renaissance, with glowing gold leaf and detailed perspective, was developed here, at a distance from the artistic centers of Rome, Florence, and Venice. The Duomo contains the altarpiece that he created for the cathedral in 1473. The massive gilt frame holds multiple panels, featuring apostles and saints with their characteristic boney feet. The central panel shows Mary holding the baby Christ, a garland of fruit and Crivelli's signature cucumber dangling above them. One of only two Crivellis that has been preserved intact and in its original frame, it also remains in its original intended home. Many of his other works were not so fortunate.

Next to the baptistery is the early 16th century Palazzetto Bonaparte, which displays a run of *cicogne* affixed to the exterior wall at the third story level. These metal brackets, which are intended to support a wooden pole, were common to a limited area of Tuscany, Umbria, and Le Marche in the 14th and 15th centuries. The name *cicogna*, "stork," apparently refers to the typical shape of the bracket, curved like a long birds' neck. Crivelli's masterpiece, "The Annunciation, with Saint Emidius" 1486, in London's National Gallery, shows two examples (see photo p. 160). One pair of *cicogne* holds a bamboo pole with a birdcage hanging from it. The other set of three supports a much longer, empty pole on a yellow brick façade receding into the distance. Various purposes have been assigned to these set-ups; you could hang out laundry to dry, mattresses and comforters to air, wool that had just been dyed, or display banners and tapestries. Maybe curtains were mounted for privacy or for protection from light, heat, or cold, in an era before glass windows became common. Maybe there was a system for hauling loads up from the street. In his delightfully obsessive book *Cicogne o Erri*, Paolo Pinti explores and debunks all these possible uses, leaving only a mystery. He includes details of Renaissance paintings depicting *cicogne* and many photos of remaining examples, from Perugia to Macerata. The birthplace of Beato Marco in Montegallo has some, the Valnerina, and especially Visso, is full of them—at least before the recent earthquakes. *Cicogne* tended to survive in isolated areas where the buildings were never renovated, and as Pinti says, once you start looking for them you can't stop.

The communes, including Ascoli, underwent a parallel development of their political structures. The consular phase was the initial stage; the concept of consul, as we have noted, harkens back to the Roman Republic. The system evolved from an older one of *boni homines*—good men; Balena points out that "good" referred to wealth, not character. Ascoli had four consuls, one for each quarter of the city. Their existence predates the full-blown commune by an unknown number of years; Balena mentions an unspecified source that says consuls accompanied Bishop Stefano to the county diocese in 1058 (Balena, p. 280).

Ascoli's consuls kept the peace and had the authority to punish with the help of twenty-five armed men for each consul. Joining the consuls was a whole cast of characters, including councilors, elders, treasurers, notaries, and trumpeters. The town council was divided into two groups: the general and the special. The general council consisted of 800 citizens elected from the twenty-four districts of Ascoli. This group convened when important matters arose, such as going to war, modifying laws, and imposing taxes. The special council was comprised of 200 councilors selected from the general council, who served for three months in rotation. Among their duties, the special council elected the four elders to their two-month terms. The elders were responsible for the maintenance and function of the city, and they set the agenda for the special council. In addition, the elders appointed the *capitano del popolo*, "the people's captain," and the *podestà*.

The office of *podestà* was instituted in communes across Italy to help resolve conflicts that inevitably arose between competing noble factions. The statutes of Ascoli, as elsewhere, required that the *podestà* not be a native of the city, had to be from noble stock, and of high character and valor. He served for six months and lived in the Palazzo Communale with his retinue, in a different part from the elders who also lived there. A *podestà* often had legal training and made a profession of serving terms in one commune after another. In the beginning, his power was limited by the bishop, but in 1242, Emperor Frederick II took away all the temporal power of the bishops, and the *podestà* became more important. Still, at this point, the *podestà* primarily represented the interests of the nobility. The rise of the *popolo* initiated a new chapter in the development of the communes and the power of the *podestà*.

These were violent times. The nobility was often caught up in murderous competitions, feuds, and neighborhood rivalries, both within the commune and with other city-states. They built towers with battlements to defend their turf and display their status, they exempted themselves from taxes, and got off lightly for crimes against commoners. Beginning with merchants, and later including craftsmen and tradesmen, the prosperous middle class began organizing themselves into guilds to protect their interests and to seek political redress, often through force of arms. The organization of guilds and neighborhoods into armed pressure groups became the *popolo*, who sought to combat the arbitrary power of the

Piazza del Popolo Ascoli Piceno ~ Photo by Alessandro Della Pietra

nobles. The *capitano del popolo* balanced the power of the *podestà* and led the armed factions of the *popolo*. The *popolo* sought a constitutional role in the government and won it in Ascoli as witnessed by *"Gli Statuti del Comune e del Popolo del 1377."*

Piazza del Popolo

Exiting the Piazza Arringo heading west you pass the Migliori store and outdoor stand (reviewed in the *New York Times)* selling local specialties such as fried stuffed olives and fried cream. Cross the Corso Trento e Trieste and choose one of the small cobblestone alleys that wind towards the Piazza del Popolo. If you are there mid-morning when everyone is on break, the rumble of voices increases like a musical crescendo as you approach the light filled space paved in travertine that glistens when it rains. The realization that this sound has been emanating from here for centuries is unavoidable as your eye confronts the Renaissance Palazzo dei Capitani across the piazza.

Here is a roll call of historical styles. This was most likely the site of the Roman forum; there are Roman foundations, paving stones, and mosaics on display beneath the Palazzo. The stone façade is a patchwork of arched windows and balconies, commemorative plaques, a great big clock, and a columned niche containing a statue of the Farnese Pope Paul III, all crowned by a 13th century belltower. The Art Nouveau Caffè Meletti, with a Roman wall in the basement bathrooms, lies to the left of the Palazzo. The Gothic Chiesa San Francesco at the far end of the piazza and the medieval colonnades on the east and south sides all unite to form a space of human scale ideal for social interaction, what author Ray Oldenburg calls *The Great Good Place*. At Carnivale chandeliers are strung overhead and masked revelers perform in the arcades. In August during the Quintana squads from each neighborhood parade through in Renaissance garb, on their way to the annual jousting matches.

Our first visit to the Piazza del Popolo was the fulfillment of youthful dreams of traveling to European cities to sit in cafés and wander ancient art-drenched streets. Ascoli was off the beaten track and it still is, but recent years have seen a greater tourist presence. Tourists help support downtown commerce which has been threatened by suburban shopping centers. Nowadays a little *trenino*, a sightseeing vehicle with a tour guide, chugs through the major thoroughfares and squares, which seems a bit Disney

Rua or Alley ~ Photo by Alessandro Della Pietra

for this marvelously walkable place. Ascoli is known for its maze of alleys—*le rue*—and almost every arch and doorway has a story to tell, sometimes spelled out in carved inscriptions. One above a window of the Palazzo dei Capitani reads, *"Difficile Placer Mvltis/* It's hard to please everybody," and a longer one on the Rua Lunga *"Chi po non vo, chi vo non po, chi sa non fa, chi fa non sa, et cosi el mvndo mal va—MDXXVIIII,"* meaning more or less—"Who can doesn't want to, who wants to can't, who knows how to doesn't do it, who does it doesn't know how to, and so the world goes badly—1529." In our early days we took pictures of every lion's head doorknocker, every lintel garlanded with pomegranates and grapes, every stone gargoyle and cherub.

A Walk Through Ascoli Piceno

Without even attempting to describe every monument, we now take a representative stroll that highlights the living tangible history of the place.

First, have a coffee and a pastry at any one of the cafés that line the Piazza del Popolo and people watch. Bells chime the quarter hour and pigeons scavenge crumbs on the travertine pavement. The regulars show up at their usual places and sit for hours talking with their friends. When the caffeine and sugar kick in, start by sauntering across this sunlit stage to the imposing Chiesa San Francesco. When St. Francis gained his thirty new followers in 1215, they first took up residence in the Benedictine hermitage San Lorenzo in Carpineto, on Colle San Marco above Ascoli, where St. Frances perhaps stayed as well. In around 1230 they moved closer to the city and in 1258 they acquired this site where they built their new church. The first stone was laid in 1262, but the structure was only consecrated in 1371. The two bell towers went up in the 15th century and the cupola in the 16th.

At the corner of the Corso Mazzini and the Via del Trivio, coming off the side of the Chiesa San Francesco, is the Loggia dei Mercanti, commissioned by the wool guild and completed in 1513. *Loggia*, as Giambattista Carducci points out, is related to the Greek word *logos*—speech, conversation, discourse (Carducci, *Su le Memorie e i Monumenti di Ascoli nel Piceno*, p. 119). Whether designed by Cola dell' Amatrice, Bramante (born 1444, near Urbino), or someone from his school, seems impossible to ascertain. With its vaulted stone ceiling and stately pillars, and a convenient ledge along the bottom of the church wall, it probably served as a place for the wool guild to exhibit their wares. A plaque on the wall dated 1568 contains alcoves defining the regulated sizes of bricks. Today as always, this is a perfect spot to socialize in the shade or to get out of the rain. A raucous scene in *"Alfredo, Alfredo"* takes place here.

Exiting the Piazza del Popolo, head north on the Via del Trivio. Just to the right will be the cloister with its medieval colonnade and vegetable market in the courtyard, and on the left the 1846 Ventidio Basso opera house with its neo-classical colonnade. (Ventidio Basso, it will be remembered, was the youngster captured with his mother during the Social War and paraded in Pompey Strabo's triumphal procession through Rome, who later went on to become a Roman consul.) The many historic theaters of Picenum are themselves worthy of study; there are seventy-three of them. The Teatro Serpente Aureo in Offida is one beautiful example, in Ripatransone, the hometown opera house of basso Luciano Neroni is tiny but lush (Neroni is the maiden name of Nathan's mother, which of course made us wonder...). Gioachino Rossini was born in Pesaro in 1792, and the city renamed its theater in his honor; its "Rossini Opera Festival" is held there every August.

Proceeding down the Via del Trivio there is even an example of '70s brutalism—unadorned, reinforced concrete construction. Next, on the second floor of an angled corner building is a 16th century shrine to the Madonna, perched above two Doric columns and wrapped with a Baroque wrought iron balcony. Now, take a left on the Via Benedetto Cairoli and proceed a few blocks to the Piazza Ventidio

Chiesa SS. Vincenzo ed Anastasio
Wood Engraving 1898

Basso. In recent years, this piazza has also been renovated, creating a larger, calmer, pedestrian zone. During this transformation, we happened to be walking past the Chiesa SS. Vincenzo ed Anastasio when we saw Luca Speranza, the archeologist, grubbing around down inside a pit next to the church foundation. He told us he was excavating some Lombard era graves and complained about the wear and tear on his knees and back.

Ascoli boasts of having more Romanesque churches than any other city in Italy, and this is one of them. The original part is said to have been built in the 11th century, and carvings on the main door indicate further work in 1309 and 1389. According to legend, a spring with healing waters was discovered when the crypt was being dug; 14th century frescoes represent the miracle of the waters. The façade of the church is especially noteworthy with its sixty-four squares, originally each one frescoed with scenes from the Old and New Testaments.

Opposite this church and anchoring the piazza is the Gothic Chiesa San Pietro Martire. Construction started in 1280 but continued into the 16th century. A portal designed by Cola dell'Amatrice was added in 1523 and the façade portal by Giuseppe Giosaffatti (1643–1731), a well-regarded, local architect who also worked on the Palazzo Arringo, was added even later. The Chiesa San Pietro contains a number of Baroque paintings by significant artists including Ludovico Trasi, Giovanni Battista Buonacuorre and Tommaso Nardini.

Exiting the piazza going north, a left on Via Trebbiani gives us a view of the Sibillini Mountains over the Porta Solestà (also called Porta Cappuccina) and the Roman bridge reconstructed in Mussolini times. The arched stone entryway—*porta* means "door"—was built in 1230, perhaps out of materials

Porta Solestà/Cappuccina with Towers, Roman Bridge ~ Photo by Alessandro Della Pietra

from a preexisting Roman structure. Across the bridge is the Tempietto di Sant'Emidio Rosso (1633) containing the stone on which St. Emidio was beheaded and a gruesome painting depicting the event (see photo p. 99). Legend has it that once decapitated, the martyr picked up his head and walked to the paleochristian catacomb where he was originally entombed. This little church is all red in memory of his blood. At the Porta Solestà a left on the Via delle Stelle and another left on the Rua Longobardo takes us to the Palazetto Longobardo, now a youth hostel, and its Ercolano tower.

Ascoli has been called the "City of 100 Towers," but only about fifty exist today. The original number has been put at 200, but Balena thought there were probably more like 150. The towers reflect the fortress mentality brought into the city by the Lombards, where the prime motive for their construction was the fear of attack. Built of travertine stone blocks, they tended to be 30–38 m high and about 21 sq.m (4.5 x 4.5 m), to 30 sq.m (5.5 x 5.5 m) at the base—100–125 ft high, 225 sq.ft (15 x 15 ft) to 325 sq.ft (18 x 18 ft) at the base.

Some years ago we were lucky enough to take a walk with Mariolina Massignani and her husband Carlo Cappelli to the Palazzo Longobardo. They explained that the label *longobardo* in this case does not refer to any specific style, but just emphasizes that the structure is very old. Some of the larger blocks of stone at the base date from Roman times. The palazzo and its tower were probably built in the mid 1200s as a home for a noble family and to protect their *consorteria*, that is, political allies. With a certain amount of relish, Mariolina pointed out openings from which the inhabitants could shoot arrows or pour boiling oil. The towers also served another function, as storage silos used instead of attics or basements. You could see definite emotion in her eyes when she recounted what had happened to the towers; Frederick II was responsible.

Holy Roman Emperor Frederick II, the grandson of Barbarossa, excommunicated four times, variously called philosopher king, poet, polyglot, a Renaissance man before the Renaissance, cuts a wide swath across medieval history. We will not go into the debunking his myth has suffered at the hands of contemporary historians. Suffice it to say, he has not been held in high regard in Ascoli for more than 750 years—and Mariolina's face showed it.

In that era, much of Italy was subjected to the ongoing conflicts between the Guelfs, supporters of the pope, and the Ghibellines, supporters of the emperor. Communes like Ascoli had to navigate between the power of these two antagonists and their warring factions while trying to maintain some semblance of independence.

Early on, many Ascolani had a soft spot for Frederick II—possibly because he was born just up the road in Jesi. But when the emperor returned from the crusade he had undertaken in order to have the pope lift his excommunication, he relinquished all territorial claims, and Ascoli went over to the Guelfs. The calm did not last long, and like any good autocrat who believes himself to rule by divine right, Frederick II could not stop himself from stepping on the pope's toes. His Constitution of Melfi, often honored for being the "birth certificate of the modern administrative state," (Kantorowicz, *Frederick the Second*, p. 228) radically declares everyone equal in the eyes of the law, and also subjects the clergy to secular law. For Frederick, the *Marca Anconetana* was a fruit too tempting to leave unplucked, especially since it served as a corridor between his various holdings.

Excommunicated again, Frederick II invaded the Papal States in 1241. In 1242, he sent his lieutenant general to besiege Ascoli. The siege went on for more than a month without success at forcing an opening. Finally, the troop commander sent messengers to the Ascolani, asking them to allow the emperor's men to offer their homage, and then they would be on their way. Apparently, the commander was invited to visit the city, which he did, admiring the buildings and monuments. They left Ascoli in the direction of Teramo, much to the Ascolani's relief. But the citizens had let down their guard. The emperor's army returned through the Porta Torricella and sacked the city for the third time in its history. In addition to pillaging and burning, they tore down 91 towers, according to local historian Gabriele Rosa, author of *Disegno della Storia di Ascoli Piceno* (p. 94).

As we strolled the streets with Mariolina and Carlo, they showed us how to identify the sites where towers had once been by the presence of flared stone bases incorporated into subsequent buildings. Some had simply been turned into church towers. Before we parted ways, Mariolina gave us a copy of an essay she had written, "Fra' Pacifico *rex versuum*," about Guglielmo di Lisciano, a poet/singer from a noble family in Lisciano, a town on the slopes of San Marco above Ascoli. In 1187, at age twenty-nine, he was chosen to be the court poet in Sicily of the soon-to-be Holy Roman Emperor, the Hohenstaufen Henry VI. Later, the young Frederick II crowned him "King of Verses;" he had perhaps played an important role in the boy's education. But in 1212, while visiting his sister in San Severino Marche, Guglielmo heard St. Francis preach and was converted, taking the name Fra' Pacifico. In 1224 or 1225, St. Francis entrusted his famous *Cantico di Frate Sole* to him. This work, also known as the *Canticle of the Sun*, and the *Canticle of the Creatures*, is the oldest example of a text written in vulgar Italian (in this case Umbrian) by a known author. It was up to Fra' Pacifico to pass it on, to teach the other Francescans to sing it, as true *"giullari di Dio*/jesters of God" (Massignani, *Esculum e Federico II*, pp. 165–180). The Marchigiano philosopher, performer, and public intellectual Cesare Catà takes it further. Since by this point St. Francis was virtually blind, did he dictate his words to his ever-present companion Fra' Pacifico? Did the highly regarded poet edit the rough draft, or perhaps supply some of the lines? And, Catà goes deeper down the rabbit-hole of centuries-old gossip when he discusses the possibility that Guglielmo, named in a document by Queen Constance as a loyal courtier, was in fact her secret lover and father of Frederick II. The story goes that the queen gave birth to her only child publicly, in the central piazza of Jesi, so that no one could dispute that the baby was indeed hers. She also swore that Henry VI was the father, but in those days before DNA testing, no one could prove that for sure (Catà, *Con l'alloro sotto il saio, ipotesi su Frate Pacifico, e il Cantico di Frate Sole*, pp. 355–395).

Once again under Frederick II, Ascoli became a Ghibelline ally. The emperor granted the city the use of a port at the mouth of the Tronto, which greatly enraged Fermo, since this land had been theirs. Ascoli remained loyal until Frederick II (and his line) expired in 1250, when it returned to playing the pope and emperor one against the other.

The communes represented the retention of local power, but with inevitable drawbacks. As historian J. K. Hyde points out, "...to some extent the problems of the communes were inherent in all small scale government, arising from the difficulty of divorcing public policy from private interests and personalities in a restricted arena where everyone knew too much about everyone else, resulting in a persistent tendency to faction and party strife" (Hyde, p. 104). The communes are easy to romanticize as some sort of force towards democracy, as many writers have done. A 29-year-old Karl Marx saw the communes as liberating the bourgeoisie from the talons of feudalism in the "Communist Manifesto." But even hard critics like Wickham, in his *Sleepwalking into a New World*, agree that the communes are notable for broadening political participation. They were not looking forward to some democratic ideal, but instead at the harsh present that had to be dealt with using the means at hand. But here, as Balena emphasizes, they had past experience to draw upon.

> The new city had an ancient spirit. Like some communes in Italy, this one was not simply the product of the feudal world nor something new that was substituted for the old order that was breaking up, but a reassertion of the autonomous way of life that preceded the dark ages, that was second nature to the Italian and Picenian civilization, that Rome tried to cancel and absorb and feudalism obscured but at this point simply resurfaced (Balena, p. 281).

The communes gave way to the *signorie*, which leads us across town to the Ponte Maggiore and the Fortezza Malatesta. The *signorie*, or rule by a lord, was a reaction to the strife and anarchy often present in the communes. A strongman entered the fray to restore order. In this case the struggle with Fermo warranted the appointment of Galeotto Malatesta as *Capitan Generale dell'Armi Cittadinesche*. His rule lasted only five years (1348–1353), but he had enough time to build his fortress on the site of a former fort.

Our walk has not taken us to every place of interest in Ascoli, but it brings us to Cecco's Bridge and the nearby statue of Cecco d'Ascoli—our next big story.

Standing on Monte Sibilla looking toward Monte Vettore and the Lago di Pilato

⁕ 11 ⁕

Cecco and the Legends

Cecco's Bridge

We lean over the balustrade of the Ponte Maggiore, the modern bridge at the eastern entrance to Ascoli, and gaze down at the Ponte di Cecco. This is one of the city's most photographed views and it is certainly picturesque. The severe stone walls of the Forte Malatesta rise above the righthand cliff. The Castellano River tumbles below, sometimes swollen with rain, as it races towards its junction with the Tronto. The footbridge itself arches over the verdant green of the riverbed, connecting the fortress with the opposite shore, once rolling farmland, now modern apartment buildings. In the middle of the double-arched span is a small roofed structure which, because the bridge is currently closed to pedestrian traffic, shelters various illicit activities.

The Ponte di Cecco first appeared as a Roman construction in the first century BC. Under Galeotto Malatesta its ruins were rebuilt in 1349, apparently by a Master Cecco Aprutino. Bombed by the retreating Germans in WWII, it was then reconstructed using the original stones. But legend claims that Cecco d'Ascoli built it in a single night with the help of the Devil. A larger-than-life statue of this local figure stands nearby, holding a book, and stretching out a finger to admonish the passersby.

Cecco d'Ascoli was born Francesco Stabili in 1269 in Ancarano, just over the Tronto River in present day Abruzzo. The date has been disputed, as have most of the details of his life. One of the earliest sources, Angelo Colocci (1474–1549) says that his mother gave birth to him unexpectedly during a religious festival at a church dedicated to the Madonna, on the site of an earlier sanctuary dedicated to the pagan fertility goddess Ancaria. Local history has it that St. Emidio, in his brief career as first bishop of Ascoli, invaded this sanctuary, smashed all the statues of pagan deities, and threw the pieces into the Tronto. Stabili, nicknamed Cecco, was the son of a wealthy noble family and grew up in Ascoli near the Porta Romana. He may have studied at the university which Pope Nicholas IV had recently founded in the city.

Cecco d'Ascoli

Pope Nicholas IV (1227–1292), born in nearby Lisciano and also known as Jerome of Ascoli, was the first Franciscan pope. One of the prime exhibits in the Pinacoteca Civica, Ascoli's art museum, is the cope that he donated to the Ascoli cathedral in 1288. The semi-circular ecclesiastical garment is heavily embroidered silk and gold. In 1797, the pearls that once covered it were stripped to provide the church with money to pay off the triumphant invader Napoleon. In 1902, the cope disappeared mysteriously, only to reappear at a museum exhibit in London in 1904, listed as belonging to J. Pierpont Morgan. The American millionaire was pressured into returning it, and in 1907, it was back home in Ascoli.

Various reports put Cecco in Salerno, Paris, and Naples. He was definitely teaching in Bologna in 1322–1324, where he was first accused of heresy. Forced to leave, he ended up in Florence in the court of the Duke Carlo of Calabria. In 1327, convicted by the Inquisition of heresy, he was burned alive along with his books in Florence's Campo dei Fiori.

If Cecco d'Ascoli had not been burned at the stake, perhaps his intellectual concerns would have been lost in the dustbin of history. The fact that the Inquisition banned and burned his books may have added to their popularity, as medieval underground best sellers.

Cecco has been variously described as an astrologer, doctor, necromancer, and magician. Except for astrologer, the other professions are apocryphal. In medieval times, astrology was considered a legitimate and respected study which many scholars today see as a gateway to modern science, very different from modern newspaper horoscopes. Astrology was an interpretive system formed in a pre-industrial civilization in which people's lives were more tightly bound to the seasons, the stars, the sun, and the moon. Trying to enter into a medieval intellectual's vision of the world is a consuming endeavor (a knowledge of Greek and Latin would help). Often credited with being the first biologist, Aristotle's view of nature is crucial, as well as how this view made its way into the European university system, not to mention the perspectives and commentaries of the Muslim thinkers who kept his works alive. Aristotle was an influential proponent of the geocentric concept of the universe where the earth is fixed and the planets revolve around it in concentric circles, as many as fifty-five in his system. In the second century AD, Ptolemy made revisions that were to dominate western thinking for 1,500 years, until Galileo and beyond; he wrote defenses of astrology that we can speculate endeared him to Cecco. Medieval natural philosophers united this system into a theological whole that harmonized with church doctrine. These cosmologies were inseparable from an astrological view of the world where the planets influence who we are and our destinies.

Cecco's most famous work is a poem, a scientific epic in five books called the *Acerba*. In a PhD dissertation (2014) entitled, "Cecco vs. Dante: Correcting the Comedy with Applied Astrology," Seth Fabian wrote "*Acerba* is intended as an ethical guidebook that explains the nature of the cosmos, the nature of humanity and proceeds to instruct his reader in the way of wisdom" (Fabian, p. 79), and that *Acerba* is "nothing less than a handbook of world peace and eternal salvation" (p. 248). For Fabian, it is a totalizing effort in grand theory of a universe bound together by love (p. 244). A recent English translation by medieval scholar Diane Murphy translates the title of *Acerba* as *The Bitter Age*. She sees the book more as a form of lecture notes, written in rhyme to aid the memory. The subject matter of *Acerba* runs the gamut of medieval concerns from astronomy, astrology, and meteorology through ethics and virtue, geology, zoology, and finally theology. This last was the topic of Book 5, which Cecco never completed; perhaps it was cut short by his death. Why would someone with such lofty ideas be burned at the stake?

The fascination with Cecco as a historical figure is magnified by how little we really know about him. He ran afoul of the Inquisition twice, leading to his execution under the two-strikes rule. However, the first charge of heresy in Bologna might have been only a corrupt shakedown for money; the second, in Florence, could have resulted from being the wrong person, in the wrong place, at the wrong time. No doubt being a Ghibilline did not help—if in fact he was one. As if blaming the victim, early descriptions of Cecco cite his abrasive personality, derived from the flimsiest historical record. His contemporary Giovanni Villani, whose *Nuova chronica* is the only first-hand account of Cecco's life and death, says "However great an astrologer he was, nevertheless he was a vain and worldly man. His learning made him so bold that he ventured into false and forbidden realms" (Fabian, p. 16).

Much is made about Cecco's relationship with Dante. Cecco claims to have had correspondence with him (*The Bitter Age*, p.88). Fabian and others say that *Acerba* is in constant counterpoint to Dante's *Divine Comedy*, that he was envious and competitive with Dante. More recent writers have tried to rehabilitate Cecco, saying his envy was that of an admirer (Castelli, *La Vita e le Opere di Cecco d'Ascoli*, chs. 12 and 13). Cecco esteemed Dante enough to find him worthy of criticism, but also praised his vast ability as a poet (*The Bitter Age*, p. 29).

Lago di Pilato (dry season) with Monte Sibilla in background

Were two horoscopes and the charge of philosophical hard determinism his real crime? In 1327, Cecco's patron Carlo of Calabria asked the astrologer for a horoscope of his daughter Giovanna, who was a little over a year old at the time. Cecco apparently predicted that the child's character was marked by wanton lustfulness; he was then expelled from the Duke's court and protection. This little girl grew up to be Queen Giovanna I D'Angio of Naples. She married four times but left no direct descendants. Her cousin, brother-in-law, and onetime heir, Carlo di Durazzo, imprisoned her in order to reassert his claim to the throne. She was assassinated in 1382, and it was Carlo's daughter who became Queen Giovanna II, whose castle still looms over the Via Salaria at Arquata del Tronto, and whose scandalous reputation lives on.

The second problematic horoscope was for Jesus Christ. The Church could not have liked the idea that the stars had determined the Savior's fate.

As the factual details of Cecco's life vanished into the mists of time, the legend of Cecco d'Ascoli flourished. The fame of the necromancer who made deals with the Devil spread far and wide. He was said to have a Book of Commands, which he consecrated with Satanic rites at the Lago di Pilato, high in the Sibillini Mountains. Nicolò Peranzoni wrote in 1510 that both Virgil and Cecco d'Ascoli had inscribed characters related to magical practices on stones at the lake. The Museo della Sibilla in Montemonaco displays a stone with incised writing brought down from the lake's shores in the 1930s, perhaps the fiendish altar of these ancient rituals.

The Sibillini Mountains were in fact a hotbed of legends. We first encountered these tales when our young Italian cousins Anna Maria, Claudia, and Stefania Ferri gave us a copy of Guiseppe Santarelli's *Le Leggende dei Monti Sibillini* (1974). Fascinated, we translated it into English and published it as *Legends of the Sibilline Mountains* (Staf edizioni, 2006). Santarelli, a Capuchin monk and director of the Universal Congregation of the Holy House at Loreto, details the wide ranging historic and literary reach of these tales. "As the Phlegraean Fields, the cave of the Cumean Sibyl, and Lake Avernus were to classical antiquity, so the Sibilline Mountains, the grotto of the Sibyl, and the Lake of Pilate were to the late Middle Ages and early Renaissance" (Santarelli, *Legends of the Sibilline Mountains*, p. 1). "There are two nuclei of the Sibilline Mountain legends, two places where they germinated as if by a magic spell. One nucleus refers to the *Grotta della Sibilla* (Grotto of the Sibyl) and the other to the *Lago di Pilato* (Lake of Pilate)" (Santarelli, p. 9).

The Legends of Pilate's Lake

The Lago di Pilato is a glacial lake, the only one in the Apennines. It sits at 1,940 m/6,365 ft in the shadow of Mt. Vettore (2,476 m/8,123 ft), the second highest mountain in the Apennines after Abruzzo's Corno Grande, encircled by a ring of peaks almost as high. Within its 9 m/30 ft deep basin is a sandbar which, in dry seasons, first partially divides the waters into the form of a pair of eyeglasses, and ultimately creates two smaller lakes like snake eyes. At times, the lake dries up completely. It is the only site in Europe where the *chirocephalus marchesoni* shrimp survives, its eggs enduring even under dry rocks. This small red shrimp, which swims on its back, was named for Vittorio Marchesoni, the scientist who originally described it in 1954.

The Lago di Pilato is first mentioned in writings from the second half of the 14th century as a destination for necromancers, though in early maps it is called the Lago della Sibilla or the Lago di Norcia. The Benedictine Pierre Bersuire wrote that since ancient times it had been inhabited by devils (did he mean little red shrimp?), and that every year the city of Norcia sacrificed one of their own to these ravenous demons in exchange for protection from devastating storms. Renaissance humanist and historian Flavio Biondo describes both legends in his *Italia illustrate/Italy Illuminated* (1453), a guide to the regions of Italy emphasizing their Roman past:

> In the high hills of the Apennine uplands… lies the town of Monte Santa Maria in Gallo. Near this town, in the Apennines themselves, is a huge cavern commonly called the Cave of the Sibyl, and a little higher up, that lake in the Norcian Apennines which is quite falsely said to teem with demons instead of fish. Yet the repute of the two places has driven many in our day (and many more in earlier centuries, as I heard) to climb these daunting hills with great effort, but all in vain, captivated by sorcery or eager to aquaint themselves with marvels (Biondo, p. 273).

He also casts some shade on Cecco d'Ascoli, "better as an astrologer than as a vernacular poet" (Biondo, p. 277). A 15th century sermon by Fra' Bernardino Bonavoglia da Foligno denounces the rites used by necromancers in this area to consecrate their magical books to the Devil, trading their souls for infinite power. It was said that Norcia built a wall to prevent people from reaching the lake, that suspected sorcerers found there were summarily executed one way or another, and that gallows loomed ominously over the path. The Florentine artist Benvenuto Cellini, in his autobiography, says that he passed up the opportunity to go with a necromantic priest to consecrate a book in the mountains of Norcia.

The association of the lake with Pontius Pilate appears soon thereafter. The story goes that after Pontius Pilate was killed in Rome his body was put into a cart pulled by two buffalos (or oxen) and set loose. Their long journey ended here—although other places in Europe also claim this honor. The beasts plunged into the water with the accursed corpse, turning the water red.

Two different hiking trails will take you to the Lago di Pilato. The shorter one starts at the Forca di Presta, the pass between Umbria and Le Marche, between Castelluccio di Norcia and Montegallo. The path winds across the high grassy slopes with sweeping views in every direction, to the Rifugio Zilioli perched on the edge of the crater that holds the lake. The summer custom is to get an early start and see the sun rise over the Adriatic from the crest. From here a steep descent ends at the waters. The *"Monti Sibillini Parco Nazionale"* guide book says it takes 2.5–3.00 hours up, 1.45–2.00 hours down,

Monte Sibilla

and includes a plea that you avoid the overcrowded months of July and August, and to not tread on the shoreline where the shrimp eggs are hidden.

The other approach is through the isolated village of Foce. Here you go up the valley, the mountains looming over you. In the early spring, avalanches still roar down these walls. The springs of the Aso River fill long stone watering troughs. Eventually you have to make your way up Le Svolte, steep gravelly switchbacks, to reach the upper valley, which finally arrives at the Lago di Pilato. (This takes 3.5 hours up, 2.0–2.5 hours down).

The Legends of the Sibyl's Grotto

On the descent back to Foce, your eyes are set on Monte Sibilla on the far side of the valley ahead of you. In October, slashes of blazing red and golden trees outline the steep slopes. The higher pastures are still green, and sheep are grazing between the veins of rock aimed skyward. Mt. Sibilla is 2,173 m/7,129 ft high; its peak is ringed by bands of rocky cliffs, resembling a crown—the crown of the Queen Sibyl. Many locals are still outraged by the white gravel road, laid down in the 60s, that zig-zags across the face. This is, however, the easiest way to get to the top. From Montemonaco, you can drive up to the Rifugio della Sibilla (post-earthquake—take a shuttle bus), walk up this road to the crest, and from there take a short hike along a knife edge to the summit (about two hours total). Further along the highly exposed path is the so-called Grotta della Sibilla. In the oldest maps, this spot is already clearly marked; only in a 1754 map is the name "sibyl" applied to the whole mountain, *la Montagna della Sibilla*, which then became the plural *Monti della Sibilla*. In 1851, the mountain chain was officially labeled the *Monti Sibillini*.

So, who was this sibyl?

The ancient Greeks described a sibyl as a female prophetess or oracle, inspired by the gods, who dwelt in a holy spot. There were a number of them. The Roman writer Varro (16 BC–AD 27, born in Rieti) lists ten—the Persian (or Babylonian, or Jewish), Libyan, Delphic, Cimmerian, Erythraean, Samian, Cumaen, Hellespontine, Phrygian, and Tiburtine—all named for the places where they lived. In the *Aeneid*, written by Roman poet Virgil in the first century BC, the Cumaen sibyl, based in a Greek settlement near Naples, guided the Trojan hero Aeneas through the underworld. It was she who offered the nine Sibylline Books to Tarquinius, King of Rome. He thought the price was outrageous, so she destroyed three and offered him six for the same price. He balked again and she destroyed three more, which convinced him to buy the last three at her initial high price. The Tiburtine sibyl was perhaps Etruscan and was added to the list by the Romans. The ruins of her temple in Tivoli sit high above the Aniene River, with a view of the waterfalls.

Scholars debate: is the sibyl a descendant of the Great Mother, of Cybele, of Ceres, of Circe, of Cupra? How is she related to Aphrodite, to Venus, to Fortuna? No definitive connection has been made. Sibyls are associated with water, springs, caves, the underworld, trees, and the rebirth of springtime. One of her functions was to teach women domestic arts such as weaving. Santarelli recalls his mother telling him the story of the sibyl who lived in mountains he could see from his childhood home in Monte Giberto; she was a queen who lived in a golden palace, "dressed all in gold, with long golden hair, who weaves and weaves an endless golden cloth… the melodious hissing of her shuttle and the harmonious strokes of her loom can be heard by putting an ear to the mouth of a grotto" (*Legends of the Sibilline Mountains*, p. 3).

Early Christians reassigned the role of the sibyls, aligning them with Old Testament prophets who predicted the arrival of Christ the Messiah. There are multiple depictions of these wise women, from the five that Michelangelo painted in the Sistine Chapel, to the twelve by Martino Bonfini (1564–1636) in the Santuario della Madonna del'Ambro (a pilgrimage site first mentioned in 1073) and the four he painted in Santa Maria Pantano di Montegallo, also known as *la Chiesa delle Sibille*. The Shrine of the Holy House in Loreto, the Virgin Mary's childhood home transported from Nazareth either by angels or returning Crusaders, is surrounded by a massive marble screen designed by Bramante. The sculptures covering its walls, created by the Della Porta brothers between 1570 and 1572, include huge statues of ten standing sibyls and ten seated prophets. However, this Christianized sibyl had a dark side. While some versions have her instructing the young Mary and assisting the pregnant Virgin, others describe her fury when she was not chosen to give birth to the Son of God.

Guerrin the Wretched

The first mention of a sibyl in the central Italian Apennines appears in *Il Guerrin Meschino / Guerrin the Wretched*, written around 1410 by the Tuscan *cantastorie* / storyteller Andrea da Barbarino. Set in the time of Charlemagne, it is the tale of Guerrin, an unfortunate knight who does not know who his parents are. After growing up an orphan and a slave in Constantinople, he searches the world for them, chasing false clues and seeking mystical advice, in a series of adventures that draw from pre-existing French, German, and Celtic folklore. The book has stayed in print through the ages, and was the most widespread Italian work until Manzoni's *I promessi sposi / The Betrothed* (1827)—which, in fact, name-checks *Il Guerrin Meschino*. It remained a staple of popular culture, carried around the world by Italian immigrants and presented in the puppet theaters of Sicily. Antonio Gramsci, one-time leader of the Italian Communist Party and political prisoner of the Fascists until his death in 1937, scathingly describes the work as appealing to the most backward, uneducated, and isolated readers, giving them a story in which all the misfortunes of the hero are redeemed by the discovery of his noble birth (A. Gramsci, *I Quaderni del Cacere / Prison Notebooks*, Quaderno 6 (VIII), p. 207).

What is the connection with the Grotto of the Sibyl? In Book 5, Guerrin Meschino travels to central Italy, tipped off that the Sibyl Alcina, who dwells in the mountains near Norcia, can tell him the secret of his ancestry. (The name *Alcina*, echoing other tales of Fairy Queens, specifically Ludovico Ariosto's *Orlando Furioso* (1532), only appears in later versions, starting with a Venetian edition printed in 1595.) In Norcia, the locals describe the grim fates of others who have gone in search of this enchantress. His innkeeper warns him of the dangers, of the guards posted to keep strangers away, and the three monks keeping watch from their monastary near the cavern. However, on hearing the reason for Guerrin's quest, the innkeeper agrees to guide him as far as this monastery. Likewise, the guards and the monks are so moved by his plight that they allow him to continue upwards, towards the maleficent grotto, alone.

After a difficult and dangerous climb, Guerrin reaches the entrance to the grotto. Here he meets Macco, the "Wandering Jew," transformed into a hideous snake, and they exchange harsh words. Beyond is an immense metal door. Carved above it is the inscription "Who enters by this door and exceeds a year will not leave again, will not die until the Day of Judgement; but then will perish in the body and be damned in the soul." The monks had warned him of this, so he recites the prayer they had taught him and knocks on the door.

The door is opened by three voluptuous damsels, and Guerrin enters the realm of the Queen Sibyl. It is noon, June 16. He soon meets the beautiful and fascinating Alcina herself. Da Barbarino identifies her as the Cumean sibyl, who, when she realized she had been passed over as mother of the Messiah, retreated to a cave in the mountains of central Italy to await the end of the world. Day after day, the enchantress leads Guerrin through an endless array of temptations, pleasures of the flesh, the lure of infinite power and wealth. With great effort, Guerrin remains pure by invoking the name of Jesus Christ. But Alcina makes it clear that she will only reveal the names of his parents if he sins. She does tell him that they are still alive, that when he was two months old his nursemaid had to flee with him by sea. Attacked by corsairs, the woman drowned and the baby was sold to a merchant in Constantinople, who raised him alongside his own son. But she will not say more, unless…

Every Friday, glittering crowds of pleasure seekers in the grotto turn pale and agitated. Guerrin soon learns that this is because every Saturday the beautiful people turn into reptiles, monsters—disgusting creatures that reflect their true sinful natures—wailing and bemoaning their lost souls until Monday. Alcina, too, becomes a horrible serpent.

Just before his year expires, Guerrin rejects the Fairy Queen's advances one last time and escapes her realm the same way he entered. After re-encountering Macco, the three monks, and the innkeeper, he makes his way to Rome to get the pope's forgiveness for ever venturing into the grotto. The pope, convinced of his purity, blesses him, and the wretched knight continues on his ultimately successful quest.

Other visitors claimed to have entered the sibyl's cave. The French courtier Antoine de La Sale, after seeing a tapestry in a royal household that he felt misrepresented the location of the grotto, decided to set the record straight. His *Le Paradis de la Reine Sibylle* is an account of the expedition he made there twenty years earlier, in 1420, with convincing details of his journey and hand-drawn maps. Whether he was acquainted with *Guerrin Meschino* is unknown. He based himself in Montemonaco and engaged a local guide to take him to the grotto. While de La Sale makes it very clear that he did not go beyond the first chamber, which contained carved stone seats and inscriptions, two young men from Montemonaco described to him their descent from there into a long tunnel. A local priest said he had accompanied two Germans deep into the cavern, across a narrow bridge, to an open space where two dragons guarded two metal doors. The Germans went through the doors; the priest did not, and waited in vain for their return. Other inhabitants of Montemonaco told de La Sale about a German knight and his groom (perhaps the same two) who ventured into the Grotta della Sibilla. There, they were welcomed by a beautiful queen and throngs of lovely young people (here, nobody ever gets old), with the understanding that if they stayed for more than 330 days they would have to stay until the end of time. The Germans were treated to all the pleasures of her domain, including ravishing consorts who, along with all the rest of the ladies, turned into snakes from midnight Friday to midnight Saturday. Eventually the knight decided he wanted to save his soul, and with his reluctant squire, departed on Day 330. They made their way to Rome, to ask the pope's pardon, but the pope withheld it. The two Germans returned to "the Paradise of the Queen Sibyl" for good. De La Sale heard several more anecdotes about gentlemen who disappeared into the grotto, and lists the names he saw inscribed on the walls of the first chamber, where he too left his mark.

As Santarelli enumerates, through the centuries various literary and artistic works have reflected this legend, culminating in Richard Wagner's opera *Tannhaüser*. Tannhaüser was a historical figure, a German *minnesinger*/troubadour and poet, born around 1205 to a noble family. He lived an adventurous life, perhaps participated in the Crusade of 1228, and died around 1268. One of the stories that grew up around him was that he disappeared into the Venusberg, the mountain where the goddess Venus ruled over a pleasure-filled realm. Repenting of his sins, he returned to ask pardon from Pope Urbano IV. The pope said he could not absolve Tannhaüser, just as his papal staff could not burst into bloom. Heartbroken, the knight returned to Venus's underworld. Three days later the Pope's staff flowered, but too late to save Tannhaüser's eternal soul.

This is, of course, remarkably similar to the story of Guerrin Meschino and the various tales collected by Antoine de La Sale. The first mention of Tannhaüser in the realm of Venus appears in a German poem, *Die Möhrin* by H. von Sachsenhelm, in 1453. Giovanni delle Piatte, a sorcerer on trial in Trentino in 1504, says he saw Tannhaüser in the Monte della Sibilla, around 1487 (Santarelli, pp. 57, 93). There are also echoes of Morgan le Fay, the Fairy Queen Morgana of Arthurian legends such as *Le Morte d'Arthur* by Sir Thomas Malory (1485). In earlier versions, Morgana was a goddess, a magician, a healer; by Malory's time she had become an evil, sexual figure.

Medieval pilgrimage routes crisscrossed Europe. For example, the Via Francigena was followed by the devout from Canterbury, England, through France, over the Alps to Rome, and then across the peninsula to Adriatic ports where ships set sail for the Holy Land. Unsurprisingly, chivalric epics and local folktales met and blended along the way, colored with a strong Christian interpretation. While scholars debate the origins of various aspects, we can attest that the story of the sibyl and her grotto is alive and well in the heart of the Sibillini Mountains. Visit the Museo della Sibilla in Montemonaco, where you can not only see the inscribed stone from the shores of the Lago di Pilato, but you can slide down a dark chute into a stone chamber.

Excavations and Investigations

Geologists and archaeologists have tried to determine whether there is, in fact, a vast cavern within this mountain. An expedition by the Club Alpino Italiano (CAI) in 1889 failed to open the grotto, but affixed a marker on top of those inscriptions that remained on the exterior wall. In 1897, Pio Rajna hiked through dense fog to find the mouth of the cave blocked by a huge boulder. In 1925, an expedition under the direction of Domenico Falzetti could not clear away the heaps of rubble that concealed the entrance. In 1930, Fernand Desonay, following de La Sale's descriptions, located a bottomless hole which he tried to plumb with a rock and a string. In 1953, he returned with Domenico Falzetti, Giovanni Annibaldi, and a diviner whose rod indicated where to excavate. They found no caverns, only carved initials (they removed the CAI plaque which had covered them), the date 1378, and a French coin from the 16th century—but by then the project had exhausted its funding (Santarelli, pp. 105–112). A 2000 geophysical investigation showed unusual horizontal karstic formations—tunnels and voids—within the mountain. For decades, there have been calls to investigate further, with no success. From the point of view of the tourism industry, it's a gamble; an attraction if there is something to visit, but less so if established once and for all that there is no enchanted grotto, no pagan cult site, no entrance to the underworld.

We, too, wanted to see the entrance to the grotto, and we chose the path that goes straight up above the Rifugio della Sibilla. This trail cuts across mountain slopes high above the tree line, skirting stands of juniper bushes. Traces of wild boar are everywhere. In spring this is a fairy land of native narcissi, crocuses, violets, and hyacinths. Several varieties of small rare orchids grow here, and also the stella alpina, a type of edelweiss. Cobalt blue gentians cling to the banks, and folds in the terrain hold swathes of crimson peonies. In this enchanted garden, with terrifying visions of how far you could fall if you slipped off the barely existent track, chamois leap without fear. Reaching the crest, with the crown of the Sibilla off to the left, you look way down into the valley of the Tenna River and on the other side, see the Eremo di San Leonardo. Padre Pietro Lavini, who died in 2015 at age 88, made it his life's work to build this hermitage, on the ruins of one dating from the 10th–11th centuries (unfortunately the construction obliterated what remained of the original structure). A popular hike threads through the Gola dell'Infernaccio up to this isolated shrine. Continuing on our breathtaking trail, with views stretching as far as Gran Sasso in Abruzzo, as far as the Adriatic Sea, we reach the grotto, only to be thwarted, like so many before us, by Mother Nature. The basin containing the possible entry is filled with snow.

Historically, this was a borderland, a refuge for Franciscan communities and other religious sects outside the rule of the Catholic Church, for hermits, and brigands. The terrain itself, with its labyrinth of mountains and valleys and caves, facilitated its use as an uncontrolled hideout; outsiders saw it as such. A list of local place names underlines its sinister, mysterious, damned, isolation—*Pizzo del diavolo, Grotta del diavolo, Fossa dell'Infernaccio, Gola dell'Infernaccio, Val dell'Inferno, Valle scura, Monte di*

La Sibilla Appenninica, Adolfo de Carolis, 1908 ~ Palazzo del Governo Ascoli Piceno

morte, Passo cattivo, Passo delle streghe... Devil's Peak, Devil's Cave, Hellacious Pit, Hellacious Gorge, Hell Valley, Dark Valley, Death Mountain, Bad Pass, Witches' Pass... (Santarelli, p.9).

Santa Maria in Pantano (see photos p. 179) was built on the slopes of Mt. Torrone below Mt. Vettore, along a *sentiero dei mietitori*, a track followed by seasonal harvesters. Local legend dates the church back to 780, but it was first mentioned, as a property of the Abbey of Farfa, in 1050. These mountains are criss-crossed with a network of roads, including the *Strada Imperiale,* which for centuries connected shepherds and migrant farmworkers with the western plains and Rome. Abundant springs with pure and refreshing mineral water made this a natural resting spot. The church was also a pilgrimage site dedicated to the Madonna; the cult of Maria contrasted with the cult of the sibyl, an outpost of Christianity in a zone known for its pagan traditions. The August 24, 2016 earthquake brought the Chiesa delle Sibille to its knees; nothing was done to shore it up, and the subsequent quake on October 30 virtually destroyed it. Only fragments of Bonfini's frescoes survived, one showing the Christ child with a donkey gazing down at him.

Olive Harvest in Piceno, 1896, "Le Olive Verdi Ascolane nell'Antichità"

Trajan's Arch Ancona, Giovanni Battista Piranesi, 1748 ~ Metropolitan Museum, New York

12

Picenum Becomes Le Marche

Picenum became Le Marche, but not all at once. The dissolution of the Roman Empire, the ensuing Gothic Wars, and Lombard invasions were major preconditions. The disappearance of the Roman administration, slowly replaced by papal authority, saw the breakup of Piceno and the creation of the Pentapolis, the Exarchate of Ravenna, and the Duchy of Spoleto.

As we have seen, Picenum was not a fixed or clearly defined area—at least, never for long. Before the Roman takeover, who knows what boundaries there were or what, if anything, the Piceni called themselves. Augustus included the Gallic lands of today's upper Marche north of the Esino River with Umbria, and around AD 297, Diocletian declared those former Gallic lands to be a part of the newly named *Flaminia et Picenum*. A fifth century administrative reorganization divided the region into *Flaminia et Picenum Annonaria*, north of the Esino, including Ravenna, and *Picenum Suburbaricum*, south to Atri and Penne near Pescara. Annona was the Roman goddess of the grain supply, typically depicted with a horn of plenty in her arm; *Picenum Annonaria* provided grain to the upper districts of Italy under Milan's administration. *Suburbaricum* means *sub urbe* or "under the city"—meaning administered by Rome. Procopius uses one Greek word, *Pikenon*, to refer to both parts (Cappelli and Vico, *Archeologia Altomediovale*, p. 5).

The word *marca*, "march," is of Germanic origin, and was probably used as far back as the sixth century to describe Ancona during the initial years of the Lombard presence in Italy. Originally, the word meant forest or wooded mountains, then a mountainous wooded territory surrounding an administrative district, and later simply a boundary. Finally, a "march" became a border area and/or an adminstrative district governed by a marquis. In the hundred some years preceding and following AD 1000, Piceno was the frontier between the Frank and Saxon holdings to the north and the southern realms of Apulia and Calabria.

As mentioned before, when Pope Stephen asked the Franks in 754 for help against Lombard aggression, Pippin pushed the Lombards back and rewarded the Pope with a large donation of land, which his son Charlemagne was later able to confirm and amplify. Although this was not the absolute beginning of the pope's temporal power, these donations were a qualitative enlargement and are often cited as the beginning of the Papal States.

After Charlemagne was declared Holy Roman Emperor in 800, portions of Piceno that had been part of the Lombard Duchy of Spoleto were broken off to become the March of Camerino and the March of Fermo. The first mention of the March of Fermo was in a document issued by Emperor Otto II in 983. It was bordered in the north by the Musone River and in the south by the Sangro in Abruzzo, and so included territory around Teramo, Chieti, Pescara, as did ancient Piceno. The Norman invasion of 1080 pushed the southern boundary up to the Tronto River. Around 1100, the northern part of the March of Fermo joined the southern part of the Pentapolis to become the March of Ancona.

The Marches/Le Marche is a plural form referring to the unification of the Marches of Camerino, Fermo, and Ancona. Guido Piovene, in his more than 900-page tome, *Viaggio in Italia* (1953–56), has another take on the multiplicity that is Le Marche:

> 'The Marches' is a plural. The north has the tint of Romagna; the Tuscan and Umbrian influence is manifested along the Apennine ridge; the province of Ascoli is an antechamber of Abruzzo and the Sabine region. Ancona, a seafaring city, is a place all its own. Even in so compact a space the language varies and has Tuscan, Umbrian, and Abruzzesi imprints according to location. Many diverse spirits and influences, manifested also in the landscape, seem to be distilled and interpenetrated in the central zone where Macerata, Recanati, Loreto, and Camerino arise… If you wanted to establish what is the most typical Italian landscape, you would have to point to Le Marche, especially Macerata and its surroundings. Italy altogether is a type of prism in which all the landscapes of the world seem to be reflected, putting in an appearance in moderate and harmonious proportion one to the other. Italy with its landscapes is a distillation of the world; Le Marche of Italy (Piovene, pp. 507–8).

Frederick I (aka Barbarosso), referring to the *marchia ancona* in a document, plotted an attack on the city in 1174. Sismondi recorded in his *History of the Italian Republics* that the people of Ancona were

> …confident in the strength of their almost unassailable position. Their town, beautifully situated on the extremity of a promontory, which surrounded a magnificent port, presented on the side open to the continent only precipitous rocks with the exception of a single causeway. The citizens had accordingly repulsed successfully for ages all the attacks of the barbarians and all the pretensions of the emperors (Sismondi, p. 47).

The people of Ancona bravely pushed the emperor's army back but remained under siege. A famine laid them low forcing them to live on herbs, shellfish, and leather.

> Such was the food on which had long subsisted a young and beautiful woman. Observing one day a soldier summoned to battle, but unable from hunger to proceed, she refused her breast to the child whom she suckled; offered it to the warrior; and sent him, thus refreshed, to shed his blood for his country. But to whatever distress the people of Ancona were reduced, they rejected every proposal to capitulate (Sismondi, p. 48).

The siege was eventually lifted. Ancona continued on as a maritime republic, second only to Venice, trading with Egypt and Constantinople, where they had a colony and warehouses, as well with the other side of the Adriatic. The March of Ancona's vaunted wealth was based on inland agriculture, particularly grain, wine, cheese, olives, and figs. Their wines were a favorite of the Venetians and their olive oil was widely exported.

Commentators have long remarked upon Le Marche's beauty and plenty. John Miley, in his *History of the Papal States*, quotes Giuseppe Michali's *Italy before the Romans*:

> "No country is more beautifully diversified than this by nature, with smiling hills and fruitful valleys, and wide-spreading fertile plains. It teems with abundance from the river Esi, at one extremity, to the Tronto, at the other." and in a later quote, "We traveled," say the Venetian ambassadors

of 1522, "from Macerata to Tolentino through the most beautiful fields; through hills and plains covered with corn: there was nothing else to be seen growing for a space of thirty miles; not a foot of uncultivated land was discoverable; it seemed impossible to gather in, not to speak of consuming, such an abundance of corn" (Miley, Vol. I, pp. 18, 20).

On an Italian trip in 1580–1581, the great French essayist Michel de Montaigne passed through Le Marche, keeping a travel journal. One leg of his journey took him from Rome to Loreto, crossing the mountains at the Colfiorito pass on the way to Tolentino and Macerata:

> In the early part of the morning we enjoyed for a time a most exquisite view of a thousand varied hills clad everywhere with the finest shady trees or by fruit trees of all sorts, or by the richest corn-fields, the ground being often so steep and broken that it seemed a marvel how horses could find their way thither…
>
> Often we could espy one village far over our heads and another beneath our feet, each well fitted with conveniences of life. What made the prospect all the more delightful was that, beyond these fertile hills, we could distinguish the rugged and inaccessible summits of the Apennines and the torrents descending therefrom, which when they have lost their primal impulse, come down into the village as gracious and gentle brooks (*The Journal of Montaigne's Travel*, pp. 191–2).

In Macerata, home of one of Europe's oldest universities founded in 1290, he mentions the *vino cotto* they served to travelers, perhaps having tried a glass himself. *Vino cotto* (cooked wine) is an ancient Marchigiano specialty, sweet and sherry-like, made from boiled down wine, and delicious with *biscotti*.

For centuries, the Marches had formed part of the Papal State, but really in name only. The temporal power of the papacy waxed and waned depending on many factors, including who was pope (and there were a lot of them). During the papacy of Innocent III (1198–1216), the pope established control over the Marches, finally achieving a goal set some four and a half centuries before with the donations of Pippin and Charlemagne. Except for the period of the Napoleonic invasions, Le Marche remained part of the Papal States until 1860.

When Innocent III consolidated papal holdings in central Italy under a centralized authority, the communes had already existed for some time with their widespread experience of autonomy. The pope divided the area into provinces and established the provincial government of rectors. His organizing efforts made space for local assemblies that retained notable independence. By the end of the 1200s, there were probably 100–200 towns organized as communes in the March of Ancona (compared to fifty in the Tuscan Papal Patrimony). The March of Ancona's unique geography and tradition of small towns facilitated their decentralized autonomy—a tradition dating back millennia. Daniel Waley, in *The Papal State in the 13th Century*, describes the March of Ancona as a province of castles. "It is a characteristically central Italian land, its scenery, a broad view of hill-top towns, most of them not at all large. Often these are situated on the tops of spurs, overlooking the eroded valleys around." The March was "par excellence a region of small towns" (Waley, pp. 87, 223). He says that the March of Ancona was often reproached by the popes as the "fickle march," for turning to the Ghibellines to side with the emperors. "The popes were to find this area of many towns the most profitable—though not most law abiding" (Waley, pp. 186, 90).

In 1353, Pope Innocent VI in Avignon sent Cardinal Albornoz to Italy to reassert his control of the

Papal States. One after another, the Spanish cardinal and his army defeated Galeotto Malatesta of Rimini and other lords of the city-state *signorie*. Albornoz, a cardinal and soldier, left a bloody trail across Le Marche but his intervention established a constitution for *la Marca Anconetana*, which became the model for the entire Papal States. His efforts, although exposing underlying papal weakness, were especially important in co-opting the autocratic tendencies of the *signorie* and keeping them within the papal orbit. At the same time, the papacy did not have the power to crush the *signorie* nor the will to alienate them. When Albornoz wrote his constitution in 1357, it marked a rather important step in the direction of statehood; the document remained in effect until 1816. But even with the constitution, which tightened control and softened the effects of the *signorie*, the quest for autonomy continued.

As for the Papal States, could they really be called states? In a sense, certainly—but not in any contemporary sense. Machiavelli, writing in 1513, had extreme doubts about the pope's temporal power. "Such princes (ecclesiastical monarchies) alone have states and do not defend them, and subjects and do not govern them. These states, though undefended are not taken from them" (*The Prince*, p. 31). But the pope was happy to collect tax receipts while the communes jockeyed for protection and autonomy. Ascoli was excommunicated by Pope Honorius (1216–1227) for wanting to elect their own *podestà*. Later, Pope Nicholas IV (Jerome of Ascoli) sold the right to do so to some communes.

The papal government, though often unsuccessful at enforcing obedience, was not nominal. In many matters—coinage, pasturage, the levying of duties—the pope could interfere, or else serve as a court of appeal. The greater communes were directly subject to papal officials, headed by a governor whose usual residence was a fortress, unless they had obtained the privilege of *Libertas Ecclesiastica*/ Liberty under the Church, which allowed them full self-government subject to the payment of a *censo* or tribute. The grant to Ascoli in 1482 of *Libertas Ecclesiastica* was to be the inspiration of one of Crivelli's greatest paintings, "The Annunciation with St. Emidius." Painted in 1486, it celebrates the brief period from 1482, when the church granted Ascoli the right to run its own affairs, until 1502, when the city elders chose to return to the church's control rather than submit to the dictatorship of a local noble family (Lightbown, *Carlo Crivelli*, p. 24).

It would be impossible to estimate the extent to which the name *Picenum* had survived the collapse of Rome. Lightbown credits Renaissance humanists, in their crusade to recover ancient texts, for bringing back the Latin *Picenum* as the Italian *Piceno*. Flavio Biondo (1392–1463) was a Renaissance historian and early archeologist, a prolific writer with a thirty-two volume history of Europe, and another three volumes on Rome as it once was—its buildings and layout. His already cited *Italy Illuminated* recounts Biondo's travels through fourteen regions of Italy; the section on our area is entitled, "Region 5: Picenum or the March of Ancona." Biondo was an early user of the three historical classifications—Ancient, Medieval, and Modern—and brought back the idea of Italy as the whole peninsula—i.e., a unified Italy. But the actual unification of Italy would not happen for another 400 years.

In the meantime, the citizens of Le Marche aquired a different sort of reputation. As subjects of the Papal State, they were the preferred job pool when the pope was hiring tax collectors. In fact, at the end of the 1500s, Pope Sisto V, from Grottammare, trusted only his co-regionals with the task of showing up at people's homes to demand the church's money. From this came the widespread proverb:

Meglio un morto in casa che un marchigiano alla porta
"Better a corpse in the house than a Marchigiano at the door"

13

The French, the Brigands, and the Unification of Italy

The French Revolution of 1789 was an epochal event that raged throughout Europe; Italy and Le Marche were not spared. The potent opposition provoked by the revolution, with its challenges to traditional authority, the entrenched interests of the *ancien regime*, and the Catholic Church, triggered an explosion of conflicts that led to the 1793 French invasion of Piedmont. In 1796, a new army commanded by twenty-seven-year-old General Napoleon Bonaparte arrived, and within three years took control of the entire peninsula. Italy was swept into the inexorable tide that swirled around France's wars with other prominent European states, including Austria, Britain, Prussia, and Russia.

Many Italian intellectuals welcomed the French, thinking that the invaders would help in the modernization of Italy. This was no longer the land of the Renaissance, when Italian culture, political organization, and business had set an example for all Europe. According to Cipolla, "From the twelfth to the fifteenth century the Italians were in the forefront not only of economic development but also of technological progress" (Cipolla, *Before the Industrial Revolution*, p. 185). By the 1700s, Italy had fallen behind. For example, Italian silk and wool were still of high quality but had lost market share due to competition from cheaper and inferior products. As yet, there was no Italian nation-state such as France, Britain, and Spain had already formed. Italy was still a decentralized collection of kingdoms, duchies, and the Papal States, mostly ruled by foreigners. Masonic lodges and republican Jacobins had been organizing underground for years, hoping to bring modernity to Italy.

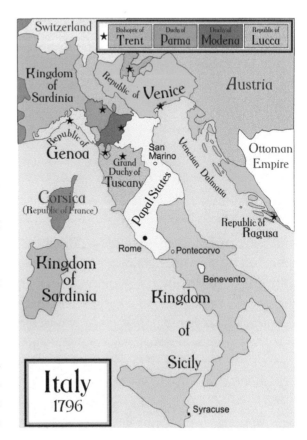

The republics set up by the French in the first phase of their occupation (1796–1799) opened the door to long-term changes in Italian government. However, in the short term, the French Directory, the five person committee governing France, viewed the Italian campaigns as a war of conquest to raise money to fund their expansionism. If Napoleon's army (and the army of bureaucrats that followed)

153

came into Italy promising liberty, equality, and fraternity, they also brought death, robbery, taxes, and a hated first-time army draft. Napoleon, the plunderer, sent massive amounts of money and loot home.

The French invasions were devastating for the papacy and the pope's temporal power. In 1796, the Papal States consisted of Rome and the surrounding region of Lazio, Umbria, Le Marche, and parts of Emilia-Romagna. The pope also controlled two towns in the south, Benevento and Pontecorvo, and Avignon in France. First, Napoleon seized Bologna, Ferrara, and Ravenna; when negotiations failed and fighting broke out again, the pope's troops were brushed aside, and in February 1797, Pope Pius VI was forced to accept the Treaty of Tolentino, named for the Marchigiano town inland from Macerata. This ceded the northern region of Romagna to France, including it in the Cisalpine Republic. The church lost Avignon after holding it for some 450 years, and took on severe financial obligations to the conquerers that basically bankrupted the papacy. The treaty also gave the winners the right to take their pick of the country's artistic treasures. The pope was kicked out of Rome; he died in exile in 1799.

Those who welcomed the foreigners and their new form of government helped overthrow the entrenched nobility and the temporal power of the Catholic Church. In urban centers, the intellectual bourgeoisie—lawyers, doctors, and teachers—seized the opportunity to gain control of local politics and to acquire expropriated properties. The farmers and mountain dwellers bore the brunt of the occupation. They were required to supply lodging and provisions to the occupying forces, and their livestock was requisitioned. Their sons were drafted into the French army and sent off to war, while the upper classes could pay to enlist a substitute. During these occupations, more than 200,000 Italians were ultimately conscripted. Of the 30,000 men sent to fight in Spain, only 9,000 returned; of the 28,000 sent to Germany, only 3,000 survived; and of the 27,000 sent to Russia, only 1,000 (Desmond Gregory, *Napoleon's Italy*, p. 136). Taxes were imposed on basic necessities—most onerously on salt and on the milling of grain. Large tracts of land owned by the church but cultivated by local farmers were sold off to private landowners. The anti-religious nature of the French Revolution was in direct conflict with the culture of the Papal States.

Brigantaggio

Resistance took many forms, but one of the most widespread was the formation of bands of so-called *briganti*, brigands, especially in southern Italy. Some were in fact highwaymen, taken on as mercenaries by the Papal States and/or the Bourbon Kingdom of Two Sicilies to fight the French in exchange for loot. But many of these *Insorgenti*, "insurgents," or *Truppe in Massa*, "popular troops," might better be described as partisans, fighting a guerilla war against invading forces. In Piceno, these groups consisted primarily of mountaineers, outsiders from marginal zones. The peasants in the productive agricultural regions, the rolling farmland between the Apennines and the Adriatic, were more firmly enmeshed in the *mezzadria*/sharecropping system and less likely to rebel.

Giuseppe Costantini, known as Sciabolone, was one of the most famous brigand chiefs in the Papal States. (The source for all descriptions of *brigantaggio* in the Marches is *Dagli Sciaboloni ai Piccioni*, Timoteo Galanti, 1990). He was born in 1758 in Lisciano, a community in the hills just south of Ascoli Piceno, which is also the birthplace of Fra' Pacifico and Pope Nicholas IV. Married at twenty to a woman from a neighboring village, he made a living as a farmer, a blacksmith, and a skilled hunter. For unknown reasons, he and his three sons took up arms against the French and gathered a band of around 200 men, beginning with relatives and neighbors. Their first encounter with the enemy took place in January 1799, at the Ponte d'Arli (still standing) in Aquasanta Terme, on the old Via Salaria. The French were planning to sack the mountain village of Talvacchia which was accused of sheltering bandits, but Sciabalone's band stopped them at this bridge. Encouraged by the victory, Sciabalone joined forces with the Abruzzese brigand and priest, Don Donato De Donatis, and others, and overran Ascoli Piceno that same month. They tore down the "Tree of Liberty" that had been planted in the Piazza del Popolo, pillaged and burned the houses of the local Jacobins, some of whom they also killed. A few days later, the French reoccupied the city, plundered the churches, executed those "brigands" they could catch, and replanted their tri-color-draped tree in the Piazza Arringo. The two sides then signed the Truce of Mozzano, but it had very little long-term effect. In fact, that April the French sacked and burned virtually all the houses in Lisciano, including Sciabalone's.

In May, Sciabalone and De Donatis took over Civitella del Tronto from the Bourbon forces. This fortress town, south of the Tronto River, on the border between the Papal States and the Bourbon Kingdom, and controlling the road between Ascoli and Teremo, was a continual bone of contention. From there, Sciabalone and now 400 or so men made their way north, occupying Ascoli again, then Ripatransone, Aquaviva, and other towns along the way, sacking and killing Jacobins. A common strategy of the brigands was to burn the town archives, thereby destroying the property records that had transferred ownership to the local bourgeoisie. The French had retreated to Ancona, where a republic had been declared on November 19, 1797, and Sciabalone headed there to meet up with the forces of General La Hoz. Giuseppe La Hoz had an illustrious career in the Austrian army and then with the Cisalpine Republic; Napoleon made him head of the Lombard Legion in 1796. But La Hoz was disillusioned with how things were going. In 1799, he deserted his post and made his way across the Sibillini Mountains, through Visso and Montegallo, to join up with the *Insorgenti* to fight for an independent, unified Italy. Leading a band of around 2,000 rebels, he named various brigand chiefs, including Sciabalone, as his generals. They took Macerata and Osima before arriving at Ancona. This strategically vital port was already blockaded by the Russo-Turkish navy, and was now put under siege on land by La Hoz.

For some, this siege was a diverting entertainment, according to Monaldo Leopardi of Recanati, father of the famous poet Giacomo Leopardi. Holiday makers from the surrounding areas came to watch the military activities; he describes seeing a Turk pass by holding the just-severed head of a French soldier, the eyes and mouth still moving (Galanti, pp. 56–57).

On the ninth of October 1799, French troops broke out and killed La Hoz, who was buried in the Holy House of Loreto. On the fifteenth, France signed a truce with Austria and they departed. Sciabalone went home to Lisciano, to his former work, now inflamed with the revolutionary ideas of La Hoz. When the French returned, he was involved in a variety of schemes to expel them that all came to naught.

The Second Coalition, consisting of Britain, Austria, and Russia, among others, had pushed the French out of Italy in 1799. The republics they had set up collapsed, and the old order was briefly restored while Napoleon was busy in Egypt. The famous 18th Brumaire (November 9, 1799) coup d'etat by Napoleon upon his return made him First Consul, i.e., dictator. The next spring, France reinvaded Italy, and on June 14 defeated the Austrians at the Battle of Marengo in Piedmont, starting the second phase of their occupation (1800–1814). In 1805, what had once been the Cisalpine Republic became the Regno d' Italia, the Kingdom of Italy, with Napoleon as King.

The French consulate had restored the Papal States in 1800, and the new pope, Pius VII, took up residence in Rome. He reached an agreement with Napoleon that reduced the church's power but did not eliminate it totally… yet. For Napoleon, the pope's temporal power was not an essential part of Catholicism. But the pope disagreed, and was displeased when Napoleon re-took Ancona in October 1805. By 1807, the French occupied Le Marche and Umbria, and in 1808 they marched into Rome. In 1809, Napoleon decreed Rome an imperial city and the Papal States part of the French empire. After excommunicating Napoleon, the pope was arrested and sent to Savona on the Ligurian coast. The Papal States were reorganized along French lines and divided into three Departments. These were named after the parallel rivers—the Metauro, Musone, and Tronto—that flow from springs high in the Apennines and debouche into the Adriatic near Fano, Porto Recanati, and Porto d'Ascoli respectively.

In 1806, Sciabalone—again as leader of the *Truppe in Massa*—was instructed by the exiled Bourbon regime of King Ferdinand IV to defend the fortress of Civitella del Tronto, the last Bourbon holdout in southern Italy. Brigands from surrounding areas—the towns along the Tronto and the Valle Castellano—were told to attack and block Napoleonic reinforcements. In return, the French sacked the nearby villages. After a two-month siege, the French succeeded in overrunning the Fortezza, where they executed civilians and soldiers, burned the archives, and displayed the impaled heads of the dead along the road. (This appears to have been common practice on both sides.) Sciabalone and his new wife were able to escape towards Ascoli. The French pursued him, but he and his band fought them off and took five prisoners, including the commander. Although Jacone di Campovalano, a fellow brigand chief, wanted to shoot them, Sciabalone spared their lives. His secret plan, in fact, was to make a deal with the enemy. In exchange for amnesty, a full pardon, and a stipend, Sciabalone and his men agreed to track down and turn over renegade brigands, including Jacone di Campovalano, whose known cruelties included slaughtering a priest and scattering his dismembered body parts around his village. Task completed, the slain rival's head was carried in triumph to Teramo, where Sciabalone, his family, and some of his band had been taken under French protection. In 1807, Sciabalone moved on to Capua with his three sons, where he died, perhaps poisoned, in 1808. In 1981, a plaque was mounted on his birthplace in Santa Maria a Corte, Lisciano, which reads (our translation):

In this house was born and lived Giuseppe Costantini 1758–1808, called "Sciabalone." Leading spirit and head of the *"Insorgenti"* he fought against the French who had invaded Piceno. He confronted the Napoleonic troops and attacked them with audacious guerilla actions inflicting notable losses. His enemies called him a "Brigand." The people exalted him as a Patriot. History remembers his deeds and courage.

Sciabalone's oldest son, Giacomo Costantini, took over his father's role. In 1809, it was he and his *Insorgenti* who ambushed French and Ascolani National Guard troops near Favalanciata on the Via Salaria. The rebels had taken control of this vital road, which the occupiers needed to reopen their connection to Rome. The mountaineers trapped the soldiers in the narrow gorge and killed around a hundred of them.

In their campaign to eliminate the brigands, the French pursued them to their villages and homes, punishing their families and anyone suspected of aiding them. This caused even more people to join the outlaws and disappear into the maze of forests and valleys and caves, rather than be imprisoned or killed. In August 1809, while Giacomo Costantini was hiding in the mountains of Montegallo and planning an attack on Ascoli, Giacomo's pregnant wife and six young daughters were seized and jailed in Fermo. The brigand chief accepted the amnesty offered by a French general of the Regno di Napoli, and in Teramo he was given the rank of captain with the task of hunting down other brigands. Like his father, he brought with him the head of another notorious leader, the one who betrayed the whereabouts of his wife and children. However, when Giacomo and his band presented themselves to the authorities in Ascoli, in the Regno d'Italia, their amnesty was denied and they were arrested. During that fall, they were executed in batches; Giacomo and several companions were shot by a firing squad in Ascoli on October 28, 1809.

In 1810, things were not going well for Napoleon in Spain, so he requested additional soldiers from Italy. Any man suspected of being a brigand or aiding them was rounded up and sent to join his army. This included the remaining two Costantini/Sciabalone brothers, Venanzio and Matteo. However, as they were being escorted to the troop ship in Naples they managed to escape back to the hills above Ascoli. There they regrouped with other fugitives—continually eluding capture, moving every night, and trusting no one, since every betrayal was rewarded with a goodly sum of money. On a map, it is almost shocking to see how close many of these places are to each other. From Montemonaco in the Sibillini Mountains to Teramo, Abruzzo is something like 40 km/25 mi as the crow flies; mountaineers who knew every secret path could move rapidly from one village to another. For army troops relying on roads, the route was much longer. Today, to drive to places like Tallacano or San Gregorio involves circuitous trips up gravel roads, descending to rejoin the Via Salaria between every stop.

In time, the Bourbon government, exiled in Sicily, and papal emissaries contacted the Sciabalones with plans to seize Ascoli. In 1813, with the brigands fighting at the gates, France sent troops to reinforce the city's defense. Thus, they maintained their control there but it weakened them in their war with the Sixth Coalition, the latest formation of European allies.

Having failed to take Ascoli, Galanti says, the brigand forces ran out of steam. Venanzio and Matteo were not as politically astute or as charismatic as their father and older brother. The social, political, and military aims degenerated into raids and petty vendettas. Along with the more political leaders, the French had succeeded in executing many of the hardened criminals and highwaymen, leaving bands primarily made up of inexperienced 18-year-old draft dodgers. Secondo Balena argues that the middle and upper classes never allied with the *Insorgenti* to repel the foreigners and insist on their liberty because, in their eyes, the brigands were lowly peasants. Whether the invaders were French, Austrian, and later the Piedmontese of the Risorgimento or German Nazis, the ruling classes preferred to collaborate rather than risk losing their class privileges (Balena, *Ascoli nel Piceno*, pp. 448–449). Venanzio was last heard of in Modena, where he had sought out the anti-Napoleonic forces. He was presumably turned over to the French and executed in 1814. That left Matteo as the only remaining Sciabalone.

The final chapter of the French Invasions took place in Le Marche. The protagonist was Joachim Murat, Napoleon's brother-in-law and right-hand man since 1795. Like Napoleon, he was a self-made man from humble origins. Napoleon had appointed him King of Naples after Napoleon's brother Joseph left Naples, where he had been in charge, for Spain. According to historian Robert Matteson Johnston, "the history of ancient Naples can show no more brilliant or romantic figure than that... of Joachim Murat" (Johnston, *The Napoleonic Empire in Southern Italy*, p. vii). Murat was noted for dashing fearlessly into battle, dressed to the nines; he was called the Dandy King. After Napoleon was exiled to Elba in 1814, Murat, fearing the loss of his kingdom, tried to strike a deal with the Austrians. When he realized they would undoubtedly renege, he declared himself in favor of Italian unification and independence. He gathered an army and marched into Le Marche to battle the Austrians at Tolentino on May 2–3, 1815. Despite his substantially larger forces, on the second day Murat, frightened by false rumors of enemy reinforcements, retreated into Abruzzo. The Austrians were left in control. When Napoleon escaped from Elba, Murat tried to rejoin him but Napoleon refused; instead he lost the Battle of Waterloo in June 1815 without his brilliant cavalry commander. Eventually, Murat mobilized a small force to seize Naples again, but he was captured and executed by the reinstalled Bourbons.

The Battlefield of Tolentino

Every year since 1996, a historic reenactment of the Battle of Tolentino has been staged. We were not going to that, but we did want to see the lay of the land. Choosing to stay in Treia, in part because of images broadcast by a weather webcam that focused on the beautifully symmetrical central piazza, we found a perfect microcosm of these hilltop towns: one street running the length of the crest and tightly packed brick buildings surrounded by massive walls. Below is the Potenza River valley. The fighting took place between here and the Chienti River to the south, in the fields and hillsides around Pollenza. The Austrians were based in Tolentino; Murat in Macerata. As we drive along country roads bordering the precisely laid out patchwork of the farms, we pass discreet markers of the villas that were fought over, and the ossuaries where the dead were burned or buried; approximately 2,000 Neapolitan soldiers and 1,000 Austrians were killed.

Today's destination is the Castello della Rancia on the Chienti River. This imposing fortress was built in the 1300s on the site of a seventh century granary belonging to the Cistercian monks of the Fiastra Abbey, and has served a variety of military and religious uses. The drawbridge has been replaced with a permanent brick span, but we still enter through the original stone archway. Once inside, we wander through the deserted halls, some used to store staging and costumes for events, climb the stairways and towers, descend into the underground storage rooms. A historic treasure in and of itself, the castle now houses a small museum which gives a quick synopsis of thousands of years of history. Most of the items were collected by Count Aristide Gentiloni Silverj (for whom the museum is named) during a series of excavations he conducted in the Tolentino area 1879–1884. (He found the previously mentioned Pebble of Tolentino, etched with an Upper Paleolithic female figure with an animal head, now in the Ancona museum). Paleolithic stone tools, Neolithic and Copper Age axes and arrowheads, two Bronze Age axes, Piceni *fibulae*, some with amber, *dischi-corazza*, a cheese grater, horse trappings, one "Lord of the Horses" handle, like those found near Treia (now at Ancona), Greek and Etruscan pottery, Roman statues and epigraphs; this is a "Cliff's Notes" of the archaeological finds of the area. Looking out from the battlements, over the expansive green and gold fluvial plain, we find it hard to picture the bloody past, but during the Battle of Tolentino the castle was conquered and reconquered, and there are tales of a cistern filled with dead bodies…

Plundered Art

The Napoleonic Era in Italy was marked not only by widespread killing and plundering, but by an organized effort to steal artworks. Napoleon (like Hitler after him) and his art experts made lists of what they wanted, and then took it. Ultimately, many were housed in the Brera Museum in Milan, which Napoleon established in 1809 as an Italian version of the Louvre. On display were masterpieces taken from all parts of Italy, especially from the churches.

On February 13, 1797, at 11 PM, Napoleon and his troops entered Loreto and ransacked the Holy House, making off with valuable contents of the shrine and its treasury (at least that which the pope had not already ordered to be spirited away), even snatching the statue of the Virgin Mary from the alter. This "Black Madonna" was exhibited at the Louvre, identified as a "Wooden statue of the Judaic–Egyptian school. Of Eastern origin." In 1800, it was returned to Loreto following the request of Pope Pius VII. At the Duomo di San Ciriaco in Ancona, Napoleon drew back from destroying the portrait of *"Maria, Regina di tutti i santi,"* said to work miracles, when he, too, saw her eyes move. On February 19, 1797, Napoleon wrote to the Directory, "The commission of experts has reaped a good harvest in Ravenna, Rimini, Pescara, Ancona, Loreto and Perugia which will be sent to Paris. That, together with what we have from Rome, will mean that we have everything that is a work of art in Italy, save for a small number of objects in Turin and Naples" (Gregory, *Napoleonic Italy*, p. 35). "The Dying Gaul" (see photo p. 76) also spent some years in the Louvre before Napoleon gave him back to Rome.

Napoleon had a family connection to Ascoli. City documents show that in 1200 a Giovanni Bonaparte was appointed the mayor of Montegallo, and later served in various posts in Ascoli before becoming the mayor of Florence. A descendant of his who stayed in Ascoli had three sons—one emigrated to Corsica, one to Tuscany, and the third was named as a canon attached to the Ascoli Cathedral in 1331. The Palazzetto Bonaparte, in the heart of the city, was perhaps so-named because it was built on land bought from the family. Napoleon, of the Corsican branch, showed no affection for the city where his relatives had lived for more than three centuries. In *Ascoli nel Piceno,* Secondo Balena cites a long list of art objects stolen from Ascoli alone. The churches were cleared out and the library of the University of Ascoli was seized. Following Napoleon's depredations, anti-clerical citizens felt free to sell off any remaining church property to international art collectors.

The works of Carlo Crivelli, one of the most prominent artists in Le Marche, were thus scattered around the globe. In 2015, the Isabella Stewart Gardner Museum in Boston mounted a Carlo Crivelli exhibit, the first ever in America. Most of the works were on loan from museums all over the US, England, and Europe; we were struck by how many of them had been commissioned for churches in towns we knew well in Le Marche. The Gardner's own masterpiece, "St. George Slaying the Dragon" was part of a 1470 multi-panel altarpiece from a church in Porto San Giorgio that was removed from there in 1803, and eventually sold off in pieces in 1876. Four of the six pieces were reunited here for the first time. Five panels from the altarpiece of San Domenico, Fermo, 1472, were present. Three of them had been sold by the Ascolano architect and art dealer Ignazio Cantalamessa Carboni to Napoleon's uncle, Cardinal Joseph Fesch, in 1826. When Cardinal Fesch died in 1839, the museum he established in Corsica held the second largest collection of Italian paintings in France, after the Louvre, around 16,000 pieces. The three main panels of the San Domenico altarpiece are still in the Pinacoteca Brera, Milan.

Carlo Crivelli, "The Annunciation" ~ National Gallery, London

Crivelli's most striking and perhaps most famous work, "The Annunciation with St. Emidius," is owned by London's National Gallery but was created for a church in Ascoli. When the Observant Franciscan friars were moved inside the city walls in 1482, the convent of the Annunziata, below the Fortezza Pia, was renovated for them and this painting was commissioned. Almost seven feet tall by five feet wide, it is a single panel—unusual for Crivelli. Mary kneels at prayer in her house, which borders a narrow street of stone and brick buildings with elaborately carved doorways and arches resembling late medieval Ascoli—and not Nazareth. She is surrounded by carefully detailed household objects and embroidered fabrics; an Anatolian rug hangs over the windowsill above her, and a peacock perches on the ledge. Plus, there are the two sets of *cicogne* brackets described earlier. From Heaven, a golden beam and the Dove of the Holy Spirit enter through a side window. Outside, Gabriel kneels on the paving stones and next to him St. Emidio holds a model of Ascoli, asking the Angel's protection from the plague. Numerous other figures go about their business in the deep perspective down the street. On the ledge right in front of the viewer sits an apple and Crivelli's cucumber, and below it the phrase *"Libertas Ecclesiastica,"* "Liberty under the Church." After the French plundered Ascoli, "The Annunciation" was taken to the Brera in Milan in 1811. Kept in storage there until 1820, it was then sold to a French art dealer, and after a series of transactions was given to the National Gallery by Lord Taunton in 1864. The painting's former home, the now deconsecrated Chiesa dell'Annunziata, has been renovated for use by the University of Camerino's School of Architecture and Design. A lecture room contains a restored fresco by Cola dell'Amatrice, which French troops had damaged when they were stationed there. Carlo Cappelli remembers standing in front of it when he, a pediatrician, instructed classes of nurses here many years ago.

The Risorgimento

The Papal States were re-established in 1815, but the issues raised by the French Revolution and the French occupation did not disappear. The idea of a unified Italy continued to ferment. Underground Republican groups such as the Freemasons and the *Carbonari* (charcoal makers) sought to further it, while the Sanfedisti fought to solidify the power of the Church. As you pass through Antrodoco, in Lazio on the Via Salaria, there is a small sign proclaiming it to be the site of the first battle of the Risorgimento. In 1821, in these steep valleys the Austrians defeated a Neapolitan army fighting for a constitutional government.

In 1822, the Vatican called for volunteers to enroll in the papal troops, soon called the Centurioni, to fight against the progressive Carbonari. In Le Marche, more than 50,000 men volunteered to serve under thirty commanders. One section of 9,000, the *Falange Sibillina*, was led by the priest Don Domenico Taliani of Montegallo. Another Centurioni leader was Giovanni Piccioni of San Gregorio di Aquasanta and Rocca Monte Calvo in the Valle Castellano, who had been a Sanfedista since 1817. After the failed revolution of 1831—yet another Carbonari attempt—Giuseppe Mazzini founded "*Giovane Italia* / Young Italy." The Risorgimento (literal meaning, "rising again") was underway.

We will not go into the full history of the Risorgimento; there are plenty of books that do. One of the most engaging, if highly anti-Catholic, remains G. M. Trevelyan's trilogy: *Garibaldi's Defense of the Roman Republic*; *Garibaldi and the Thousand*; and *Garibaldi and the Making of Italy*, published in the early 1900s. This biography of the charismatic hero reads like a novel. And Garibaldi did make several notable appearances in the Papal States.

Giuseppe Garibaldi was born in Nice in 1807, a sailor from a family of sailors. In 1833, he joined Mazzini's *Giovane Italia*. After taking part in an unsuccessful revolt, he was condemned to death but escaped to South America. In Brazil and Uruguay, he participated in a series of revolutionary republican movements, leading guerilla forces of locals and Italian immigrants in the cause of liberty. He also found Anita, an 18-year-old Brazilian with an abusive husband. Their immediate and overwhelming love kept them together, often fighting side by side, until Anita's death. (This is a movie that Brad Pitt and Angelina Jolie should have made. A 1952 version, *Camice rosse*, stars Anna Magnani and Raf Vallone.) In 1848, already hailed as "The Hero of Two Worlds," Garibaldi returned to Italy on Mazzini's invitation with his Italian Legion, or Red Shirts. Anita, now his wife, had preceded him with their three children. It was she who designed the distinctive garment worn by the fighters.

Italy, like the rest of Europe, was boiling with nationalist struggles. Garibaldi first went to Lombardy, where they were trying to expel the Austrians. When that failed, he escaped to Switzerland. The Austrians regained control of northern Italy, except for the Republic of Venice. The Kingdom of Two Sicilies, under the Bourbon king Ferdinand II, ruled the Regno di Napoli, southern Italy, and Sicily. Between them lay the Papal States. The Republican leaders posted the Italian Legion to various outlying cities, keeping them away from Rome. Garibaldi, too, was often called a brigand and his troops dismissed as uncontrolled outlaws.

By the winter of 1848, Garibaldi and his Red Shirts were in Macerata, hoping to enlist more volunteers. Originally, they planned to go to Ascoli to patrol the boundary with the Regno di Napoli. However, Count Ludovico Saladini Pilastri, *Gonfaloniere*, did not like the idea of 10,000 men descending on the city, partly because of the cost and difficulty of lodging them and because it might cause trouble with the "mountaineers." In fact, the anti-Republican bands of the Piccioni brothers of San Gregorio di Aquasanta and of Don Domenico Taliani of Montegallo were strongly supported by the local clerical faction. So only Garibaldi and an escort of six horsemen paid a visit. (Serafino Castelli has gathered all the details of the trip in *Garibaldi in Ascoli*.) One of the six was Andrea Aguyar, also called *il Moro*. Born a slave in Uruguay before slavery ended there in 1842, he and Garibaldi fought on the same side during the Great Siege of Montevideo. When Garibaldi was called back to Italy, Aguyar accompanied him as comrade and bodyguard. Contemporary reports often commented on the sight of the general with his flowing, red-gold hair and beard on a white horse next to a massive black man on a black horse.

Taking the coastal road through Porto San Giorgio, they spent the night of January 24–25, 1849, in San Benedetto del Tronto. Garibaldi stayed at the Casa Neroni (to reiterate, this is Nathan's maternal family name) in via Rossini, where he left a thank-you note now preserved in the Museo del Risorgimento in Macerata. The next afternoon, they arrived in Ascoli to an enthusiastic welcome; Garibaldi was immediately recognizable by the poncho he always wore. From a window in the Palazzo del Capitano, Garibaldi exhorted the crowd below in the Piazza del Popolo to fight for independence against clerical oppression. (Eight years later, this window was reconfigured as a balcony, possibly to erase the memory of his appearance. Currently, there is a plaque in his honor.) In the evening, Garibaldi went to a performance at the Teatro Ventidio Basso, at the end of which he made another speech. At the dinner held in his honor, one of the guests was Matteo Costantini / Sciabalone, now captain of the Civil Guard. Paid for by the city, the receipts suggest that the menu included fried olives, pasta with truffles, spinach, and pigeons *alla ascolana*. This same menu could undoubtedly be eaten today in Ascoli, with chicken *ncip-nciap* standing in for the pigeon version. Garibaldi spent the night at the Casa Tranquilli, 182 corso Mazzini; Aguyar slept across the doorway so nobody could enter. Of course, there is a plaque on the exterior wall.

The next morning, the little band set out for Rieti. Matteo Costantini wanted to accompany them as far as Arquata but Garibaldi refused the offer, despite warnings that he might be attacked by the Piccioni-Taliani bands who controlled the Via Salaria. The two men parted at the Mozzano crossroads with hugs and kisses. Garibaldi, in recognition of the anti-French actions of the Sciabalones, and the deaths of the two brothers, gave Matteo his sword. From there, Garibaldi proceeded to Aquasanta Terme, where he famously smoked a cigar in front of the Bar dello Sport—marked by another plaque. After spending the night in Arquata, the band took the road that goes up through Piedilama, Pretare, over the pass at Forca di Presta to Castelluccio, Norcia, and finally Rieti. In his autobiography, Garibaldi describes it thus:

> We crossed the Apennines by the rugged heights of Monte Sibilla, meeting with severe snow-storms, in consequence of which I suffered from rheumatic pains, which detracted greatly from the picturesqueness of the journey. We were well received by the stalwart mountaineers, feted everywhere, and enthusiastically escorted on our way. The precipices resounded with their cheers for Italian liberty; and yet a few days later that brave and energetic people, corrupted and instigated by the priests, rose against the Roman Republic, wielding arms furnished for the purpose by those black traitors (Garibaldi, *Autobiography of Giuseppe Garibaldi,* p. 310).

From the end of January to the middle of April, Garibaldi and his Legion of approximately 1,000 men were stationed in Rieti, near the border of the Regno di Napoli. Anita joined him there briefly, leaving their children with his mother in Nice. The Roman Republic was declared on February 8, 1849, and led by a Triumvirate with Mazzini in charge. Garibaldi was elected to the Constituent Assembly as a representative of Macerata. The liberals of Ascoli supported the new republic, and in many towns the new Italian flag was raised in triumph. But the pro-papal forces struck back. In April, Piccioni, Taliani, and 200 mountaineers temporarily reclaimed Arquata and Aquasanta Terme, and then moved to surround Ascoli. It was during this phase that a skirmish between Piccioni's band and Republican soldiers resulted in his name being attached to the *Albero del Piccioni*, an ancient plane tree along the Via Salaria. The Triumvirate considered sending Garibaldi to secure the city, but a bigger problem was developing. Louis Napoleon, the French President and soon-to-be Emperor Napoleon III, had decided that he wanted to return the exiled Pope Pius IX (born in Senigallia) to power in Rome. On April 25, French troops landed at the nearby port of Civitavecchia. Mazzini sent for Garibaldi and his Legion, who entered Rome on April 27. On April 30, they turned back the French at the San Pancrazio Gate on the Janiculum Hill. After a pause that allowed French reinforcements to regroup, the foreign invaders laid siege to the city on June 3. At this point, the Republican troops, including Matteo Costantini/Sciabalone and his family, left Ascoli, Ancona, and other Marchigiani towns where they had been stationed, and made a secretive retreat towards Rome.

In Rome, the constant skirmishes took their toll, as did the relentless bombardments. Andrea Aguyar was killed by a shell near the Church of Santa Maria in Trastevere on June 30. Anita had returned to Nice before Garibaldi marched on Rome, but at the end of June she made her way through enemy lines, disguised as a Spanish noblewoman, to rejoin her husband. She was four months pregnant and ill with a fever, perhaps malaria, which she had caught in Rieti.

An armistice was declared on July 1. The Roman Republic surrendered, and the French troops were to take control of the city on July 3. On July 2, Garibaldi, Anita (dressed as a man, with her hair cut short), and about 4,000 Garibaldians left Rome through the Porta San Giovanni. Their plan was to get to the besieged Republic of Venice, still holding out against the Austrians. But first they had to elude the French, Neapolitan, Spanish, and Austrian forces that were hunting them down. Well skilled in guerilla warfare, Garibaldi succeeded in evading them through a series of feints and false starts. His path led from Tivoli to Monterotondo to Terni and Todi, then looping through Tuscany, Orvieto, and Arezzo, before crossing back into the Papal States at San Sepolcro. They crossed the Apennines in the northern reaches of Le Marche and into the Foglia River valley. Trevelyan has a great description, still valid today:

It is one of the strangest regions of Italy: the higher mountains, naked peaks and tables, rear themselves on the sky-line in fantastic fortress shapes, hard to distinguish, except by their size, from the works of man—the old robber castles perched on their summits. The aspect of the lesser hills, skeleton ridges, washed bare of soil and corrugated by the rain-torrents, baked by the sun into a hard white grey, with patches of brown or of sparse verdure, is well known in the backgrounds of Piero della Francesca and other painters of the Umbrian school. The broad valley bottoms are white as snow-drifts, being filled from side to side with the polished stones of the dried-up river courses… Such was the country through which the Tyrolese sharpshooters followed on the heels of the Garibaldians from Sant'Angelo in Vado to San Marino, killing all whom they caught, and sometimes treating even the wounded with revolting brutality (Trevelyan, *Garibaldi's Defense of the Roman Republic*, p. 261).

Men had been deserting, as well as being killed, all along the way; only 1,500 Red Shirts remained when they arrived at San Marino on July 31. San Marino was, and still is, the last remaining medieval city-state in Italy, perched on a mountaintop with a view out to the Adriatic. In this independent republic, surrounded by Austrian troops, Garibaldi disbanded the Legion, telling his men they could lay down their guns here and go home, or continue with him to Venice. He begged Anita, who was in great pain and fading fast, to stay where she could be taken care of, but she refused to be separated from him. In the middle of the night, Garibaldi, Anita, and 200 men set out on a 22-hour trek to the seacoast town of Cesenatico, between Rimini and Ravenna, where they commandeered thirteen fishing boats. In the morning they set sail, but their enemies were too close. The Austrian fleet captured most of the boats, with 162 Garibaldians on board. Three boats made it to shore further north in the Po River delta. Garibaldi and Anita were on one of them. This was the heartrending end of their love story, as "The Hero of Two Worlds" ferried his dying wife through the lagoons of Comacchio, where a last few loyal supporters provided a hideout for them. Anita died in his arms on August 4, 1849. Garibaldi escaped to America—to fight and win another day. A statue of Anita, an Amazon on horseback with a gun in one hand and a baby in the other, rears on the Janiculum Hill in Rome.

Now, the big question was, who would take over the Papal States, the Austrians or the Bourbons? The Austrians got there first, and in June they had re-established the pope's government. Matteo Costantini was arrested in Ascoli, despite a safe-conduct pass he had been given after an earlier encounter with the Austrians in Force. He and other Republican fighters were accused of common crimes so that they could not take advantage of the amnesty offered for defeated political opponents like the liberal bourgeoisie. The last of the Sciabalones was given a life sentence and sent to the prison in Ripatransone, where he died of an illness in November 1849. The papal government also turned its back on the mountaineers. The tax on milling grain was reimposed, and the requests by Don Taliani and others for reparations for damages done by the Republicans were denied or belittled. Giovanni Piccioni and his son Leopoldo asked only for an audience with Pope Pio IX when he visited Ascoli in 1857, but the pope refused to see them.

In 1860, the pendulum swung the other way. The new Savoy king, Victor Emmanuel II, with the help of Napoleon III, had pushed the Austrians out of Piedmont, leaving them in possession of only Mantua and Venice. All the regions of northern Italy voted to join his Kingdom of Sardinia. Garibaldi and his Thousand invaded Sicily in May. The Austrians had also exited the Papal States, sailing out of Ancona in June 1859. The liberals of Ascoli and other cities were again preparing to rise up and join the expanding united Italy. So, the church turned again to the mountaineers and asked Giovanni Piccioni to recruit and organize a new legion of "Papal Auxilleries."

After conquering Sicily (except for Messina) and declaring himself dictator, Garibaldi and his army crossed over to Calabria and made their way north. They were welcomed in Naples on September 7, and the Bourbons retreated to the fortresses of Gaeta. By the 17th, Garibaldians had crossed the Tronto from Abruzzo and occupied San Benedetto, Grottammare, and Monteprandone. The Piedmontese, who already controlled Umbria, realized they had better hurry if they wanted to stop Dictator Garibaldi from getting to Rome ahead of them. On September 18th, the Battle of Castelfidardo took place, between the Piedmontese invaders and the remnants of the papal army, who lost. The towering monument commemorating the battle stands in the town of Castelfidardo, though the encounter itself took place closer to the sea. When word of the victory reached Ascoli, the papal government and its supporters fled to Rome. The liberal faction declared a new government. The Papal Auxilleries led by Piccioni were again left in the lurch; many took up the new government's offer to surrender their arms and go home. The Piedmontese troops entered Ascoli on September 25, 1860, and occupied the territory, controlling the road to Rome. The definitive defeat of the Bourbon army by the Garibaldians took place on October 1–2 at the Battle of Volturno in Campania.

Garibaldi and Mazzini had fought for a republic, not a kingdom, but in the end they accepted unification under the constitutional monarchy of Victor Emmanuel II. Garibaldi ceded his dictatorial power to the young king on October 26, at Teano, near Caserta; both men on horseback shook hands on the deal. (However, Garibaldi was not happy when Prime Minister Cavour gave his birthplace Nice to France.) The first-ever democratic vote in Le Marche took place soon afterwards; a "yes" vote was in favor of joining the constitutional monarchy of Victor Emmanuel II; "no" meant staying with the pope. The election was deeply flawed, but the king was named the overwhelming victor. The pope held on to Rome and the surrounding region of Latinium, despite the fact that the Kingdom of Italy had declared Rome as its capital.

While Naples and Teramo fell to the Garibaldians, the Bourbon soldiers retreated to Civitella del Tronto, locking the doors, and declaring it under siege. Popular uprisings were taking place throughout the south, including around Teramo and the region bordering the Tronto River, with cries for the return of their own king—now Francis II, after the death of his father Ferdinand II in 1859. The Piedmontese rounded up all suspected "brigands" and surrounded the fortress of Civitella with the aim of starving out those inside. The Bourbons appealed to the Piccionis and other reactionary bands, asking them to divert the Piedmontese forces by attacking them in other places. Accordingly, the pro-papal Auxilleries once again took over Aquasanta and Arquata, controlling the Via Salaria as far as Amatrice from the heights above it, and threatened Ascoli and Castel Trosino.

In January 1861, Piedmontese troops arrived to defend Ascoli, and engaged in a bloody battle at Mozzano for control of the crossroads and the bridge over the Tronto. The reactionaries held their ground but in retaliation, the Piedmontese laid the surrounding territory to waste. With every back-and-forth, innocent bystanders were raped and slaughtered, property was stolen, and houses were burned. When the Piedmontese ultimately re-took the Via Salaria, they torched every church from Aquasanta Terme to Ascoli, after removing anything of value. In Aquasanta, a painting by Cola dell'Amatrice was slashed with bayonets. By February, the pro-papal "brigands" were effectually defeated, and nearly all the mountain villages of the upper Tronto had been reduced to piles of rubble. The last full-on battle in the Ascoli area between the anti-unitarian bands, including the Piccionis, and the Piedmontese took place on February 10. It ended when the mountaineers, realizing they could not defeat the army, retreated into the Valle Castellano and surrounding mountains, and the army, fearing ambushes, retreated to Ascoli.

On February 3, the fortress of Gaeta, abandoned by the French, finally surrendered, and King Francis II formed a government in exile in Rome. On March 12, Messina gave up. The Piedmontese intensified their bombardment of Civitella del Tronto. King Francis II sent orders for his soldiers to surrender, and on March 20, 1861, this last remaining Bourbon holdout capitulated. Despite earlier offers of amnesty, many of the defenders were executed or imprisoned. The fortress was dismantled, the walls torn down, and all its artworks taken or destroyed. Over the decades, it was used as a dump for construction debris before eventually being partially restored as a historic site and museum.

From this point on, the Italian state concentrated on wiping out what remained of the brigands, and anyone who supported them. Their hard line reflected the disrespect and hatred of the aristocratic Piedmontese generals for the rebellious "scum of the earth." Government soldiers served basically as bounty hunters, with constant patrols combing the outlaws' territory. For example: in September 1861, a troop of Piedmontese and Ascolani soldiers attempted to root out brigands hiding in the Valle Castellano. The brigands, however, got the best of them, taking four Ascolanis to be executed and re-leasing four injured Piedmontese. The Piedmontese reached the village of Forcella, where the women bandaged their wounds and fed them a dinner of farro. During the night, the soldiers experienced severe stomuch pains, and convinced they had been poisoned, were on the verge of killing their hosts. Fortu-nately, their symptoms abated, and the Piedmontese realized they were simply unaccustomed to eating the coarse wheat grains. They returned to their base in Aquasanta, and the outraged Piedmontese sent 300 soldiers back to the villages of Vosci and Forcella, where they spent three days burning down the houses of everyone in the area suspected of having ties to the brigands, including the house that had taken in the injured soldiers.

Many "brigand chiefs" had made their way to safety in Rome, including Leopoldo Piccioni, who received a salary as a captain in the papal forces. In March 1862, a mass trial of brigands was held in Ascoli; 96 of those charged, including six clerics, were prisoners in the Forte Malatesta, and an addi-tional 76, including three priests, were tried in absentia. Although not present, Leopoldo, Giorgio, and Gregorio Piccioni were condemned to death, and their father Giovanni was given a life sentence of hard labor. In September 1863, 27-year-old Giorgio was killed by government soldiers near Aquasanta, betrayed by spies. His brother Gregorio killed the suspected informer at his home in Piedicave and then joined his brother Leopoldo in Rome. They were both awarded medals in 1867 for leading elite papal Zoave contingents against Garibaldi and his troops at the Battle of Mentana, southeast of Mon-terotondo off the Via Salaria, defending the pope's territory against a larger attempt to occupy Rome. The patriarch Giovanni was disillusioned with his former comrades, who had turned from religious pa-triotism to a fight for survival, vendetta, and plunder. He hid in an Ascoli monastary while plans were made to smuggle him into Rome with a false passport. But he and three monks were arrested at an inn by the train station in San Benedetto, where they were presumably going to catch a train to Rome. He had perhaps been set up, betrayed in an elaborate plot by relatives for the substantial price on his head. Sentenced to a life of hard labor, and charged a large fine, he died in the Fortezza Malatesta in 1868.

On September 20, 1870, with the symbolic breaching of the Porta Pia, the Italian government finally took over Rome, and the pope retreated to Vatican City—a situation only formalized with the Lateran Treaty of 1929, under Mussolini. The "brigands" who had sought shelter in the city were now fair game. Gregorio Piccioni was captured as he performed sentinel duty at the Castel Sant'Angelo on

December 21, 1870; his brother Leopoldo was arrested at his home in Rome on January 8, 1871. After being taken back to Ascoli to be re-sentenced, Gregorio was sent to prison in Liguria, where he died a few years later. Leopoldo did 25 years of hard labor and then returned home to Rocca Monte Calvo, where he died on April 14, 1898. Piccioni descendants still live there. When we take the twisting winding road to San Gregorio, birthplace of Giovanni Piccioni, a man working in his garden points the way to the house. "You call him a brigand," he says, echoing the marker on Sciabalone's home, "We call him General."

By the end of the 1870s, the citizens of the new Italy, willing or not, were forced to submit. Galanti remarks on the enormous amount of Italian blood shed on both sides in this struggle, saying it was probably more than was lost in the military battles of the Risorgimento and the partisan resistance during WWII (Galanti, p. 348). The undocumented civilian deaths of women, children, and the aged can never be fully determined. Only the countless reports of villages that were destroyed, with most or all inhabitants slain, have come down to us.

Some "brigands" found a place in the new order. One morning at the Bar Zocchi in Montemonaco, we have coffee with Antonio Capponi, who runs the nearby Agriturismo La Baita di Pilato. He is descended from a brigand family—Giovanni Piccioni married Angela Capponi. He tells us that after the Unification of Italy, the government handed over the management of the grist mills of Montegallo to his family; the last to close was the Mulino di Capponi in Interprete in 1976. Instead of seizing the mills to protest state-imposed taxes, the outlaws were now running them.

Not surprisingly, the legends of the brigands live on in folklore, literature (including Alexander Dumas's *La Sanfelice*) and in the emerging art of cinema. Silent films featuring the Sanfedista brigand/patriot Fra' Diavolo (born in Itri, Lazio, 1771; executed in Naples, 1806) include one made in Mexico in 1906, and a couple of Italian versions from 1924 and 1925. The 1933 Laurel and Hardy comedy *Fra' Diavolo/The Devil's Brother* was based on the 1830 French operetta by Daniel Auber. Sardinian heartthrob Amedeo Nazzari starred in multiple brigand movies, including one in which he played Fra' Diavolo, and another in which he played the French Colonel Hugo (Victor Hugo's father) in charge of capturing the outlaw. Perhaps the most intriguing representation of this history can be seen in the internationally beloved "Spaghetti Westerns," transposing the Italian conflicts of the 1860s to Civil War era America. Sergio Leone's masterpiece trilogy, *Fistful of Dollars* 1964, *For a Few Dollars More* 1965, and *The Good, the Bad, and the Ugly* 1966, stars Clint Eastwood wearing a Garibaldian poncho and chewing on a cigar. Scenes in these movies were filmed at Campo Imperatore, a plateau high in the mountains near L'Aquila, and around Castelluccio. The stories share a moral wilderness, without law or government, where no one is really a good guy, an emphasis on bounty hunters and betrayals, the threat of ambush around every rock, riding into a town that has been destroyed, escaping across the border, whether between the Papal States and the Regno delle Due Sicilie, or between the US and Mexico. The parallels are striking; the renegade southern Confederates against the Union troops, the defeated Bourbons against the northern Piedmontese. On one side, were they brutal outlaws or freedom fighters? On the other, democratic liberators or one more invasion of murderous overlords?

The Neroni family on their farm, Mather, Pa., circa 1928

14

The Legend of Decenzio Neroni

Somewhere in Italy, a boy struggles up a steep donkey path to a remote mountain village. He stops at the first house and knocks on the door. Someone opens it and the inhabitants take him in. He becomes almost like a son and when he grows up, he marries the daughter of the family.

The boy's father, a nobleman, had been killed in a war with the French. His mother left him with his father's family near the seacoast, and ran away with a French soldier. These relatives raised him to a certain age, and then informed him they would no longer treat him as one of their family. He would have to live with the servants and earn his keep. Rather than submit, Decenzio Neroni ran away.

Decenzio Neroni was Nathan's great-great-grandfather, and this is Nathan's tale to tell.

I grew up hearing this story, but I never really knew where in Italy it was supposed to have taken place. My family's relatives were somehow different from other Italian immigrants; we were told they were from northern Italy, not the south of Naples and Palermo. Our thin spaghetti sauce was made without tomato paste or bottled sauce, just whole tomatoes with garlic, olives, and canned tuna. At Thanksgiving and Christmas, my grandmother and mother fried up green olives stuffed with hamburger.

Some decades back, before I knew that there was a Land of Piceno or where it was, I took a college course in Renaissance Intellectual History. Reading Machiavelli's *The Prince* led me to his *History of Florence*; Book 3, Chapter 2, which discusses the Neroni Conspiracy. It caught my eye because "Neroni" is my mother's family name. I remembered vague reports about the noble origins of my maternal grandfather's family—reports that I always thought were absurd, even pathetic. People who wanted to build themselves up with boasts of ancient nobility or civil war heroes seemed like lost souls with their obsessive charting of family trees. In fact, going back ten generations puts one on an equal footing with potentially millions of people to claim one notable ancestor. We are all the descendants of princes and slaves. But this was Machiavelli! That summer after graduation, book in hand, I took a trip to the Pennsylvania farm where my grandmother lived. Nonna Lia's assurance that there was a connection did not assuage my doubts, nor did Aunt Lucy's statement some years later, that Lia (short for Elia) claimed to have accompanied her father-in-law Pietro Neroni to an office in Ascoli Piceno to renounce his title of "Count" because he was tired of paying the fee on it.

The reality of the Neroni dairy farm cut a stark contrast to the idea of nobility and a family crest. My mother often complained about how poor they were. My grandfather Amedeo could neither read nor write, because his stepmother had pulled him out of school to work—a common fate in that era. At age 19, he landed in New York City on July 4, 1900. The docks were filled with revelers celebrating Independence Day and the new century. Someone handed him a firecracker. He did not know what it was, it exploded and destroyed three finger tips. He then joined his older brother Domenico in western Pennsylvania and married Elia Orazi, who had immigrated later from the same village. Once they were able to purchase the farm, Nonno Amedeo drove a cart delivering milk to the coal-mining hamlets. The money he made during Prohibition, selling homemade wine concealed behind the milk bottles, sent five of their six children to college.

Amedeo died in 1942, and after their youngest child, my mother, finished high school, Nonna Lia closed up the farm and moved to Brooklyn to work in her niece's shirt factory. She was an extremely accomplished seamstress having learned the trade from the nuns in Ascoli Piceno. In 1966, in her mid-seventies, she moved back to Pennsylvania to grow her own food, complaining about the poor quality of what you could get to eat in New York.

By the time Lia died in 1979, quite a few years had passed with scant contact between the American and Italian branches of our family. Pietro Neroni, son of Decenzio, had twelve children, four with his first wife and eight with his second, who was the first wife's sister. Eleven went to America, of whom only one, the oldest son Domenico, returned to Italy. The oldest daughter Rosa stayed in Abetito, barred from entering America because she was lame, having slipped and broken her leg at the village laundry trough. The descendants of these two are the people we got to know over the years.

We had no idea where Abetito was. In an early trip to Italy, Phoebe and I failed to locate it. Later, my older brother John got the necessary information from our uncle Albert, who was born in Abetito when my grandparents returned to Italy on an extended honeymoon (extended, because the US would not let the now-pregnant bride back into the States). In the 1930s, Albert took advantage of his Italian birthright to return there to attend medical school; unfortunately, citizenship also made him subject to the draft. Rather than serve in the Fascist army, he came back to the States; until his death he kept in touch with his cousin Fabio, Rosa's son. Albert even knew how to spell Abetito, as my mother's dialect pronunciation was more like *"Abuhdida."* It turned out that Abetito is one of some twenty-two mountain villages in the *comune*, or township, of Montegallo, in the Province of Ascoli Piceno, in Le Marche.

"I am the Neroni from America," my brother announced at the first door he knocked on when he got there. The Italians got a big kick out of that and still quote him in their thick Italian accents—to much raucous laughter. They also had a good idea of who he was and where he fit in the family tree.

Phoebe and I went three years later, in 1989, and were stunned by the beauty of Abetito with its spectacular views of Mt. Vettore and Mt. Sibilla, and its proximity to Ascoli. We have been going back ever since, every other year at first, then every year for a month or two, practicing a kind of micro-tourism and learning all the local paths and Marchigiani back roads. Now that we are retired, we go twice a year, spending four months of the year there and the rest in Cambridge, Massachusetts. (This should explain our fondness for historical anecdotes with Boston connections.)

Only two relatives with the Neroni name were still living in Abetito, Iva and Iolanda, the daughters of my grandfather's older brother Domenico. He had gone to America first, Amedeo, the second son, joined him, and they worked together at a dish factory in western Pennsylvania. After receiving threats from the local Mano Nera/Black Hand mob, Domenico returned to Abetito sometime after 1918, and married a woman he had last seen as a baby in her mother's arms. The big Neroni house in Abetito, built by their father Pietro, still belongs to Domenico's granddaughter. Above the front door is a stone carving inscribed *N.P.* (Neroni Pietro), *1909*, and above that a sculpture of a rooster, the mascot of Monte-

Pietro Neroni's Rooster, Symbol of Montegallo

Pietro Neroni and some of his family, Abetito, circa 1900

gallo. Bob Neroni, a far-flung American cousin whom we eventually met, told us a family story about this figure. According to him, the local priest had commissioned Pietro Neroni to make a series of animal sculptures to decorate the Chiesa di SS. Pietro e Paolo in Abetito. But when Pietro delivered the completed order, the priest expected him to donate them. Pietro hemmed and hawed, and eventually did give him the critters for free—all except his favorite, the rooster, which he mounted on an exterior wall for everyone to admire.

Pietro's descendants have handed down their pride in his skill as a sculptor and stonemason. The church's belltower is his work, dated 1874, built onto a probably medievel structure with interior renovations marked 1570. Our cousins point out the details he added around the main door, which include St. Peter's keys to Heaven and a sturdy fist hefting a sword, symbol of St. Paul. In the 1950s, some of the American Neronis donated two wooden statues of the saints, currently stored in an attic awaiting the post-earthquake repair of the church.

Inside the Neroni house is a massive kitchen fireplace, large enough to sit inside, its tufo stone mantel stained black and carved with *P.N, 1901*, religious motifs, and more little birds. In the dining room, the cabinets contain a full service of monogrammed china made by Amedeo and Domenico in Pennsylvania. A framed picture of my grandfather as a young man hangs on the wall in the "schoolroom," alongside formal photos of his parents, of Domenico and his wife, and of other brothers. Iva and Iolanda were both teachers, and this room in the big house was where all the local people of our generation went to elementary school. Old leather suitcases stacked on a side table are filled with family photographs and postcards from America, from the first half of the 20th century.

We met cousins whom my mother had never met or known about. One cousin she did know was Rosa's son Gino, Amedeo's favorite nephew and Fabio's brother. Gino served in the Italian army in WWII and was captured as a prisoner of war; he eventually ended up in England in a POW camp. Amedeo sent him $500 while he was there, but the Brits returned the money, saying they would provide him with everything he needed. After the war, Gino worked first in Venezuela and then in Canada as a miner, and stayed for a while with Lia in Brooklyn on his way back to Italy. He later bought my grandfather's share of the family property and chestnut groves in Abetito from my widowed grandmother.

None of our relatives had any knowledge of a familial connection to Machiavelli's Neroni Conspiracy; a few had heard vague reports of a noble title.

Diotisalvi Neroni, as recounted in Machiavelli's *History of Florence,* may not have been someone you would want to claim as an ancestor. As a trusted advisor to Cosimo di Medici, he had occupied the pinnacle of Florentine society. Nerone Neroni, his father, had been instrumental in the rise of the Medici family. His brother Giovanni was archbishop of Florence and his brother Francesco was a very wealthy merchant, entrepreneur, and business genius, specializing in silk and wool. Before Cosimo died and his son Piero (the Gouty) took over, Cosimo recommended his trusted advisor Diotisalvi Neroni to Piero for the management of his personal finances and city government.

An audit of Piero's finances soon after his father's death indicated much disarray. As a solution, Diotisalvi recommended that Piero call in some loans, an approach that was toxic, angering some, ruining others. The way Machiavelli tells it, Diotisalvi seriously misled Piero and set him up for a big fall that Diotisalvi hoped to profit from. With three other men, Diotisalvi formed a conspiracy that attracted other dissidents. When they could not accomplish their goal of deposing Piero, they allegedly formed a plan to murder him in a plot frustrated by an informant. Diotisalvi and his family went into exile, first in Venice and then Ferrara. He died in Rome in 1482, and is buried in the Santa Maria Sopra Minerva church, just steps away from the Pantheon; his crypt is on display by the door.

The transhistorical slandering of Diotisalvi Neroni is relevant to our story only as an aside. Contemporary historians are not content, as Ten Hove was in his 1797 *Memoirs of the House of Medici,* to say that Diotisalvi Neroni joined "ambition to a great meanness of soul." They point out that a confession signed by his brother Francesco, obtained only through "light torture," does not mention a murder plot, and they balk at calling this a conspiracy (Rubenstein, pp. 373–387). Our goal was to find out if there was a connection between this 15th century Florentine family and my mother's family.

In 2007, we rented an off-season apartment in Porto d'Ascoli, just a block from the beach. We knew that even if we could not find what we were seeking, the bowls of *brodetto* (seafood stew) at a table looking across the Adriatic would make it all worthwhile. The proximity to the coastal super highway would allow for quicker trips up to northern Le Marche and south into Abruzzo. Above all, it would be easy to explore nearby seaside spots like San Benedetto del Tronto and Grottammare, as well as inland towns such as Ripatransone, Acquaviva, and Monteprandone, without the forty-minute trek from Montegallo (plus our one-hour stop in Ascoli for a cappuccino on the Piazza del Popolo).

The old Via Salaria sets off from Ascoli on the northern bank of the Tronto River, the longtime border between northern and southern Italy. The *autostrada* on the Abruzzo side is quicker, but the old Salaria is like something out of an early Fellini film, lined with canopied plane trees. Up at the top of the olive tree and grapevine covered slopes, villas from another era signify the wealth and prosperity of bygone times. Modern development has cost the Via Salaria much of its elan—worst of all is the industrial development on the Tronto flood plain—but it is still possible to see, with a little imagination, what it once was.

We did not choose this coastal area blindly. There were still phone books then, and those we consulted from this area had Neronis listed. At a town curiously called Centobucchi (Hundred Holes), about 4 km/2.5 mi inland from Porto D'Ascoli, the Neroni-Cancelli family had a villa with the top story serving as drying rooms for tobacco. Zia Iva said she went to school with a Neroni from Spinetoli, halfway between Ascoli and Porto d'Ascoli. We also knew that the old upper town of San Benedetto has a Via dei Neroni and a Palazzo Neroni, with a plaque commemorating Garibaldi's overnight stay. A previous excursion to nearby Ripatransone had revealed a "Bianca Neroni" on a mailbox—the Italian version of my mother's name. Most important for us was the tape my brother had made (no longer in existence), in which Nonna Lia told him the story of Decenzio Neroni and the relatives on the coast. On the tape, she also said that every Christmas a box of citrus would arrive in Abetito, a gift from family in Grottammare.

Offida, a hilltown about 8 km/5 mi north of the Salaria and maybe 16 km/10 mi inland, is dominated by the Chiesa Santa Maria della Roccia, built over an older church and set on a dramatic promontory. During WWII, a bomb fell in the churchyard but did not explode, indicating divine intervention according to local believers. My cousins, the sisters Luana and Maria Grazia Lappa, live nearby. Luana is an expert on local art and architecture and we were lucky to have her show us many local gems. Maria Grazia is a journalist for the newspaper Il Resto del Carlino and teaches politics at the University of Macerata. They had heard something of Decenzio from their grandfather Fabio, a first cousin of my mother and my Uncle Albert's pal. Their version was a little different—they had not heard the part about his mother leaving him with relatives. But we all wondered what had propelled him to Abetito. Luana thought he may have been avoiding being pressed into military service, as young men and boys often were in the time of the Napoleonic occupation. We decided that Ripatransone was a good place to start our investigation; Maria Grazia agreed to accompany us to town offices there.

Ripatransone is a short drive northeast of Offida with a lovely panorama of vineyards, farmlands, and the belltowers of walled hill towns near and distant. No Saracens coming from the coast would have had an easy time capturing these fortresses. The old town of Ripatransone is not much more than a main street with piazzas and a few side streets, one of which claims to be the narrowest in Italy. Locals also claim that the *calanchi* here are the most striking to be seen in the area, but the competition is stiff.

We arrived at Ripatransone to find the archive closed but, hoping to make the most of the situation, we went into the tourist office for information about the Neroni family. The older gentleman in charge was delighted to help us out. He knew Padre Giuseppe Santarelli, author of the book we had translated, and of course he was familiar with the Neronis. He took us upstairs and showed us a picture of hometown opera singer Count Luciano Neroni (1909–1951), a basso profondo. Luciano Neroni died young, but not before making his mark in the opera world by singing with stars like Maria Callas and local tenor Beniamino Gigli, to name a couple. Despite two significant interruptions in his career, one for military service in Sicily and the other due to WWII and its aftermath, had he lived he would have appeared at the Met in New York, which had already offered him a contract. The tiny Teatro Luigi Mercantini opera house is across the street; performing here, amidst its ornate gilded decorations, must have felt very intimate compared to the more cavernous theaters in larger cities.

Back downstairs, our guide brought out a book from the back office that got us excited, *Le Famiglie Nobili Ripani / The Noble Families of Ripatransone*, by Giuseppe Boccabianca—the same last name as Luciano Neroni's mother. Page 43 begins a section entitled, "Neroni." Boccabianca says nothing with certainty but supports the idea that the Ripatransone Neronis, a family in exile, are likely connected with Diotisalvi. The Neronis first came into this region under the protection and in the service of the Duke of Atri, in northern Abruzzo. Further, he records a Simone Neroni, probably a grandson or nephew of Diotisalvi, who in 1553 was the *castellan* of the castle at Aquaviva Picena, 8 km/5 mi southeast of Ripatransone. A certain Tomasso from Acquaviva was the first Neroni in Ripatransone. He married a Ripane woman who was the last of her line, so Tomasso came to live with her family and manage her affairs.

With so much information but nothing definitive about Decenzio, we knew we had to visit Acquaviva Picena. We went the next morning and admired its castle, but the visit turned out to be a bust. First, Sciabalone had torched the archives, and then during the French occupation of the area, many town and church offices were destroyed. We were hoping to find a church archivist to tell us if anything pertinent had been spared, but to no avail.

Disappointed but not defeated, we spent the rest of the day walking the seaside promenade, the *lungomare* of San Benedetto del Tronto, out the long curving jetty with its sculpture dedicated to Jonathan Livingston Seagull, and admiring the Art Nouveau villas set among the reinforced concrete hotels and apartments. That night, we decided to drive the forty minutes back up to the mountains—we never could stand to stay away for long.

We had already asked Don Vincenzo, the longtime parish priest of Abetito and other villages of Montegallo, for help. He brought us copies of the local church archives, but only from the 20th century, nothing we did not already know. On a rainy afternoon we were having a glass of wine at the Bar Babbalò in Balzo with Francesco Eleuteri, an actor, playwright, and novelist. We translated and published his crime novel, *The Blood of the Sibillini*, and try to attend his one-man shows whenever we can. He grew up in Rome but his family is from Montegallo, and he and his mother moved back here some time ago. We told him what we were up to and he suggested we consult Don Elio Navighari, the other parish priest serving Montegallo, who knew a lot about local heraldic traditions.

"I know Don Vincenzo," Don Elio said. "Ask him to let you see the archives for yourselves." So we did. One day, while Don Vincenzo performed Mass for the elderly ladies in the San Savino church of Uscerno (the village at the bottom of the hill from Abetito), we were in the back room poring over the tattered ledgers and notebooks recording births, deaths, and marriages written in a very even and legible priest's hand—in almost impenetrable Latin.

It did not take long to find what we were looking for, the record of Decenzio's marriage to Maria Perotti. (Several Perotti families still live in Abetito.) When mass was over, Don Vincenzo came back and very generously helped us with the Latin. Parish priests are busy people!

Decenzio was from Monteprandone, about 36 km/22 mi from Abetito. His father's name was Pietro. Traditionally, names would skip a generation, so it made sense that Decenzio's son was also named Pietro. *"Che cazzo di nome e questo Decenzio?* What the f**k kind of name is Decenzio?" asked our friend Emilio, who ran a grocery store in Balzo, when we were discussing our quest. Not a common name to be sure. Decenzio was a Christian martyr and saint who together with his brother Germano was killed on October 28, 320, in Pesaro, on the northern edge of Piceno. The basilica there is dedicated

Monteprandone

to the two of them and was probably constructed on the place they were martyred; their sarcophagi are now preserved in a local church museum.

Decenzio and Maria were married in 1835 with a special permission from the church because they were distant relatives (third or fourth cousins); the document said that he had been living in Abetito for ten years. We also found his death record. He died in 1889 at age 78; therefore, he was born in 1811, and had come to Abetito in 1825 at age fourteen. The church permission provided a tantalizing clue as to why he had chosen this particular place.

We were already well aware of Monteprandone. One of our favorite wine cantinas, Il Conte, is there, where a pleasant young woman always welcomes us back. Therefore, a trip to stately Monteprandone was never a loss, but it took us a few visits over several years to find archivist Saturnino (Nino) Loggi, a writer and local historian. He went into the church's archive and brought back a tremendous treasure trove of information. Decenzio was born December 3, 1811. His father Pietro Neroni was born May 31, 1782, to a Nicola Neroni whose father, also named Pietro Neroni, was from Acquaviva—an obvious link to the Acquaviva branch of the Neroni family. Crivellucci, in his 1893 book about Acquaviva, *Una comune delle Marche nel 1798–1799*, lists a Nicola Neroni on the town council of Acquaviva.

Interestingly, the town of Acquaviva was named for the Acquaviva family, a southern Italian noble family who were also the Dukes of Atri. Were the dukes somehow related to the presence of the Neroni family in Acquaviva? Possibly? Probably? At any rate, the Acquaviva family sold the town to Fermo in 1438 as an outpost against Ascoli, twenty-eight years before the Neroni Conspiracy of 1466.

But for us, the best part of Loggi's report was that Decenzio's mother was from Abetito di Montegallo, and her name was Maria Nicola Salvucci, another family name still present in Abetito. We had already shared many glasses of wine with our friend Alessia Salvucci. Now we understood why Decenzio showed up in an obscure mountain village; he probably already knew relatives there, or was at least aware of a family connection.

There are no death records for Pietro Neroni or Maria Salvucci in Monteprandone. All we know about them is through family legend. Fairy tales depicting Maria as a beautiful peasant girl from the mountains and Pietro as a coastal nobleman, who met through his relatives or economic interests he had in Montegallo, are unverifiable fantasies. Their fate is lost to us in the vortex of history. But we do know some of their dates, which place them squarely in the era of the Napoleonic invasions. Pietro was fourteen when Napoleon entered Italy in 1796.

A previously unknown fact came to light with Loggi's information. Apparently, Decenzio had a little brother—another Pietro—born on May 28, 1814, which indicates that his father Pietro was still alive around nine months previously, in September 1813. Once we had a more concrete idea of Pietro the elder's dates, we wondered if he was killed at the battle of Tolentino (May 1815). Although we found no mention of him in relation to that battle, we came across interesting facts about his Ripatransone cousins. During the Napoleonic Era, when the Department of the Tronto was created, Giuseppe Neroni-Cancelli had served as captain of the National Guard, mayor of San Benedetto, and vice prefect of San Ginesio (near Tolentino). After Murat was defeated by the Austrian general Bianchi, the Austrians kept Giuseppe Neroni-Cancelli as vice commissioner of Tolentino. When the edict of July 1816 resurrected the Papal States, he turned down the governorship of San Ginesio in order to return to San Benedetto. Giuseppe's brother, Emidio Neroni, died in the retreat of Napoleon's army from Moscow. Two letters that he wrote to their father, Pietro Paolo Neroni, are in the Risorgimento museum at Macerata. Their father, also of Ripatransone, was eulogized in a poem by G. Gioachino Belli (1791–1863), *In Morte del Cavaliere Pietro Paolo Neroni.* Nino Loggi generously gave us a tall stack of books he had written about the area, and an eight-volume boxed set of *Memorie Storiche di Monteprandone,* by Don Giuseppe Caselli (1937).

It was heartening to learn as much as we did about Decenzio, given the historical cataclysm he lived through. But after reading Margaret Collier's 1886 *Our Home by the Adriatic,* we realized that one of the larger stories was the decline of the nobility, a centuries-long process in its death throes. Margaret Collier—aka Madame Galletti di Cadilhac—was herself a British noblewoman, who married an Italian nobleman, Arturo Antonio Gaetano Maria Galletti di Cadilhac. She was the grandmother of Massimo "Max" Salvadori and his sister, Joyce Lussu, two important Marchigiani scholars and writers. The book recounts her experiences setting up house near Porto San Giorgio in Le Marche and deserves reading by anyone interested in the region. She describes the poor conditions there in the late 1800s. "It is in these remote villages that the specimens of decayed nobility... are mostly to be found—people bearing grand names and retaining considerable pride in their ancient lineage, whom generations of idleness and unthriftiness have reduced to extreme poverty" (Collier, p. 98). Collier scorns one count, a housepainter, as having scarcely better manners than the peasants. (If you decide to read Margaret Collier's book, do not let her upper-class British attitudes discourage you. Many of our contemporaries have similar views, but know how to keep them under wraps.)

This led us to think about our own count and great-grandfather, stone mason Pietro Neroni, ancestor of so many Italian and American cousins; he was no slacker. And we wondered about the fate of his father, the original Decenzio. Were the relatives who so cruelly demoted him to servant themselves already decayed nobility? The fact is, the post Napoleonic economy in Le Marche was a disaster, and perhaps played no small role in his widowed mother's fleeing with a French soldier... if that is what really happened. We will probably never know, but it would make a great historical novel.

Our research brought to light another strong tradition—the local histories written by the above-mentioned parish priests and hometown scholars. Don Vincenzo di Vincenzo wrote a booklet about the history of the Chiesa San Savino (1568) of Uscerno—where he had let us rummage through the archives—and the rectory (1569) across the piazza. We had poked around this now empty building, admiring the stone work and inscriptions. The imposing house attached to it was used briefly in 1943 as headquarters by the retreating Germans as they fought the partisans sheltered in the surrounding mountains. He includes a description of the nearby Chiesa Madonna del Carmine (1600), with a photo of its newer tower that is inscribed "S.M. 1903 P. N." (Pietro Neroni). In a second booklet (both co-authored with Giuliano Ghighi), he recounts the story of Domenico Orazi, a 19-year-old soldier from Abetito who died of pneumonia in a Bergamo hospital during WWI. Domenico's pure spirit touched the heart of the military chaplain attending him, the priest Don Angelo Roncalli, who became Pope John XXIII. Don Vincenzo was instrumental in having the boy's remains brought home to the Abetito cemetery in 1994. Our interest here is that Domenico Orazi was a cousin of my grandmother. Nonna Lia always said her family did not leave Italy because they were poor, like the Neronis, but because her father wanted to get away from his older brother, maybe Domenico's father... but that is a whole other story—or novel.

One of our first exposures to the history of the region was *Leggende dei Monte Sibillini* by Father Giuseppe Santarelli. The director of the Santa Casa of Loreto, about which he has also written extensively, Santarelli grew up in Monte Giberto, between the Aso and Tenna river valleys, with a view of the Sibillini mountains. Another specific source was *Memorie di Montegallo* (1903), by the local priest Arcangelo Rossi Brunori. We had seen mentions of it but had not been able to locate a copy, when someone told us that a relative of the author lived nearby and had a copy we could look at. A meeting was set up. At the appointed hour we knocked on the door. To everyone's delighted surprise, the man who opened it was someone we had chatted with over the years at the Bar Gallo dei Sibillini in Balzo, where he played cards with friends every evening.

And finally, the Cappelli family has been a major resource. Mariolina Massignani and her husband Carlo Cappelli, their son Furio, daughter Flavia and her husband Giuseppe Vico, have written extensively about many aspects of local history. Their small family press, *Lamusa*, has published a series of highly focused booklets. Over the years, we have had many enjoyable conversations with all of them. We have attended their lectures and shopped at the bookstore they ran for a while in Ascoli. Furio has his own long list of publications; he is an expert on medieval art and architecture in Picenum, tracking down every church, every crypt. In *Beni Ambientali Beni Architettonici* (p. 209), he describes the Casone Bonelli di Corbara, a massive stone fortress/house built in the late 1500s. A photo shows the carved inscription above one window, which reads *"Mensurata Durant*/Measured Things Last." We had explored this isolated, abandoned building in the valley below Abetito many times over the years, after Zia Iva told us that Pietro Neroni had worked on it. Unfortunately, the recent earthquakes reduced it to a pile of blocks surrounded by sheep. At least we always have Furio's documentation of it and of so many other historic art treasures.

When we first imagined this book, our aim was to produce something compact and readable like the works published by *Lamusa*—but the project got out of hand. To quote another inscription from the Casone Bonelli, *"Non Senza Fatiga*/Not Without Effort."

Abandoned Mill near Santa Maria in Lapide, Montegallo

𝕠𝕞𝕨𝕠 15 𝕠𝕞𝕨𝕠

La Terra Trema

On August 24, 2016, a 6.1 temblor struck central Italy; 299 people died, 388 were injured. Amatrice was practically levelled, and at Arquata del Tronto, little more than Regina Giovanna II's castle remained standing. The devastation spread over 3,500 square miles, stretching from Fabriano to L'Aquila and from Rieti to Ascoli Piceno. Castelluccio and towns to its north suffered severe damage.

On October 26, there was a 5.9 shock, and four days later on October 30, a 6.5 shock accompanied by twenty aftershocks greater than 4. On January 18, 2017, there was a 5.5 and a 5.4 coupled with eleven aftershocks greater than 4. At the same time, the region was hit with a record-breaking snowfall of more than 2.5 m/8 ft. The world heard about dramatic rescues at the ski resort of Rigopiano in Abruzzo, where an avalanche on Gran Sasso killed twenty-nine. Friends on Colle San Marco told us about opening their front door to escape and having to dig a tunnel through a wall of snow to reach the road. The sclerotic bureaucracies failed to accomplish the most obvious tasks, such as building temporary shelters for livestock; thousands of cattle and sheep died in the cold. The ancient Santa Maria in Pantano church, which was badly damaged in August, was not shored up and collapsed in the subsequent quakes, taking with it what was left of Bonfini's frescoes of the Sibyls.

Santa Maria in Pantano

Santa Maria in Pantano after the 2016–17 earthquakes

In the year after the initial shocks, there were more than 12,000 aftershocks over 2, and 70 over 4. "It was like we were in a war," Stefano Valentini told us. From his window in Balzo di Montegallo, he had watched 400-year-old buildings shaking and swaying, their roofs touching over the narrow main street. He is a third-generation chef who grew up in Rome, where his cousins have a restaurant near the Pantheon, but his family is originally from Amatrice. His mother was at home there on August 24 and suffered serious leg injuries; at least 230 people out of the town's population of 1,200 were killed. This terrible tragedy was covered by major media outlets, but it is only part of the story. As Stefano's wife Antonella Rovedi said, "What's worse than the earthquakes is the government. They don't know how to manage the situation, and they don't have the will to make this area rise again." Antonella grew up in Montegallo; Zia Iva Neroni was her second grade teacher. The couple and their teenage son are among the thousands of *terremotati*, people displaced from their homes by this natural disaster. They run the local restaurant "Lo Spuntino," formerly housed on the main terrace of Balzo, now open in a modular unit in the *cittadella*, the temporary town center set up on the soccer field below.

Cousin Gianna described seeing the earth rippling like the ocean, Mt. Vettore seeming to rise up like a cresting wave. "All day and all night, too, it was rumble, rumble," Gianna said, shaking her hands above her head. Fortunately, after the August tremors her extended family of thirteen had already moved into tents and no one was hurt. Unfortunately, their two-family stone house was declared uninhabitable because of narrow cracks running from corner to corner, inside and out. Gianna's father Gino had rebuilt the house in the 1970s. At the time, he was required to make the roof out of reinforced concrete to withstand possible earthquakes; now they say its weight has compromised the walls. Unlike some nearby villages, nothing collapsed in Abetito—although several houses require extensive work before they are habitable, and the church is shuttered in scaffolding. Local lore states that long ago Abetito was further uphill on Mt. Ceresa, but after a severe earthquake its inhabitants moved down to its current location, where the ground is more solid. The patchwork of damage and destruction suffered by the hilltowns and mountain villages followed a geological rationale of fault lines that were not necessarily visible to the eye. Ascoli Piceno, on its prow of rock, was relatively unscathed.

"The problem is just too big," Emilio Rossi, retired math teacher, one-time candidate for mayor, and local grocer told us. Ten years is the number we keep hearing of how long rebuilding will take. When we asked Gianna's husband Sergio where that number came from, he said it is based on what happened after the 2009 earthquake in L'Aquila, 6.3, 300 dead. (We had arrived in Balzo the next day and were woken by a sudden boom in the middle of the night, an aftershock that sounded like someone had set off a bomb nearby.) Berlusconi promised a quick turnaround but the work remains unfinished. In L'Aquila, 75,000 buildings were affected. This time there are 208,000 that have to be examined and classified according to level of damages.

The earthquakes of 2016–2017 were among the many historical seismic events to affect Piceno. Amatrice was destroyed in 1639 by a 6.2 earthquake with hundreds dead. Afterwards, the earth continued to shake for two years. A series of quakes followed, including the years 1672, 1703, 1859, and 1883. The Colfiorito/Asissi quake of 1997, also felt here, attracted worldwide attention because of damage done to art works in the Basilica of St. Francis in Assisi.

Years ago, we described the drive above Arquata like this:

Behind the Hotel Regina Giovanna, the road turns right and begins the jagged climb into the Sibillini Mountains. The timid traveler says, "I hope there's not much more of this," but there is; curve after curve, looking down on the red tile roofs of the villages, dwarfed by the open mountain slopes. White splashes of wild cherry trees bloom against the gray cliffs. In Piedilama, where brand-new additions are being built onto centuries-old houses, the people turn warily to see who is in the car creeping along their street. In Pretare, the Bar Vettore and the Bar Sibilla pay homage to the nearby mountain peaks; the village is celebrated as a place where the fairies from the Grotto of the Sibyl came down to dance with the local boys, running back up the mountain on their "feet which clattered like goat's hooves" before dawn could catch them. The sculptor Anthony Caponi wrote a poetic memoir, *Voice from the Mountains,* describing his childhood in Pretare and his return there as an American soldier during WWII:

> "Monte Vettore bore the village on its lap
> Like a mother sitting with parted legs
> Holds her baby in the hollow of her skirt" (p. 5).

The fortress tower of Arquata, swathed in protective scaffolding, still watches over the Via Salaria, but the stone houses that once clung to the cliffs below it are largely gone. Pretare and Piedilama lie in ruins, the shells of a couple of churches propped up amidst piles of rubble. The road was closed for two years until the shattered houses lining it could be cleared away. The void left behind is devastating. Modular housing has been set up in a field nearby, including a space where our distant cousin Vittoria and her husband have reopened the cafe they used to run in Piedilama. On that August 24, the villages were packed with people, many of them families returning to their ancestral homes for summer vacation. Vittoria's little girl was spending the night with an aunt in Pescara del Tronto, perched above the Via Salaria, but she called her parents complaining that she wanted to come home. Her father went and picked her up. At 3:36 am the first earthquake ripped through the unstable ground underneath Pescara del Tronto, sending the entire village down the steep hillside, killing fifty people including the aunt. Massive concrete barriers now edge the Via Salaria to hold back the debris.

The drive to Castelluccio di Norcia, at 1,452 m (almost a mile) the highest settlement in the Apennines, is still a sight to behold. Tumbled-down ruins of stone buildings from previous centuries sit in fields of rocks. In the spring, these slopes are carpeted with primroses and violets, windflowers and cyclamen, intensely scented forget-me-nots, wild orchids, gentian, and a multitude of wildflowers that are smaller, stranger, and rarer the higher you go. When you round Mt. Vettore at Forca di Presta, the breathtaking openness of the Piano Grande is now marred by the destruction wreaked on Castelluccio, where only a few buildings survived. And, the Path of the Fairies, which the sprites ran down to dance with the local boys, is now recognized as one of a parade of faults up and down the Sibillini to Gran Sasso and beyond.

Social Fault Lines

Terra Picena had already experienced a roller coaster of disasters and rebirths long before the recent earthquakes. Our chapter's title, *"La Terra Trema* / The Earth Trembles," refers not just to earthquakes, but to other major upheavals of the last century. Luchino Visconti's film of the same name portrays the doomed struggles of Sicilian fishermen trying to break free from an oppressive system; "the mythical dimensions of the fishermen's daily struggle to survive" (Bondanella, *Italian Cinema: From Neorealism to the Present*, p. 71). Visconti, a Roman aristocrat who aided fugitive POWs and partisans during WWII, was rounded up after the Ardeatine Caves massacre of 1944 and sentenced to death. Once he escaped, the Americans had him film the trial and execution of the man who had interrogated him in prison.

The Unification of Italy, which ruptured so many traditional social connections, set off a massive wave of emigration. One third of the country's population left, mostly from the south. Between 1880 and 1924, more than four-and-a-half million Italians had emigrated to the US, 80 percent of them from the *mezzogiorno*/southern Italy. Interestingly, more than half of them eventually returned to Italy (Mangione and Morreale, *La Storia*, pp. 32–33, 159). Le Marche was the fourth most affected region after Calabria, Abruzzo, and Sicily. Survival was difficult in these predominantly agricultural areas; government policy was encouraging the industrial revolution to take hold in the favored north. Single men, followed by their families, went to North and South America, Canada, and Australia, emptying out many Italian villages. In Kenosha, Wisconsin, there is a neighborhood known as "Little Montegallo," where immigrants from our area settled. When Nathan's grandparents went to America, more than 5,000 people lived in Montegallo; in 2016, there were fewer than 600 year-round residents—and this was before the earthquakes. Between the turn of the century and 1914, often more than 200,000 Italians a year were entering the States. However, in 1917 the US Congress passed a bill restricting immigration from eastern and southern European countries. The xenophobic Immigration Act of 1924 set a yearly quota of fewer than 6,000 Italians, giving the English and other northern Europeans preference over the so-called "inferior races"—Slavs, Russians, Poles, Greeks, and Italians (*La Storia*, pp. 315–316).

The frontline of WWI was well to the north of Le Marche, though Ancona was bombed in 1915 by the Austro-Hungarian navy, damaging the Duomo di San Ciriaco. The nearby ports of Senigallia and Potenza Picena were also targeted. But Galanti points out that the infantry was overwhelmingly made up of central and southern Italians—one-time "brigands"—fighting in the Alps with northerners. For the first time, a united Italian army repelled foreign invaders (Galanti, *Dagli Sciaboloni ai Piccioni*, p. 349). Every little town has its monument to their war dead. Corridonia, near Macerata, has more than that. Once called Pausula, in 1931 Mussolini renamed it in honor of his socialist friend Filippo Corridoni, who was killed in battle above Trieste in 1915. A statue depicting the moment the Austrian bullets hit the local hero stands in the center of a piazza, ringed by stark white Fascist era buildings.

The political and economic turmoil that followed the "War to End All Wars" enabled the rise of the Fascist party. Benito Mussolini was born in 1883 in Predappio, a village near Forli-Cesena just north of the border between Le Marche and Emilia-Romagna. Early in his career, he was an ardent Socialist, and appointed editor of the Socialist newspaper *Avanti* in 1912. As such, he was against Italian involvement in WWI, but he changed his mind and was expelled from the party. While he had once moved to Switzerland to evade the draft, he now enlisted and was injured in battle. After the war, he gained power as a charismatic rabble-rouser, with a message of returning to the glory days of the Roman Empire. His Fascists battled the Socialists and Communists in the streets, with violence and the financial support of classes threatened by the left-wing parties. In 1921, Mussolini was voted into Parliament. In 1922, as hordes of his Blackshirts threatened a March on Rome to combat a general strike, King Vittorio Emanuele III appointed him Prime Minister. By the end of 1925, the growing Fascist Party had rewritten the laws, making Mussolini, as head of the government, answerable to no one but the King.

Il Duce set out to remake Italy according to his ideas, with the state controlling all aspects of citizens' lives. Mayors and other local officials were replaced with Fascist functionaries, political opponents were banned, tortured, and killed. New emigration rules made it almost impossible to leave the country legally. Mussolini, however, had widespread support, in part because of his much publicized programs of public works. Propaganda proclaimed that housing and highways had been built, swamps were drained, "the trains ran on time." In Montegallo, people still cite an example of this. In the winter of 1934, an avalanche destroyed Casale, a mountain village on the slopes below Mt. Vettore. Eight villagers were killed; the rest survived because they were safely sheltered in their church (built in 1580) while attending the funeral of a little girl who died the night before. Two descendants of the "brigand" Capponi family were outside shoveling snow off the road and were swept away; their gristmill was severely damaged. The government quickly rebuilt Casale Nuovo at a nearby, better protected location. Today this story is retold as a bitter comment on the slow pace of post-earthquake reconstruction.

Mussolini's expansion into Abyssinia and Albania, and his involvement on the side of Franco in the Spanish Civil War, primarily affected Le Marche in terms of the draft. But in 1936, he signed the Axis Pact with Hitler, which led in 1938 to the antisemitic National Racial Code.

Jewish Communities in Le Marche

Jews have a long history in Le Marche (Silvia Agnoletti, *"Gli insediamenti ebraici nella Marca altomedievale/*Jewish Settlements in Medieval Le Marche," pp. 231–250). Legend has it that St. Ciriaco, the patron saint of Ancona, was a Jew who converted to Christianity after he helped Constantine the Great's mother, Helena, locate the True Cross during her tour of the Holy Land 326–328. His remains were brought to Ancona in 418 and can still be seen in the Duomo. Jewish inhabitants of Ancona are mentioned before 900, and in 1300 the city was second only to Rome in the size of its Jewish population. The Adriatic ports, which were connected with Ragusa/Dubrovnik, the Ottoman Empire, the Mediterranean, and the Holy Land, were obvious sites for merchants, but by the end of the 1200s there were also numerous Jewish communities documented in many inland cities and hilltowns. Ascoli Piceno first records a Jewish presence in 1297. For the most part, Jews were confined to the business of moneylending, a necessary service which Christians were forbidden to perform. In some places they were also involved in other trades, dealing in fabrics (especially silk), wine, olives, and foodstuffs. Medical doctors were often Jewish. In the Papal States, their treatment depended much on the whims of the local nobility and on who was pope. For example, in 1569, Pope Pio V expelled the Jews from every city under his rule except for Rome, Ancona, and Avignon. The entire community in Ascoli Piceno moved to Pesaro, at that time part of the Duchy of Urbino, because their rabbi was from there. In some places, Jews were subject to various restrictions, segregated in ghettos, and required to display identifying markers (usually yellow) on their clothing and properties; in other places, they were more integrated into the local social and economic scene. The early Jews were primarily from the Levant, later joined by Ashkenazi Jews expelled from Germany, and then Spanish and Portugese refugees fleeing forced conversion to Christianity during the Inquisition. Many of these last, disparagingly called *marrani*, settled in Ancona where twenty-five were burned at the stake for heresy in 1556.

In the 1400s, a Christian form of moneylending called the Monti di Pietà was established. Some key figures in this movement were Marchigiani: Beato Marco da Montegallo, born in Fonditore; S. Giacomo della Marca of Monteprandone; Frate Domenico da Leonessa (either he or his parents were from San Severino Marche). These Franciscan brothers went from town to town preaching the advantages of this nonprofit Catholic credit organization, often in antisemitic terms. The idea was to preempt the Jewish pawnbrokers and travelling Lombard moneylenders, who charged high interest rates. Donations to the church would be loaned out at low or zero interest; borrowers pawned valuable objects as security. Many towns responded by setting up a local Monti di Pietà; Ascoli Piceno's was founded in 1458. But the donations were not always enough to meet the demand for loans, and sometimes even the church had to borrow from the Jewish bankers.

When Napoleon invaded, his troops destroyed the ghetto walls in every city they occupied, but when the French left, the segregated quarters were re-established. In 1859, the Savoy king proclaimed the emancipation of the Jews. With the Unification of Italy, the secular government did away with restrictions on Jews, who for all intents and purposes now became simply Italian citizens. The Papal State, which had limited Rome's Jews to dealing in second-hand clothes, followed suit in 1870. In his book, *Benevolence and Betrayal*, Alexander Stille writes "Italian Fascism was in power for sixteen years before it turned anti-Semitic in 1938. Until then, Jews were as likely to be members of the Fascist Party as were other conservative-minded Italians" (p. 12). Mussolini, who once had a Jewish mistress, scorned Hitler's racist obsessions—and Italy's Jews were largely unprepared for what was to come.

During WWI, a prisoner-of-war camp had been established at Servigliano in the Tenna River valley. (The original hilltop town had suffered so many landslides, capped by earthquakes in 1747 and 1751, that in 1771 Pope Clemente XIV had it rebuilt on the plains below.) In the beginning, the camp held Austrian POWs, but with the rise of Fascism, Mussolini's political opponents were imprisoned there. After 1938, it also served as a holding pen for Jews who were being sent to their deaths in German concentration camps. The Villa Morpurgo sits in the center of San Benedetto del Tronto, a lovely Art Nouveau building with an impressive wisteria arching over the entrance to an art gallery. Its original owner was Oscar Morpurgo, a Jewish businessman born in Ancona and deported to Auschwitz, where he died in 1943. Giorgio Fuà (1919–2000), also Jewish and from Ancona, as a college student fled the Italian racial laws for a safe haven in Switzerland. After the war he returned home, making a career as an economist. It was he who originated the economic model *"modello marchigiano,"* as well as founding the economics department at the Università Politecnica delle Marche in Ancona.

The Devastation of World War II

The war had been taking place far away from Le Marche, but everything changed in the summer of 1943. The Allies invaded Sicily and the King dismissed Mussolini on July 25. *Il Duce* was arrested and imprisoned in a hotel on the Campo Imperatore in the mountains of Abruzzo. A window of opportunity opened, later called the Forty-five Days: political prisoners were released and Fascist officials were overthrown. However, this gave the Germans time to move substantial forces into Italy. On September 8, the new government of Prime Minister Badoglio and King Vittorio Emanuele III announced an armistice with the Allies and immediately fled to their headquarters in Brindisi, leaving the population to fend for themselves. British enmity towards the Italians, personified in British Foreign Secretary Anthony Eden, had thwarted moves to prevent the German occupation. The Brenner Pass was not bombed, and Eisenhower abandoned plans to land north of Rome. The war would be fought up the boot of Italy. On September 9, the Allies landed in Salerno and the Germans seized Rome, splitting the peninsula at the level of Naples. On September 11, German paratroopers snatched Mussolini away from Gran Sasso and set him up as head of a Fascist state, the Republic of Salò, in northern Italy. The Italian army disintegrated without clear orders from above. Most troops headed for home, but the Germans captured and disarmed many others. More than a half million were sent to German labor camps. Italian soldiers stationed on the Greek island of Cephalonia refused to surrender; of 10,000 men, 9,600 were killed. In the zones controlled by the Republic of Salò, the Jews were rounded up and deported to extermination camps. The Nazis and their Fascist collaborators set about taking full control.

On the morning of September 12, 1943, the German troops entered Ascoli Piceno. As he describes in *Bandenkrieg nel Piceno/Guerilla Warfare in Piceno*, historian and partisan Secondo Balena was in the Piazza Roma when the enemy, in full battle gear and armed to the teeth, rolled into the city on their way to the central Umberto I barracks. The Italian soldiers there fought them off, with losses on both sides. Under fire from townspeople, the German jeeps drove on. A larger convoy, on the Piceno-Aprutina road to Teramo, was ambushed by partisans in front of the secondary barracks on Via Erasmo Mari. The recruits stationed there launched an attack, bombing the enemy trucks and blocking the road at a railway overpass. The Germans retreated towards the seacoast, leaving behind about one hundred prisoners in the hands of the Italians. That evening they returned under a white flag and negotiated an exchange of prisoners and the burial of the dead. Ascoli claims to be the only city in Italy where the Germans were forced into a truce of this sort. For the time being, Ascoli remained a *città libera*, a free city.

Between September 13 and 17, the capitals of all four provinces in Le Marche were occupied by the Germans. The Italian military disbanded, adding to the numbers of young men taking refuge in the surrounding mountains. Civilians had not been supplied with arms to defend themselves or their country. Their main recourse, as happened in Ascoli, was to raid the abandoned army posts and make off with as much weaponry as they could. It was up to the partisans to fight the Germans. They were a mixed lot, including: long-time opponents of the Fascists like the Communists; former Fascists who did not want to fight for the Republic of Salò or to be sent to Germany; young draft dodgers of every stripe; and a raft of escaped POWs and/or deserters from every army fighting in Italy. Like the brigands before them, they hid out in the labyrinthine mountains and relied on the support of the locals. Zia Costanza told us how she and other women of Abetito took food to a covey of English soldiers hidden in caves on the slopes of Mt. Ceresa. In a house in the village, there is a hiding place in the ceiling where villagers concealed the prosciuttos, salamis, and cheeses from German confiscation.

The first open battle between the Germans and the partisans took place at Bosco Martese on September 25. Around a thousand men had gathered in this remote area in the Monti della Laga; antifascists from Abruzzo, military officers, students, and Anglo-American and Slav ex-prisoners. That morning the Germans had taken over Teramo, to the east, and now sought to stamp out any resistance. Although poorly armed, the partisans were able to stop the enemy trucks and force their retreat back to Teramo. The Germans returned early the next morning to bombard the area, but the guerilla fighters had already melted away towards the Valle Castellana and Aquasanta. The Germans massacred a number of civilians in reprisal.

In Ascoli, after the battles at the barracks, the anti-Fascist rebels had taken refuge on the 694 m/ 2,277 ft Colle San Marco, which overlooks the city and the Via Salaria and backs up on the Monte dei Fiori. (Colle San Marco has a long history as a haven for monks and hermits, including the 13th century Eremo San Marco hermitage carved into the cliff face.) Around 250 men, with a core of fifty seasoned

Caciara-Stone Shepherd's Hut

fighters, came and went, searching for food, supplies, and weapons, helped by their families, citizens of Ascoli, and farmers and shepherds around them. Poorly armed and poorly organized, they hoped to hold out until the Allies got there. As requested by the partisans of Bosco Martese, a small band of them destroyed the bridge over the Castellano River at nearby Castel Trosino, with the aim of blocking a German advance.

The partisans expected to be attacked from Ascoli, especially after they exchanged fire with an enemy convoy near Porta Cartara. But the highly seasoned Nazi troops, with information provided by Fascist spies, had completely encircled Colle San Marco. At dawn on October 3, they pounced. As mortar fire rained down on their encampment, the rebels had little choice but to escape as best they could. An earthquake tremor at mid-morning paused the battle but did not stop it. The *Sentiero della Memoria*, a hiking trail, retraces the tragic events of the day. Here, the Germans burned down the house where they found and killed a young man. Here is the *caciara*, an archaic stone shepherd's hut, where three partisans fought to the death to give the rest of their band time to get away. Further along, there is a spur where others set up a machine gun to mow down the advancing enemy, and then another larger *caciara* where partisans and English POWs took cover. Many men were able to escape, but more than thirty died on Colle San Marco, and many more were taken prisoner. Seven prisoners were forced to carry German supplies for three days and nights before they were killed. Others were taken to Forte Malatesta, where the Germans executed sixteen and sent the rest to concentration camps. On one of our visits, cousin Sergio took us to the annual memorial on San Marco, where his uncle is among the honored dead. It takes place on April 25—Liberation Day—which is also St. Mark's name day; there is a longstanding tradition of making a pilgrimage on foot to the summit.

On October 5, the Nazis took over Ascoli, and on October 30, King Vittorio Emanuele III finally declared war on Germany. After the Allies landed at Anzio in early 1944, Le Marche became the battlefield. The Germans had constructed the Gothic Line from La Spezia on the Tyrhennian coast, over the Apennines, and down the Foglia River valley to the Adriatic coast near Pesaro. Fifteen thousand slave laborers had cleared a swath 16 km / 10 mi wide, destroying farmhouses, felling trees, mining the fields, and building a defensive line of trenches, machine gun nests, bunkers, and observation towers. The Nazi-Fascists planned to stop the Allies here.

The various partisan groups realized that, despite their political differences, they had to organize a united front under the command of the CLN (Committees of National Liberation). Around Ascoli, the *Brigate Garibaldi* paramilitary bands aimed to create a network connected with the Allies to the south, and to impede the Germans with acts of sabotage and harassment. In response, the Germans, kept up to date by their local spies, intensified their brutal repression. Troops combed the countryside, rooting out the opposition and punishing anyone suspected of aiding them. Despite the winter's heavy snows, they stormed through the towns surrounding Mt. Ascensione above Ascoli, scattering the partisans sheltered there. On March 11, they descended on the isolated villages of Pozzo and Umito in the deep valleys near Aquasanta. A tortuously winding road led to huddled groups of stone buildings, some built into the rock faces of the cliffs. At dawn, the Nazis and their Fascist collaborators surprised the civilians of Pozzo, dragging eight young men from their beds to be shot in front of their parents, looting provisions and weapons, and torching the homes. All the men were rounded up, but before they could be executed, word arrived that the real partisans were in Umito, the next village over, and the killers moved on. A large group of partisans was indeed based there, many of them Montenegrans who had escaped from POW camps in Colfiorito and Servigliano (the infamous Camp 59), as well as veterans of the Bosco Martese battle. In the course of a desperate fight, the group's leader and a majority of his men made it to safety in the heights of the Monti dei Fiori, but twenty-six partisans, including one woman, died. Before retreating, the Germans also killed ten civilians, one of them a baby girl who was burned alive in the family home. Their bodies were buried in a common grave until 1974, when a cemetery was built to honor them. This shrine was badly damaged by the earthquakes and snows of 2016–17, but has now been fully restored. One can read the tombstones of thirteen Italians, twenty-one ex-Yugoslavian/Montenegrans, and five English and Greek Cipriots. Along the narrow paths between the houses, there are plaques on the walls that name the inhabitants executed here. Even the most remote little town seems to have a memorial to its partisan dead. In Montemonaco, we were struck by the family names of people we know, who still run businesses here. Stone markers along rural roads honor native sons where they died.

Time was running out for the Germans. The Allies entered Rome on June 4, 1944. As the Nazis retreated north, they left a trail of destruction. On June 16, they blew up the bridges of Ascoli—the 14th century Ponte Maggiore, the Ponte di Porta Cartara with its irreplaceable double-arched aquaduct, and the legendary but tiny Ponte di Cecco. Ascoli was liberated shortly thereafter, on June 18. The Allies bombed Ancona on June 16–18, destroying or badly damaging 60 percent of its buildings, including the museum and its Piceni artifacts. The bombing razed much of the medieval center and laid bare a Roman amphitheater underneath. Like Syracuse and Palestrina, many of the Roman sites we admire today had been submerged under centuries of habitation, revealed only by the devastation of WWII; call that a silver lining if you will. Macerata was liberated on June 30, Fabriano on July 13, and Osimo, which had served as the temporary capital of Le Marche, on Aug 18. The Allies and partisan brigades fought their way up the coast. On August 25, they launched a full-on attack on the Gothic Line, crossing the Metauro River at Fano, and blasting German positions with heavy artillery fire. The Germans retreated and Allied planes unleashed tons of bombs on strategic points around Pesaro and on the city itself, targeting bridges, railways, and factories. The Allied forces were largely made up of soldiers from Britain, Canada, and other Commonwealth countries, Poland, and the partisan brigade *Maiella* from Abruzzo. After days of intense battles, they occupied Pesaro and drove the Germans north, out of Le Marche and towards a major battle near Rimini. This area hosts a cluster of military cemeteries for thousands of Commonwealth dead at Coriano, Montecchio, and Gradara, and for a thousand Polish dead buried at Loreto.

Mussolini had tried to escape from Milan to Switzerland, but he was captured near Lake Como and executed on April 28, 1945. His body, along with that of his mistress and other Fascists, was hung up on display in Milan, in a square where fifteen dead partisans had been exhibited the previous year. One of the British intelligence officers who had tracked his movements was Massimo "Max" Salvadori (1908–1992), grandson of Margaret Collier (author of *Our House by the Adriatic)*, with family ties in Fermo and Porto San Giorgio. In 1924, he and his father had been beaten up by Blackshirts for their political beliefs and the family had moved to Switzerland. Max returned to Italy in the early '30s, but was arrested for anti-fascist activities and sent to prison. However, because both his grandmothers were British, he had dual citizenship and was permitted to go into exile rather than serve out his sentence. With the onset of WWII, he joined the British Special Operations, and was involved in joint British and partisan efforts, including organizing the escape of historian and philosopher Benedetto Croce from Sorrento to Allied safety in Capri. He gives an account of these years in his books, *The Labor and the Wounds* and *Breve storia della Resistenza italiana*. After the war he moved to America, where he taught political economy at Smith College for many years. His sister Joyce Lussu (1912–1998) was also deeply involved in the Resistence, specializing in forging passports and other vital documents. She was imprisoned for helping the Jewish anti-fascist socialists Vera and Giuseppe (older brother of the painter Amedeo) Modigliano cross the French/Swiss border. Her companion and later husband was the Sardinian partisan Emilio Lussu, one of the founders of the *Giustizia e Libertà*/Justice and Liberty movement. She became a politically active writer and translator, focusing on anti-colonialism, the Third World, and feminism. Later in life, she returned to her Marchigiani roots, writing and editing books on local history and traditions, including the Sybil, and an introduction to the Italian translation of her grandmother's book, *La nostra casa sull'Adriatico*. Her experiences during the war are described in her memoir, *Portrait*.

In Italy, WWII ended on April 25, 1945. The monarchy was voted out on June 2, 1946, and Italy became a democratic republic. Now it was time for the woodpecker, symbol of the Piceni, to rise from the ashes.

The *Mezzadria* and the Economic Miracle

Italy and Le Marche emerged from WWII under the shadow of widespread destruction and economic dislocation. By the late '40s, however, production had reached pre-war levels, and by 1953, production was double the 1938 rates. From 1951 to 1973, economic growth averaged 5 percent and more every year. The much touted Italian economic miracle was in progress, but Le Marche continued as a primarily agricultural zone in these years. In the '50s, Abetito finally received modern services such as electricity and telephones, as well as a paved switchback road where once there was just a donkey path. This expansion could not last forever; by the late '60s, the economy was in decline, and with the Arab oil embargo of 1973 the boom was over… except possibly in Le Marche.

For more than 700 years, the *mezzadria* system of sharecropping had been the dominant agricultural institution of this zone, mostly in the lower hills and on the coast. Le Marche had one of the highest concentrations of *mezzadria* of all the regions of Italy. Landowners, including the church, provided the farmer with a place to live—and often more, including equipment, tools, livestock, seeds, etc. Peasants provided the labor and other contractual obligations. The share was often fifty-fifty, thus the name *mezzadria—"mezza"* meaning one half. After the Unification of Italy in 1861, the new government dissolved the vast property holdings of religious organizations like the Abbey of Farfa and the Benedictine monasteries. Much of this land was sold to private owners; this privatization of common lands also abolished traditional rights to wood-lands and pastures. In the former Papal States, this redistribution led to a larger, non-noble, rural middle class that controlled its own farms, instead of working for others. By the 1950s, the *mezzadria* system had been in decline for more than a hundred years, but sharecropping still accounted for 55 percent of farms and 70 percent of arable land in Le Marche. In the early years of that decade, agriculture employed 60 percent of the workforce. A 1964 law abolished new sharecropper contracts and phased out those existing, leaving a few long-term contracts that lasted into the early 1980s. In the meantime, with the help of government mortgages, many sharecroppers bought land, as did some returning emigrants. But at this point, agriculture did not pay enough to surpass bare subsistence. Farmers took jobs in town or brought piecework into their homes. The *mezzadria* had a long tradition of cottage industries; the estate was more than just a locus of food production. When there was no work in the fields, the peasants made things for their own use or to be sold or exchanged, including brooms, chairs, rope, farm tools, and straw baskets. In addition to helping in the production of the above items, women took on every step of textile manufacturing. The *mezzadro* was a multi-skilled person, not only a cultivator but also a carpenter, mason, metal worker, weaver, and so on, as a part of an autonomous and self-sufficient production unit seeking to minimize cash outlay.

The *mezzadria* and agricultural opportunities in general were in decline. In a countryside dotted with little towns, people who were unwilling or unable to emigrate, but who had savings, skills, family workshops or stores, created an economy of family-based artisanal production. Starting in the 1950s, there was a slow movement toward these sorts of small and medium scale enterprises, employing fewer than fifty people and often less than ten. By the 1960s, this trend was hitting its stride, and from the mid '70s it took off. As Giorgio Fuà relates:

> In some cases, change starts with the arrival of homework contracts from firms a long distance away. After a while, the most enterprising home workers start to work on their own. In other cases, resettling emigrants are the bearers of change: they have been able to acquire industrial experience in foreign lands, to establish contacts with external manufacturers and markets, and to put aside savings. On their return home they exploit all this by setting up small businesses of their own (Fuà, *The Environmental Basis of Diffuse Industrializaton*, p. 8).

Here is the famous *modello marchigiano*.

A popular book from the 1970s declared that *Small is Beautiful* (E.F. Schumacher, 1973); others would argue that the *modello marchigiano* is a myth and that another book, published in Le Marche, *Quando piccolo non è bello / When Small Isn't Beautiful* (ed. G. Vagnarelli, 2008) is more accurate. The economic crisis beginning in 2008 took a heavy toll in Le Marche, as in all of Italy, and many think the only way forward is to join the inexorable march of centralization and globalization.

The emphasis on *mezzadria* may make it seem as if Le Marche never had industry, but this is not accurate. Fabriano has been manufacturing paper since the 12th century. At the Fabriano paper museum, it was amusing to see a piece of paper—sumptuous, premium paper—watermarked with the name of a wealthy Chicago bank. Ascoli, too, had a paper industry, centered at the 16th century Cartiera Papale. The shoe industry here dates back to medieval times and was mentioned by Boccaccio. The slipper manufacturers of Le Marche specialized in a product that found an international market. Copper work in the town of Force, musical instruments in Castelfidardo, hats in Montappone—these industries and more existed before and into the 20th century and beyond. Throughout northeast and central Italy, the foundation of family-based, small and medium size enterprises comprise the "Third Italy," as scholars call it to distinguish it from first, the industrial triangle of Milan, Genoa, and Turin, and second, the economically backward southern Italy. According to Fuà:

Poster for the silk industry of Ascoli Piceno

An important initial factor defining the NEC (northeast central) model is the environmental framework within which the process of industrialization starts. In evocative but hurried terms, the environment of origin is l'Italia dei Commune, the Italy of the city-states, thus named to distinguish the area from the old kingdom of Naples (Fuà, p. 7).

The silk industry in Piceno had deep roots in the *mezzadria* system. Women and girls on the estates grew cocoons by feeding mulberry leaves to the silk caterpillars. Silk manufacturers bought the cocoons, which provided extra cash. Ascoli had mulberry trees for silk production dating from the 15th century, although the industry did not reach its peak until the 19th and early 20th centuries, when Italy produced 90 percent of Europe's raw silk. Jesi was an important center with the first silk factory in 1837. Ascoli had as many as fifty workshops processing cocoons, and supplied a third of the national total. But then Japan and China, where silk was invented in the Neolithic Era, reconquered the market. Unable to compete with the cheaper imports, the last factory in Ascoli closed by the 1960s. In Piazza Roma, the once imposing headquarters of a major silk company now houses one of our favorite bookstores, the Libreria Rinascita.

Not only silk, but cotton, wool, and flax were processed, largely in rural farmhouses where almost everybody had a loom. Here was a classic women's cottage industry, widespread and diffuse, of spinning, weaving, tailoring, and embroidery. Tablecloths, sheets, blankets, dresses—entire doweries were created. Offida was famous for its lace and even today you can find lacemaking, *merletto a tombolo*, there. The education and training of young women in these skills was institutionalized. The fine products they made were sold all over Italy to the well-to-do. As we mentioned, when Nathan's grandmother Lia was a girl she trained with the nuns in a convent next to the San Gregorio Magno church in Ascoli Piceno. After Nonno Amedeo died in 1942, Nonna Lia worked in her niece's shirt factory in Brooklyn, producing uniforms for the US military. She made winter coats that she sent back to relatives in Italy after WWII, and made our winter coats as well, among many other items. We possess examples of her hand-embroidered linens, which we cherish.

The agricultural products of Piceno have a deep past. Winemaking in this region predates the Romans, who reputedly liked Piceno's wine—as did the Venetians. Pliny the Elder, an ancient wine critic, says that the wine of Picenum was enjoyed beyond the Alps (*Natural History*, Book IV, Chap. 4). Rosso Piceno, Passerina, and Verdicchio, to name a few, have made their way into today's international wine market. Most curious of all is Pecorino—the wine. Cheese lovers will know that *pecorino* is a sheep's milk cheese. Why was the wine also named "little sheep?" Legend has it that grazing sheep (*pecore*) loved to eat this grape, native to the Sibillini Mountains. An indigenous species, it grows at a higher altitude than many grapes, according to Lalli and Eupizi in their book *Il Vino Pecorino (u pecuri) di Arquata del Tronto*. In the late 1800s, a disastrous wine blight devastated the industry; imported American grapevine roots had brought with them a fast-reproducing aphid that killed the vines throughout Europe, especially in France. Eventually, by grafting and hybridizing species native to America that were naturally resistant to the aphid, growers were able to surmount the plague. The Pecorino grape, growing higher on the mountainside and thereby capable of withstanding colder weather, escaped the blight, which could not tolerate the low temperatures. The Pecorino grape is one of the very few autochthonous (indigenous) European grape species still in existence.

Castelli touts Mazzochi's famed green olives

The agricultural products of Piceno are many and of high quality, but we have not yet addressed olives, probably the most famous of all. Amedee Coutance in his 1887 book, *L'Olivier/Olives,* writes, "Picenum was the promised land of olives." The much-adored *oliva ascolana*, pitted, stuffed with meat, and deep fried, is the signature dish of Ascoli Piceno. The olives of Picenum were especially prized by the Romans. A late 1800s pamphlet by Giuseppe Castelli, *"Le Olive Verdi Ascolane Nell'Antichità*/The Green Olives of Ascoli in Antiquity,"* recounts what several ancient writers had to say about them. A curious combination of scholarship and publicity for M.Mazzocchi, a local Ascoli olive producer, Castelli's pamphlet states that "The Romans didn't realize the wealth of Picenum until they conquered it."

The Roman poet Martial says that the olives from Picenum began and ended meals. Apparently, Romans thought the olives would soothe a too-full stomach when the meal was over. Of the many quotes from Latin writers that Castelli includes, we choose this one from Martial:

If after all this Bacchus perchance rouses
An appetite, as his way is,
Fine olives will come to your aid,
Recently borne by the branches of Picenum.
(Book V, Epigram 78, trans. D.R. Shackleton)

That the olives of Picenum had an international following is confirmed by the archeological record. An amphora typical of the Le Marche region, marked *Oliva Picena* and dated to AD 275, was found in Bliesbruch, France, near Metz on the German border.

Castelli underlines the economic importance of Picenum to the Romans and lists the many other products—especially the apples, figs, grapes, and pears—that made their way along the Via Salaria to the markets of Rome. One type of red apple, the esteemed *mela rosa dei Sibillini,* merited special attention; they were not much to look at but they tasted better than others. Recent nutritional studies have shown them to be twenty-five times more powerful in antioxidants than the average apple.

In modern times, agriculture only accounts for a small percentage of employment in Le Marche, having gone from 6.85 percent in 1993 to 2.8 percent in 2010. Manufacturing had taken off, moving briskly from the mid-1970s well into the 1980s. Four types of products dominated: furniture, textiles, shoes and leather, and mechanicals, including machine tools and appliances. Concentrated in their respective districts, they made Le Marche one of the most industrialized regions in Italy, with the highest concentration of manufacturing as a portion of overall employment in Italy. The '90s and early 2000s witnessed considerable headwinds from mature markets, restrictions imposed by the Maastrict Treaty, and the introduction of the highly valued euro. And then came the Great Recession.

In 2008, after the notorious collapse of Lehman Brothers Holding, the international banking crisis struck Italy and Le Marche. *La Grande Recessione* took hold. Unemployment in Le Marche sailed from 4.7 percent in 2008 to 10.6 percent in 2019, peaking at 12 percent in 2016. Youth unemployment, including people from 15–24 years of age, went from 12.5 percent in 2008 to 22 percent in 2018, peaking at 36.4 percent in 2014. Between 2008 and 2014, Le Marche lost 4,500 small artisanal businesses, with more to follow (Dini, Blim, and Goffi, *"Il decline dei distretti industriali tradizionali,"* p. 12). In the ten years following the onset of the Great Recession, Italy's economy went into recession three times. According to Blim and Goffi, Le Marche's unemployment rate had historically been much lower than the national rate; by 2017 it was only 0.6 percent lower.

Some social scientists of the late '70s and early '80s thought that the small-scale artisanal production model of central Italy might be part of a solution to the economic problems that beset the world in the 1970s, especially urban poverty. Stagflation, high unemployment, factory closings, deindustrialization—many thought that the system of mass production/standardized goods that brought so much wealth to some had reached its limit. Markets were saturated and international competition was narrowing profit margins. Yet, here was a small and beautiful, nimble and flexible alternative. Others were less sanguine. Here was a nest of problems: too much under-the-table work with no pension contributions, child labor, and family tensions that could be a huge impediment to forward thinking. Household production has traditionally been a peripheral activity, ripe for exploitation, and frequently a dead end. And now, children were getting college degrees and often did not want to participate in the family business.

For decades, the depopulation of the mountain zones had been an ongoing concern. The farms and pastures one sees in old photographs have reverted to forests. The remains of flour mills dot the river banks, some converted to making electricity. Wherever we go in Montegallo, we meet older men who had emigrated after WWII to find work. Recognizing us as Americans, they tell us about their decades in New Jersey or Montreal. Some had returned long ago to their family properties; others were just visiting on their yearly vacation—often with a foreign wife. The next generation down, our generation, had also spent time abroad. In the '60s and '70s, several of our cousins worked in factories in Switzerland and Germany, and one as an electrician in Saudi Arabia. Those we know best returned to local factory jobs or private businesses, to raise their families and be near their parents. However, many have siblings who stayed in Germany or Belgium—or at least Milan or Rome.

Weaknesses had been apparent in the Marchigiano industrial system before the Great Recession. The problems include lack of infrastructure, low-skill work, an uninterested younger generation, lack

Monte Ascensione seen from Montefalcone

of foreign investment, and too many enterprises stuck in traditional or mature industries. The economic meltdown of 2008 raised fears about the notable Marchigiano quality of life, where economic inequality is low and food and housing are affordable. Frugal families were able to survive the Great Recession through their savings. By the middle teens, economic conditions were starting to improve… but then came the earthquakes of 2016–2017.

What Lies Ahead?

"Montegallo is finished," Alessandro Rossi says. "Rigo, Castro, Migliarelli, Colle, Astorara—all those houses in ruins…" Alessandro is a veteran of the Italian army, of the *Alpini*—tough men trained to fight in mountainous conditions. We have known him for years as a happy guy always quick with a joke, hanging out in Balzo's two bars. When we encounter him on a deserted back road, he tells us how he dragged his three daughters from his crumbling house, one under each arm and the youngest clinging to his neck while he held onto her t-shirt with his teeth. Forced to move to a town eleven miles away, the girls are in school there and it is closer to his wife's factory job. "Why would they ever move back?" he asks. But, here he is in Montegallo every day. This is home, where he grew up and his family has lived for generations—and also where he works. He is a woodcutter, and while there are lots of trees to chop down, not many people are buying firewood. Four years after the earthquake, the house his family fled still stands on the hillside, one corner missing, tumbled mattresses visible inside.

The beauty of this area is its timeless way of life, agricultural, pastoral, the steep hills studded with medieval fortress towns, villages cresting slopes covered with vineyards or chestnut trees. The mountains, the beautiful hills with their dramatic *calanchi*, the Adriatic Sea, all merge to form a place where people can live well, nested in an inherently romantic landscape. Many of the stone houses were built (with no anti-seismic code) by the great-grandparents of families who still cultivate the land. These towns and villages contained Romanesque churches where family weddings were celebrated, bars where men played cards every evening, restaurants that served road crews and hikers, little grocery stores selling the local cheeses and salamis. The destruction of this social network is one of the most painful effects of the earthquakes. In 2016–2017, about 41,000 people in the *"cratere"* were evacuated; 22,000, the majority of them from Le Marche, were settled elsewhere. "We can't let our way of life die," we hear repeatedly. Many inhabitants are fighting hard to move back into their homes and reopen their businesses. But if rebuilding is put off too long, people will have to start over elsewhere, and these sparks of life will flicker out. A common fear is that this is a deliberate strategy, the "politics of exasperation," that the government wants to empty the zone because it is cheaper to run it as a national park than as an inhabited area with schools and post offices. A regional representative of Le Marche suggested that funds raised to help the earthquake zone be used to build a bicycle path from Civitanova Marche on the coast to Sarnano, up in the hills. This, of course, is a nice idea, but how can it take precedence over making people's houses and towns livable?

Le Marche has never been at the top of the list of Italian tourist destinations. First, there is Rome-Florence-Venice; then on the next trip maybe the Amalfi Coast, Pompei/Capri, Cinque Terre, Turin/Milan, the Dolomites, Sicily... Back in 2005, the *New York Times* published a travel article asking, "Is Le Marche the Next Tuscany?" Some years later the question became, "Is Le Marche the Next Umbria?" For many American travelers, the only place they recognize in Le Marche is Urbino, home of the Renaissance painter Raphael. The *Lonely Planet 2020* travel guide declared Le Marche to be the second most desirable region to visit that year (after the Central Asian Silk Road), citing the 500th anniversary of Raphael's death. Before 2016, there were signs that the tourist industry was taking off. Local families opened B&Bs and *Agriturismi*. After a change in the law, traditional cafés like Bar Babbalò in Balzo, Chicco Bar in Uscerno, and Bar Zocchi in Montemonaco were allowed to serve food, too, and delicious, cheap meals became available everywhere.

Castelluccio, on the Umbrian side of Mt. Vettore, has long been one of the main destinations. Hoards of tourists from all over the world come every spring to see the *fioritura*, the flowering of the fields in psychedelic colors. Franco Zeffirelli shot part of *Fratello Sole, Sorella Luna*, his 1972 hippie biopic of St. Francis, on the Piano Grande. After the quakes, the roads were closed to all traffic. The following spring, protesting farmers drove a convoy of tractors over the mountains from Norcia, demanding the right to plant the lentil fields—their major crop. Now, modular units have sprung up to provide restaurants and other tourist services, while the rubble of the town's heart is slowly removed. Even four years later, the road into Le Marche from Castelluccio through Visso was only open on the weekends.

Tourism cannot be the only answer to Piceno's economic problems, with its seasonal fluctuations and low wages. (And, the long-term effects of the Covid-19 pandemic are yet to be seen.) The model should not be Disneyworld, or even Tuscany. A friend spoke admiringly of a town in the Italian Alps where the workers wear traditional garb, lederhosen and aprons. Please, no! There are also inherent problems dating back to the dawn of time. Except along the coast, the mountains and river valleys impede rapid north-south travel. There are no vast plains available for more airports or large-scale developments. No direct trains connect Rome and Ascoli Piceno, despite proposals going back more than a hundred years.

Some want to minimize the damage done, labeling the ruined houses as mostly second homes, occupied only during vacations. In many of the cases we have seen, these places have been in the family for generations. In their youth, the current owners might have been forced to emigrate elsewhere for work, but this is where they wanted to return. They spent summers and holidays here with their extended families and childhood friends, they kept the farms and the chestnut groves going. When they retired, they fixed up the old homestead and moved back for good... or so they hoped.

With today's resources, surely people should be able to build a good life here. The Internet makes working from home possible and the international marketplace accessible. One young mother is selling the family's harvest of prized Abetito potatoes online. In Balzo, an enterprising couple planted fields of lavender, which they turn into a range of wonderfully perfumed products, *La Lavanda dei Sibillini*. Mario Alessandri runs the *Agrimusicismo B&B&B* in Astorara, high on the slopes below Mt. Vettore, where one can eat, drink, and enjoy music and theater. Our three cousins, as *La Casetta di Marzapane Bijoux*, make jewelry in a village workshop that we helped renovate. At Camping Vettore, Qi Gong classes in a field surrounded by a breathtaking mountain panorama are followed by lunch at the campground's pizzaria.

We cannot prescribe a plan for the future, but we are always struck by how many products and places that are rare and costly in America are simply how things are here. Any one of these ancient hilltop towns would attract visitors from hundreds of miles away in the States, would have billboards along the highways, and be featured in travel magazines. Here, however, there are so many that you forget which is which, and you say, "Oh, another gorgeous medieval fortress. Is this the one where we had those delicious fruit tarts in that café built into the wall?" Farm-to-table is how much of the food chain works here. The supermarkets are full of items you might search for in our high-priced gourmet boutiques, with organic wine and olive oil from the nearby vineyards and groves. Locally milled flour is made into bread and pasta by the *Azienda Agricola Michele*. The herds of sheep that regularly block the roads produce the cheeses you buy at the deli counter.

In the spring, we walk along country tracks where primroses and violets bloom and later, wild strawberries. Cuckoos mock us from the trees, the swallows swoop around their nests built under the eaves of the stone houses. Summertime brings cherries and blackberries. Everybody plants big kitchen gardens with rows of tomatoes, beans, and potatoes. In the fall, the woods are full of *porcini* mushrooms, if you know where to look, and truffles are a local industry. We eat walnuts that have fallen on the road—but never venture onto private property to steal this abundance, the result of continual caretaking! The chestnut groves are heavily laden with prickly husks, the nuts raining down. Cousin Gianna makes us chestnut ravioli with chocolate, dusted with powdered sugar. And so, we end here with this winter treat and dreams of the next springtime in Piceno.

Figs and Grapes

Bibliography

Adornato, Francesco, and Cegna, Annalisa. *Le Marche nella Mezzadria: Un Grande Futuro Dietro la Spalle*. Macerata: Quodlibet, 2013.

Agnoletti, Silvia. "Gli insediamenti ebraici nella Marca altomedievale," in *Ascoli e Le Marche: tra Tardoantico e Altomedioevo*, a cura di Menesto, Enrico. Centro Italiano di Studi sull'Altomedioevo, Spoleto, 2004.

Alesi, Alberico, and Calibani, Maurizio. *Monti Sibillini Parco Nazionale*. Folignano (AP): Società Editrice Ricerche, 1992.

Alfieri, Nereo. "Le Marche e la fine del mondo antico," *Atti di Memorie, Istituzioni e Società nell'Alto Medievale Marchigiano*. Ancona-Osimo-Jesi: Atti di Convegno, October 1981.

Allevi, Luigi. *Piceno Religioso nell'Antichità*. Ascoli Piceno: Casa Editrice Giuseppe Cesari, 1940.

Anderson, Perry. *Passages from Antiquity to Feudalism*. London: Verso, 1974.

Anselmi, Sergio, a cura di. *Il Picchio e il Gallo*. Jesi: Cassa di Risparmio di Jesi, 1982.

Atti del XXII Convegno di Studi Etruschi ed Italici, *I Piceni e l'Italia Medio-Adriatica*. Pisa/Roma: Istituti Editoriali e Poligrafici Internazionali, 2003.

Azzara, Claudio. *I Longobardi*. Bologna: Il Mulino, 2015.

Appian. *The Civil Wars*. London: Penguin Books, 1996.

Appian. *History of Rome: The Samnite Wars (2)*. Trans. by Horace White. livius.org.

Badian, E. *Foreign Clientelae*. Oxford: Clarendon Press, 1968.

Baldelli, Gabriele. "Civiltà Picena: *Safini, Peicentes*, ed *Asculum caput gentis*." *La Salaria in Età Antica*. Roma: L'Erma di Bretschneider, 1999.

Balena, Secondo. *Ascoli nel Piceno*. Folignano AP: Società Editrice Ricerche, 1999.

Balena, Secondo. *Bandenkrieg nel Piceno Settembre 43-Giugno 44*. Ascoli Piceno: G. Cesari, 1965.

Bar-Yosef, Ofer, and Pilbeam, David. *The Geography of Neandertals and Modern Humans in Europe and the Greater Mediterranean*, Cambridge MA: Harvard University, Peabody Museum of Archeology and Ethnology, 2000.

Beales, Derek. *The Risorgimento and the Unification of Italy*. New York: Barnes and Noble, 1971.

Beard, Mary. *Confronting the Classics*. New York: Liveright Publishing Corporation, 2013.

Bertini, Franco, a cura di. *Storia delle Marche*. Bologna: Poligrafici Editoriale, 1995.

Biondo, Flavio. *Italia Illustrata/Italy Illuminated*. Trans. by Jeffrey A. White. Cambridge, MA: Harvard University Press, 2005.

Blim, Michael, and Goffi, Gianluca. "The Long and Short of It: The Value of the Concept of *longue duree* in the Analysis of Contemporary Development and Decline." *Economia Marche Journal of Applied Economics*, Vol. XXXIII, No. 1 (June 2014), pp. 84-104.

Blim, Michael, and Goffi, Gianluca. "Marche, a Region between Success and Decline." *Research Gate*, Essays in honor of the 50 year anniversary of ISTAO, (June, 2018).

Blim, Michael. *Made in Italy*. New York/Westport/London: Praeger, 1990.

Boccabianca, Giuseppe M. *Le Famiglie Nobili Ripane*. Ripatransone nel Piceno: A. Barigelleti, 1929.

Bondanelli, Peter. *Italian Cinema from Neorealism to the Present*. New York: Ungar Publishing, 1999.

Braccesi, Lorenzo, a cura di. *La Pirateria nell'Adriatico Antico*. Roma: L'Erma di Bretschneider, 2004.

Bradley, Guy; Isayev, Elena, Riva, Corinna, edited by. *Ancient Italy: Regions without Boundaries*. Exeter, UK: University of Exeter Press, 2007.

Brunt, P.A. "Italian Aims at the Time of the Social War," *The Journal of Roman Studies*, Vol. 55, No. 1/2 (1965), pp. 90-109.

Brunt, P. A. *Social Conflicts in the Roman Republic*. New York: W.W. Morton and Co., 1971.

Bury, J.B. *History of the Later Roman Empire* Vol. I, II. New York: Dover Publications, 1958.

Buseghin, Maria Luciana. *L'Ultima Sibilla*. Pescara: Carsa Edizioni, 2012.

Cappelli, Carlo. *ASKL*. Ascoli Piceno: Lamusa, 2001.

Cappelli, Carlo. *I Barbari*. Ascoli Piceno: Lamusa, 2002.

Cappelli, Carlo. *La Civiltà Egeo-Appenninica*. Ascoli Piceno: Lamusa, 2009.

Cappelli, Carlo. *La "Zattera" di Guglielmo Allevi*. Ascoli Piceno: Lamusa, 2009.

Cappelli, Flavia, and Vico, Giuseppe. *Archeologia Altomedievale: I "Secoli Bui" tra Marche e Abruzzo*. Ascoli Piceno: Lamusa, 2011.

Cappelli, Furio. *La Cattedrale di Ascoli nel Medioevo*. Ascoli Piceno: Lamusa, 2002.

Cappelli, Furio. *La Via Salaria in Piceno*. Ascoli Piceno: Lamusa, 2003.

Caponi, Anthony. *Voice from the Mountains*. St. Paul, Minn: Ruminator Books, 2002.

Carducci, Giambattista. *Su le Memorie e i Monumenti di Ascoli nel Piceno*. Fermo: Saverio Del-Monte Editore, 1855.

Castelli, Giuseppe. "The Green Olives of Ascoli in Antiquity." Trans. by Nathan Neel and Phoebe Leed. Unpublished translation of "Le Olive Verdi Ascolane nell'Antichità." Ascoli Piceno: Enrico Tassi, 1901.

Castelli, Giuseppe. *La Vita e le Opere di Cecco d'Ascoli*. Bologna: Ditta Nicola Zanichelli, 1892.

Castelli, Serafino. *Garibaldi in Ascoli (25-26 Gennaio 1849)*. Ascoli Piceno: Author Publisher, 2007.

Catà, Cesare. "Con l'alloro sotto il saio. Ipotesi su Frate Pacifico and il Cantico di Frate Sole." *Picenum Seraphim. Rivista storici di studi storici e i francescani*, XXV (2006-2008), pp. 355-395.

Cecco d'Ascoli, *Acerba/The Bitter Age*. Trans. by Diane Murphy. Ascoli Piceno: Capponi Editore, 2015.

Childe, Gordon V. *The Dawn of European Civilization*. New York: Vintage Books, 1957.

Cianfarani, Valerio; Lollini, Delia G.; Zuffa, Mario. *Popoli e Civiltà dell'Italia Antica*. Roma: Biblioteca di Storia Patria, 1976.

Cicero. *The Orations of Marcus Tullius Cicero*, Vol IV. Trans. by C.D. Yonge. Gloucester: Dodo Press, 2008.

Cipolla, Carlo M. *Before the Industrial Revolution*. Trans. by Marcella and Alida Kooy. New York: W.W. Norton and Co., 1976.

Collier, Margaret. *Our Home by the Adriatic*. London: Richard Bentley and Sons, 1886.

Collucci, Giuseppe. *Antichità Ascolane*. Fermo: Published by the Author, 1792.

Colonna, Giovanni, et al. *Eroi e Regine: Piceni Popolo d'Europa*. Roma: Edizioni De Luca, 2001.

Cook, S.A; Adcock, F.E; Charlesworth, M.P. edited by. *The Cambridge Ancient History*, Vol. IX. Cambridge: Cambridge University Press, 1951.

Cornell, T.J. *The Beginnings of Rome*. London / New York: Routledge, 1995.

Cornell, T.J. "The Samnite Wars." *The Encyclopedia of Ancient Battles*. Hoboken: John Wiley and Sons, 2017.

Coutance, Amedee. *L'Olivier*. Paris: J. Rothschild Editeur, 1877.

Crivellucci, Amedeo. *Una Comune delle Marche nel 1798 e 1799 e Il Brigante Sciabolone*. Ripatransone AP: Maroni, 1893, 1992.

Dardari, Manuela-Coordinator Editoriale. *Guide al Piceno in 5 Vol.: La Storia, Sibillini, L'Arte, Civiltà e Territorio, La Val di Tenna*. Ripatransone AP: Maroni, 1992.

Dench, Emma. *From Barbarians to New Men*. Oxford: Clarendon Press, 1995.

Dench, Emma. "Sacred Springs to the Social War: Myths of Origins and Questions of Identity in the Central Apennines." *Gender and Ethnicity in Ancient Italy*. Ed. by Tim Cornell and Kathryn Lomas. London:Accordia Research Insitute, Univ. of London, 1997.

De Sanctis, Gaetano. *La Conquista del Primato in Italia*. Firenze: La Nuova Italia, 1960.

De Vecchi, Pierluigi, a cura di. *Beni Ambientali, Beni Architettonici: Atlante dei Beni Culturale dei Territori di Ascoli Piceno e di Fermo*. Ascoli Piceno: Assessorata alla Cultura, 1998.

Devoto, Giacomo. *Gli Antichi Italici*. Firenze: Vallecchi Editore, 1931.

Di Fillipo Balestrazzi, Elena. "Attorno a un fiume, Riflessioni su *Truentum* e *Castrum Truentinum*." *La Pirateria nell'Adriatico Antico*. Rome: L'Erma di Bretschneider, 2004.

Diodorus of Sicily. Trans. by Francis R. Walton. London / Cambridge MA: William Heinemann, Harvard University Press, 1967.

Ellis, Peter Berresford. *Celt and Roman*. New York: St Martin's Press, 1998.

Eutropius. *Abridgement of Roman History*. Trans. by Rev. John Selby Watson. London: Henry G. Bohn, 1853. www.forumromanum.org.

Fabian, Seth Boniface. "Cecco vs. Dante: Correcting the *Comedy* with Applied Astrology." New York: Ph.D. dissertation, Columbia University, 2014.

Francke, Linda Bird. *On the Road with Francis of Assisi*. New York: Random House, 2005.

Fuà, Giorgio. "The Environmental Basis of Diffuse Industrialization." Trans. by J. Irwing. *International Studies of Management and Organization*, Vol. 21, No. 1 (Spring 1991), pp. 5-20.

Fabiani, Giuseppe. *Ascoli nel Quattrocento*. Ascoli Piceno: Società Tipolitografica Editrice, 1950.

Fanning, Steven C. "Lombard Arianism Reconsidered." *Speculum*, Vol. 56, No. 2 (April, 1981), pp. 241-258.

Finley, M.I. *The Ancient Economy*. Berkeley CA: University of California Press, 1973.

Friedlander, Paul J.C. "Excursion into Tranquility." New York: The New York Times, August 13, 1961.

Frontinus, Sextus Julius. *Strategems*. Chicago: Lacus Curtius, penelope.uchicago.edu, 2018.

Gabba, Emilio. *Republican Rome, the Army and the Allies*. Trans. by P.J. Cuff. Berkeley: University of California Press, 1976.

Galanti, Timoteo. *Dagli Sciaboloni ai Piccioni*. Roma: Edigrafital, 1990.

Garibaldi, Giuseppe. *Autobiography of Giuseppe Garbaldi*. Trans. by A. Warner. London: Walter Smith and Innes, 1889.

Geary, Patrick. *The Myth of Nations*. Princeton: Princeton University Press, 2003.

Gellius, Aulus. *Attic Nights*. Trans. by John C. Rolfe. Cambridge MA: Loeb Classical Library Harvard University Press, 1927.

Gibbon, Edward. *The History of the Decline and Fall of the Roman Empire*. Edited by J.B. Bury. London: Methuen and Co, 1901.

Ginsborg, Paul. *A History of Contemporary Italy: Society and Politics 1943-1988*. London / NewYork: Penguin Books, 1990.

Giovanelli, Rita. *Rieti Underground*. Rieti: Universo Editoriale, 2005.

Goffi, G. "Il sistema economica delle Marche. Artigianato e mercato del lavoro dagli anni Novanta alla crisi attuale." *Economia Marche Journal of Applied Economics*, Vol XXXII, No. 1 (June, 2013), pp. 97-125.

Gregory, Desmond. *Napoleon's Italy*. London: Associated University Presses, 2001.

Guida Illustrata del Museo Nazionale di Ancona con Estesi Ragguagli sugli Scavi dell'Ultimo Decennio Preceduta da uno Studio sull'Origine dei Piceni. Ancona: Stabilimento Tipografico Cooperativo, 1915.

Hearder, Harry. *Italy in the Age of the Risorgimento 1790-1870*. London: Longman, 1983.

Hodgkin, Thomas. *Italy and Her Invaders*. Oxford: At the Clarendon Press, 1895.

Holland, Tom. *Rubicon*. New York: Anchor Books, 2003.

Homer. *The Iliad*. Trans. by W.H.D. Rouse. New York: Mentor Book, 1938.

Hyde, J.K. *Society and Politics in Medieval Italy*. New York: St. Martin's Press, 1973.

Johnston, R.M. *The Napoleonic Empire in Southern Italy*. London: MacMillan, 1904.

Keaveney, Arthur. *Rome and the Unification of Italy*. London and Sydney: Croom Helm, 1987.

Kantorowicz, Ernst. *Frederick the Second*. New York: Frederick Ungar Publishing Co. 1957.

Laffi, Umberto. *Storia di Ascoli nell'Età Antica*. Pisa: Giardini Editore, 1975.

Lamb, Richard. *War in Italy 1943-1945: A Brutal Story*. New York: St. Martin's Press, 1993.

Leach, John. *Pompey the Great*. Dover NH: Croom Helm, 1978.

Lightbown, Ronald. *Carlo Crivelli*. New Haven / London: Yale University Press, 2004.

Livius, Titus. *The History of Rome, Books 9-26*, Trans. by D. Spillan and Cyrus Edmonds. London: Henry G. Bohn, 1899.

Livy. *Rome and Italy: The History of Rome from its Foundation Books VI-X.* Trans. by Betty Radice. London: Penguin Books, 1982.

Livy, *The Early History of Rome. Books I-V.* Trans. by Aubrey De Selincourt. London: Penguin Books, 1960.

Lollini, Delia G., a cura di. *La Civiltà Picena nelle Marche.* Ancona: Maroni, 1988.

Luporini, Annalisa, and Prigi, Bruno. "Multi-Task Sharecropping Contracts: The Italian Mezzadria." *Economica* Vol. 63, No. 251 (August,1996), pp. 445-57.

Lussu, Joyce. *Portrait.* Roma: L'Asino D'Ora, 2012.

Machiavelli, Niccolo. *History of Florence and the Affairs of Italy.* Trans. by Christian E. Detmold. Teddington, Middlesex: The Echo Library, 2006.

Machiavelli, Niccolo. *The Prince.* Trans. by Thomas G. Gergin. New York: Appleton Century-Crofts, 1947.

Malone, Caroline. "Italian Neolithic: a Synthesis of Research." *Journal of World Prehistory,* Vol. 17, No. 3 (September, 2003), pp. 235-312.

Maltese, Curzio. "Il Successo Nascosto del Modello." *La Repubblica,* 6/17/2007.

Mangione, Jerre and Moreale, Ben. *La Storia.* New York: Harper Perennial, 1992.

Mariotti, Cesare. *Il Palazzo del Comune di Ascoli Piceno.* Ascoli Piceno: Giuseppe Cesari, 1905.

Massignani, Mariolina. "Fra' Pacifico *rex versuum.*" *Esculum e Federico II.* Spoleto: Centro Italiano di Studi sull' Alto Medievo, 1998, pp. 165-180.

Menestò, Enrico. *Ascoli e Le Marche tra Tardoantico e Altomedioevo,* Spoleto: Centro Italiano di Studi sull'Alto Medioevo, 2002.

Micali, Giuseppe. *L'Italia Avanti il Dominio Romani.* Milano: Giovanni Silvestri, 1826.

Miley, John. *The History of the Papal States: from their Origin to the Present Day,* Vol 1. London: T.C.Newby, 1850.

Milliken, Sarah. "The Earliest Occupation of Italy," *The Journal of the Accordia Research Center,* Vol. 7 (1997-1998), pp. 7-36.

Milliken, Sarah. "Neanderthals, Anatomically Modern Humans, and 'Modern Human Behavior' in Italy." *Oxford Journal of Archeology,* Vol. 26, No. 4 (2007), pp. 331-358.

Milliken, Sarah. "The Neanderthals in Italy." *The Journal of the Accordia Research Center,* Vol 8 (1999-2000), pp 11-82.

Modugno, Giuseppe. "*La Battaglia del Maggio 1815 in Provincia di Macerata.*" Macerata: Istituto per la Storia del Risorgimento Italiano Comitato di Macerata, 2005.

Mommsen, Theodore. *History of Rome,* Vol. 3. London: Richard Bentley, 1863.

Mommsen, Theodore. "Petrarch's Conception of the Middle Ages." *Speculum,* Vol. 17, No. 2 (1942). Chicago: University of Chicago Press, pp. 226-242.

Montaigne, Michel De. *The Journal of Montaigne's Travels in Italy.* Trans. by W.G. Waters: London: John Murray, 1903.

Moorhead, John. *The Pope and the Church in Late Antiquity.* New York: Routledge, 2015.

Mussi, Margherita. *Earliest Italy: An Overview of the Italian Paleolithic and Mesolithic.* New York: Kluwer Academic/ Plenum Publishers, 2001.

Naso, Alessandro. *I Piceni: Storia e Archeologia delle Marche in Epoca Preromana.* Milano: Longanesi and Co. 2000.

Niebuhr, B.G. *Lectures on the History of Rome from the Earliest Times to the Fall of the Western Empire.* London: Taylor, Walton, and Maberly, 1849.

Noble, Thomas F. X. *The Republic of St. Peter: The Birth of the Papal State, 680-825.* Philadelphia: University of Pennsylvania Press, 1984.

Orosius. *The Anglo-Saxon Version by Alfred the Great.* Trans. by Daines Barrington. London: W. Bowyer and J. Nichols, 1773.

Ovid. *Metamorphoses.* Trans. by Rolfe Humphries. Bloomington: Indiana University Press, 2018.

Paroli, Lida, a cura di. *La Necropoli Altomedievale di Castel Trosino. Bizantini e Longobardi nelle Marche.* Milan: Silvana Editoriale, 1995.

Paget, R.F. *Central Italy: an Archeological Guide.* Park Ridge NJ: Noyes Press, 1973.

Pagnani, Alberico. *Sentinum: Storia e Monumenti.* Sassoferato: Istituto Internazionale di Studi Piceni, 1954.

Pallottino, Massimo. *A History of Earliest Italy.* Trans. by Martin Ryle and Kate Soper. Ann Arbor: The University of Michigan Press, 1991.

Partner, Peter. *The Lands of St. Peter: The Papal State in the Middle Ages and the Early Renaissance.* Berkeley/Los Angeles: University of California Press, 1972.

Paul the Deacon. *History of the Langobards.* Trans. by William Dudley Foulke. New York: Longmans, Green and Co., 1907.

Peet, Thomas Eric. *The Stone and Bronze Ages in Italy and Sicily.* Oxford: At the Clarendon Press, 1909.

Pelgrom, Jeremia, and Stek, Tesse. "Roman Colonization under the Republic: historiographical contextualization of a paradigm." *Roman Republican Colonization,* ed. by Tesse Stek and Jeremiah Pelgrom. Rome: Palombi Editore, 2014.

Percossi, Serenelli, a cura di. *Museo Archeologico Nazionale delle Marche: Sezione Protostorica, I Piceni.* Ancona: Ministero per i Beni Culturali e Ambientale, 1991

Percossi, Serenelli, a cura di. *Museo Archeologico Nazionale delle Marche: Sezione Preistorica, L'Eneolitico.* Ancona: Ministero per i Beni Archeologici delle Marche, 1991.

Percossi, Edvige, and Frapiccini, Nicoletta, a cura di. *Non Solo Frivolezze.* Ancona: Soprintendenza per i Beni Archeologici delle Marche, 2004.

Perowne, Stuart. *Death of the Roman Republic.* New York: Doubleday, 1968.

Pinti, Paolo. *Cicogne o Erri.* Centobuchi (AP): Linea Grafica, 2008.

Pinto, Giuliano. *Ascoli Piceno.* Spoleto: Centro Italiano di Studi sull'Alto Medioevo, 2013.

Piovene, Guido. *Viaggio in Italia.* Milano: Baldini and Castaldi, 1993.

Plutarch. *Plutarch's Lives.* Trans. by John Dryden. New York: The Modern Library.

Plutarch. *Roman Lives.* Trans. by Robin Waterbridge. Oxford: Oxford University Press, 1999.

Polybius. *The Histories.* Trans. by William Roger Paton. Cambridge: Harvard University Press,1922-27, Lacus Curtius, penelope.uchicago.edu.

Procopius. *The Anecdota or Secret History*. Trans. by H.B. Dewing. Cambridge MA: Harvard University Press, 1935.

Procopius. *The Buildings of Procopius*. Trans. by H.B. Dewing. Cambridge MA: Harvard University Press, 1940.

Procopius. *History of the Wars (Gothic Wars)* Vol. I-VIII. Trans. by H.B. Dewing. Cambridge MA: Harvard University Press, 1919, 1992.

Puglisi, Salvatore. *La Civiltà Appenninica*. Roma: Bonsignori Editore, 2005.

Radmilli, Antonio M. *Guida della Preistoria Italiana*. Firenze: Sansoni Editore, 1978.

Rath, John R. *The Fall of the Napoleonic Kingdom of Italy (1814)*. New York: Columbia University Press, 1941.

Riall, Lucy. *The Italian Risorgimento*. London/New York: Routledge, 1994.

Riall, Lucy. *Risorgimento*. New York: Palgrave MacMillan, 2009.

Ridgeway, David. "Nestor's Cup and the Etruscans." *Oxford Journal of Archeology*. Vol. 16, No. 3 (Nov. 1997), pp. 325-344.

Riva, Corinna. "Keeping up with the Etruscans? Picene Elites in Central Italy during the Orientalising Period." *The Accordia Research Papers*, Vol. 9 (2003-4), pp. 69-91.

Robinson, Cyril E. *History of Rome*. New York: Thomas Y. Crowell Co., 1965.

Rubenstein, Nicolai. "La confessione di Francesco Neroni e la congiura antimedicea del 1466." *Archivio Storico Italiano*. Vol. 126, No. ¾ (452/460) (1968), pp. 373-387.

Rosa, Gabriele. *Disegno della Storia di Ascoli Piceno*. Bologna: Arnaldo Forni Editore, 1979.

Rosen, William. *Justinian's Flea: Plague, Empire and the Birth of Europe*. New York: Viking, 2007.

Rossi-Brunori, Arcangelo. *Memorie di Montegallo*. Ascoli Piceno: Grafia Economica di Enrico Tassi, 1903.

Rostovtzeff, M. *The Social and Economic History of the Roman Empire*. Oxford: Oxford at the Clarendon Press, 1926.

Sabatier, Paul. *The Road to Assisi: The Essential Biography of St. Francis*. Ed. by Jon M. Sweeney. Brewster, MA: Paraclete Press, 2003.

Sabatina, Tommaso, and Silvestrini, Mara. *Potere e Splendore: Gli Antichi Piceni a Matelica*. Roma: Erma di Bretschneider, 2008.

Sallust, Florus, and Velleius Paterculus. Trans. by Rev. John Selby Watson MA. London: George Bell and Sons, 1889.

Salmon, E.T. "The Cause of the Social War." *Phoenix*, Vol. 16, No. 2 (Summer, 1962), pp. 107-119.

Salmon, E.T. *Samnium and the Samnites*. Cambridge: Cambridge University Press, 1967.

Salmon E.T. *Roman Colonization under the Republic*. Ithaca: Cornell University Press, 1970.

Salmon, E.T. *The Making of Roman Italy*. Ithaca: Cornell University Press, 1982.

Santarelli, Giuseppe. *Legends of the Sibilline Mountains*. Trans. by Phoebe Leed and Nathan Neel. Amandola (AP): Staf Edizioni, 2008.

Santarelli, Giuseppe. *Le Origini del Cristianesimo nelle Marche*. Loreto: Edizioni Santa Casa, 2009.

Santarelli, Giuseppe. *Loreto: History and Art*. Trans. by Andrea Lukianowicz. Ancona: Edizioni Aniballi, 1998.

Salvadori, Massimo. *Breve Storia della Resistenza Italiana*. Firenze: Vallecchi Editore, 1974.

Salvadori, Massimo. *The Labor and the Wounds*. Trans. by Giacinta Salvadori-Paleotti. London: Pall Mall Press, 1958.

Schwarz, Jeffrey, and Tattersall, Jeffrey. *Extinct Humans*. New York: Westview Press, 2001.

Scullard, H.H. *From the Gracchi to Nero*. London: Routledge, 1959.

Scullard, H.H. *A History of the Roman World*. London: Methuen and Co LTD, 1935.

Sessa, Kristina. *The Formation of Papal Authority in Late Antique Italy*. Cambridge: Cambridge University Press, 2012.

Sismondi, J.C.L. de. *A History of the Italian Republics*. New York: Anchor Books, 1966.

Suetonius. *Lives of the Twelve Caesars*. Trans. by Robert Graves. New York: Welcome Rain Publishers, 2001.

Smith, Denis Mack. *Mussolini: A Biography*. New York: Vintage Books, 1983.

Sparapani, Sergio, a cura di. *Lezione di Storia*. Ancona: Il Lavoro Editoriale, 2013.

Strabo. *The Geography of Strabo*. Trans. by Horace Leonard Jones. Cambridge: Harvard University Press, 1960.

Tabacco, Giovanni. *The Struggle for Power in Medieval Italy*. Trans. by Rosalind Brown Jensen, Cambridge: Cambridge University Press, 1989.

Ten Hove, Nicholaas. *Memoirs of the House of Medici: From its Origins to the Death of Francesco the Second, Grand Duke of Tuscany*. Trans. by Sir Richard Clayton. London: G.G. and J. Robinson, 1797.

Tiberi, Carlo. "Nuova e Vera Relazione del Terribile, e Spaventoso Terremoto Successo nella Città della Matrice, e suo Stato." Roma: Domenico Marciani, 1639.

Trump, D.H. "The Apennine Culture of Italy." *Proceedings of the Prehistoric Society*, Vol. 24 (December, 1958), pp. 165-200.

Trump, D.H. *Central and Southern Italy before Rome*. New York/Washington: Praeger Publishers, 1966.

Trump, D.H. *The Prehistory of the Mediterranean*. New Haven/London: Yale University Press, 1980.

Trevelyan, G.M. *Garibaldi's Defense of the Roman Republic*. London: Cassell, 1988.

Vermeulen, Frank. "Roman Colonization and Early Urbanization in Central Adriatic Italy: The Valley of the River Flosis." *Roman Republican Colonization*. Ed. by Tesse Stek and Jeremiah Pelgrom. Roma: Palombi Editore, 2014.

Waley, Daniel. *The Italian City Republics*. London/New York: Longman, 1988.

Waley, Daniel. *The Papal State in the Thirteenth Century*. London: Macmillan and Co., 1961.

Wallace-Hadrill, Andrew. *Rome's Cultural Revolution*. Cambridge/New York: Cambridge University Press, 2008.

Wickham, Chris. *Early Medieval Italy*. Ann Arbor: The University of Michigan Press, 1989.

Wickham, Chris. *The Inheritance of Rome*. New York: Penguin Books, 2009.

Wickham, Chris. *Sleepwalking into a New World*. Princeton: Princeton University Press, 2015.

Woolf, Stuart. *A History of Italy 1700-1860*. London/New York: Routledge, 1979.

Photo Credits and Wikimedia Licenses

Acknowledgments

As well as everyone already mentioned in the book, the following is a partial list of those who have been so helpful, generous, and kind to us in our research: Tito Antonini; the Cappelli family; Carlo, Mariolina Massignani, Furio, Flavia, and Giuseppe Vico; Alessandro Della Pietra; Francesco Eleuteri, Sergio Fabiani; Anna Maria, Stefania, and Claudia Ferri and their parents Gianna Guerrieri and Sergio Ferri; Antonello Guerrieri and his parents Anna Bastiani and Alessandro Guerrieri; Luana and Maria Grazia Lappa; Saturnino Loggi; Nora Lucentini; the Morganti family; Artemio, Ada Guerrieri, et al., Andrea Morra; Diane Murphy; Anna Maria Piccinini and family; Nunzio Piotti; Alessia Rossi; Guerriero Rossi Brunori; Giuseppe Serafini; Luca Speranza; Gioia Stevens; Jane Tenenbaum; Stefano Teodori. We are grateful to all our family and friends in Le Marche, especially for humoring us over the years.

Unless otherwise noted, the photos and translations are our own.

Phoebe Leed and Nathan Neel are writers living in Cambridge, Massachusetts, when not in Montegallo, Ascoli Piceno. Their translations include *Legends of the Sibilline Mountains* by Giuseppe Santarelli and *The Blood of the Sibillini* by Francesco Eleuteri.